Dr. John Mitchell

Dr. John Mitchell

THE MAN WHO MADE THE MAP

of North America

by Edmund Berkeley
and Dorothy Smith Berkeley

The University of North Carolina Press
Chapel Hill

Manufactured in the United States of America
Printed by Heritage Printers, Inc., Charlotte, N.C.
ISBN 0–8078–1221–8
Library of Congress Catalog Card Number 73–16162

Library of Congress Cataloging in Publication Data

Berkeley, Edmund.
  Dr. John Mitchell: the man who made the map of North America.

  Bibliography: p.
    1. Mitchell, John, d. 1768.   2. Botany—United States—History.
I. Berkeley, Dorothy Smith, joint author   II. Title.
QK31.M48B47   570'.92'4 [B]   73–16162
ISBN 0–8078–1221–8

This biography is respectfully dedicated to the American Philosophical Society which continues today to encourage and inspire scientific investigators as it did John Mitchell and his friends in the eighteenth century.

Contents

Illustrations

Acknowledgments

The research on which this biography is based has extended over a number of years, during which many people have been very helpful in a variety of ways. We have, we hope, expressed our appreciation to each of them individually, but it is also a pleasure to emphasize here that each of them had some part in the production of this biography. If it has any merit, the material and encouragement which they have provided is, to a great extent, responsible. Its faults must be credited to us.

Dr. Gordon W. Jones, of Fredericksburg, Virginia, was something of an authority on John Mitchell before we came on the scene, and probably should have written this biography. Instead, he and Mrs. Jones gave us every encouragement and assistance which they and their very fine library could provide. Mr. James F. Lewis, of Callao, Virginia, had established the correct place and date of Mitchell's birth, prior to our investigations, correcting a great deal of previous error of others. He did much to get us started on the right foot.

Dr. Whitfield J. Bell, Jr., Mrs. Gertrude D. Hess, and Mr. Murphy D. Smith, of the American Philosophical Society, kept us continually in their debt, as they have so often done in the past. Dr. Bell introduced us to Miss Mary Cosh, of London, which proved very fortunate for us. Miss Cosh entertained us most cordially there, and gave us the benefit of her own extensive research on the life of Mitchell's friend, the Duke of Argyll. She provided references to Mitchell which she had found, suggested manuscript collections which we might have missed, and introduced us to Miss M. Veronica Stokes, Archivist and Curator of Coutts & Company, London bankers. Miss Stokes presides over the records of that venerable firm which establish its existence as early as 1692. She gave generously of her time and patience in assembling for us a large array of enormous ledgers compiled in the mid-eighteenth century, and shared her office with us as we pored over them for records of Mitchell and his friends. We are grateful, not only to Miss Stokes, but to the Directors of Coutts & Company.

Miss Catherine Armet, Archivist to the Marquess of Bute, Isle of Bute, Scotland, very kindly sent us copies of Mitchell items which she found among the papers of the third Lord Bute. Thomas I. Rae, Assistant Keeper of Manuscripts, National Library of Scotland, was helpful above and beyond the call of duty. R. J. F. Carnon and R. W. Thomson, of the University of Edinburgh Library, did everything possible to assist us there, in the absence of that perennial helper, Charles P. Finlayson, who still managed to help by correspondence.

Since neither of us was well informed in the area of cartography, we feel especially indebted to several people who made a noble effort to educate us! A particular note of thanks must go to Dr. William P. Cumming, Professor of English at Davidson College; Dr. Richard W. Stephenson and Dr. Walter W. Ristow, Geography and Map Division, Library of Congress; and Dr. Helen Wallis, Superintendent of the Map Room of the British Museum.

Dr. A. Rössler, of the Erlangen-Nurnberg University Library, very kindly provided copies of a number of manuscripts from its important collections. Dr. H. DeVries, Institute of Biological History, University of Utrecht, once again supplied us with many useful references from the indexes of that remarkable institution. Mr. R. Desmond welcomed us to the fine new library at Kew and gave generously of his time and good advice.

In addition to those mentioned above, we are grateful to Mary Clapinson, Department of Western Manuscripts, Bodleian Library; E. J. Miller, State Papers, British Museum; Phyllis I. Edwards, British Museum (Natural History); G. S. Rousseau, University of California at Los Angeles; H. J. R. Wing, Christ Church College, Oxford; Mrs. H. N. Clokie, Pinner, Middlesex, U.K.; Dr. W. B. McDaniel 2nd, Library of the College of Physicians of Philadelphia; Mrs. Robert A. McGregor, Colonial Williamsburg, Inc.; Nicholas B. Wainwright, the Historical Society of Pennsylvania; H. M. G. Baillie, Historical Manuscripts Commission; Harriet McLoone, Henry E. Huntington Library; Taylor Milne, Institute of Historical Research, University of London; John Jacob, the Iveagh Bequest, Kenwood, London; Edward A. Hughes, Jr., and Mrs. William Tonkin, Library Company of Philadelphia; Theodore O'Grady, Linnean Society of London; Diana Haskell,

The Newberry Library; P. A. Penfold, Public Record Office, London; Mrs. C. McNamara, Post Office Records, London; D. G. C. Allan, The Royal Society of Arts, London; I. Kaye and L. P. Townsend, Royal Society of London; Joseph and Nesta Ewan, Tulane University; Mrs. M. Evans, the Rt. Rev. J. K. Russell, and Peter Wells, Tunbridge Wells; William Moll, Medical Library, University of Virginia; Mrs. Virginia R. Hawley, Western Reserve Historical Society; Pamela Bell and Judith A. Schiff, Yale University; and T. J. Hopkins, Archivist, Central Library, The Hayes, Cardiff.

All of the following have very kindly given permission to quote from manuscripts in their collections: City of Cardiff Public Libraries, Cardiff, Wales; Department of Western Manuscripts, Bodleian Library, Oxford; Edinburgh University Library; Lord Bute, Mount Stuart, Rothesay, Isle of Bute; National Library of Scotland; Public Record Office, Chancery Lane, London; Scottish Record Office, Edinburgh; The Historical Society of Pennsylvania, Philadelphia; The Huntington Library, San Marino, California; The Linnean Society of London; The Royal Society, London; The Trustees of the Will of the Late J. H. C. Evelyn, Christ Church Library, Oxford; and University Library, Erlangen, Germany.

Abbreviations

The following abbreviations are used in the notes:

Libraries:

BM	British Museum
CPL	Cardiff Public Library
ENU	Erlangen-Nurnberg University Library
HSP	Historical Society of Pennsylvania
LC	Library of Congress
LCLS	Linnean Correspondence, Linnean Society
LS	Linnean Society of London
NL	National Library of Scotland
OU	Oxford University
PRO	Public Record Office, London
RSL	Royal Society of London
UE	University of Edinburgh
VSL	Virginia State Library

Publications:

APR	*The American and Philosophical Register*
CLO	James Edward Smith, *A Selection of the Correspondence of Linnaeus and Other Naturalists* (London, 1821)
LPCC	*Letters and Papers of Cadwallader Colden* (New York, 1910)

Introduction

*". . . few men rival Mitchell as a key to the problems of the intellectual
life in the colonies. He has a place in the early history of American botany
zoology, physiology, medicine, cartography, climatology, and agriculture, to
say nothing of politics. He was for a time perhaps the ablest scientific investi-
gator in North America, and is credited both with the authorship of the earliest
work on the principles of taxonomy to be written in what is now the United
States and with making of what has been called the most important map in
American history."*

Theodore Hornberger

It might be expected that the name of a man about whom such a statement as that above could be accurately made would be a very familiar
one to natives of that state and nation from which he came. This is not
the case, however, with John Mitchell. Neither Americans in general,
nor Virginians in particular, are familiar with his career. This is not to
say that he is unknown. Curators of map rooms at such institutions as
the Library of Congress and the British Museum know him very well
indeed. Botanists with a taxonomic interest usually know that Linnaeus
named our Partridge Berry *Mitchella repens* in his honor. Here and there
are people who know much more about him, but he has not received
the recognition that he deserves. One reason for this may be that he
had, until very recently, been believed to have been an Englishman
who lived for a few years in Virginia.

Although the British colonies of southern North America offered a
vast opportunity for discovery in natural science, a relatively small
number of men seem to have made significant contributions to the

---

1. Theodore Hornberger, "The Scientific Ideas of John Mitchell," *Huntington Library
Quarterly* 10, no. 3 (1947):277.

history of scientific discovery there in the period prior to 1750. Among these John Mitchell appears to have been the only one born in the colonies, and he was long thought to have gone to Virginia from England. Thomas Glover spent only a few years in Virginia. Three seventeenth-century clergymen, John Clayton, John Banister, and Hugh Jones, were sent from England with the definite purpose of conducting scientific investigations in addition to their clerical duties. Under the auspices of the Temple Coffee House Botany Club, William Vernon and David Krieg were dispatched as collectors. John Lawson, who made discoveries in Carolina, was an Englishman, as was Mark Catesby, the best known naturalist of the later period. John Clayton, the botanist, lived in Virginia for more than half a century, but he too was born in England. William Byrd II was born in Virginia, but it is difficult to classify him as a scientist, either in terms of training or accomplishment in science.

There is then a particular interest in the scientific career of John Mitchell. He was born in Virginia to parents whose families had been there for several generations. His early life was therefore influenced by people who knew the area well and who could teach him a great deal about its natural history. He grew up among men who had learned how to farm in a wilderness, how to cultivate the Tobacco plant, how to make use of the Indian maize, how to supply their families with meat by hunting and with necessities made by their own ingenuity when England's ships were delayed or lost. From the women, Mitchell learned their favored prescriptions for the ill in a land where there were few doctors and few of these with any real medical training. From the slaves and Indians, he learned other remedies as well as the proper plants for dyeing cloth or hypnotizing snakes. From friends and neighbors he heard of the great areas of the west yet to be explored. He spent the invaluable early years of curious boyhood discovering for himself the wonders of his birthplace, storing up the knowledge of which he later made great use. It was this familiarity with his native land, absorbed from birth, which gave him an advantage over the English-born scientists who came to America. It is also true that Mitchell was somewhat unique in that he was born in Virginia, educated in Scotland, practiced medicine in Virginia, but lived the last twenty-two years of his life in England. He was particularly well qualified to influence British thinking about North America.

All of the foregoing would serve to make Mitchell worthy of study, but the more important reason is that he was a scientist of considerable ability, who had an important influence on British-American relations in the middle years of the eighteenth century. Much has been written about him but this is the first full-length biography.

Dr. John Mitchell

I ❧ Family Background and Education

"You'll still keep in mind what has been said on another occasion, that a Teacher can propose to do little more than draw the outlines of a Science; it's the Learner's part to do the rest by his own application."

Charles Alston to his Materia Medica students, 1736[1]

John Mitchell was born April 13, 1711, son of Robert Mitchell and Mary Chilton Sharpe Mitchell, of White Chapel Parish, Lancaster County, Virginia.[2] The Mitchells were not newcomers to Lancaster for John's grandfather, also a Robert, first appeared in county records in 1683. There had been Mitchells in the Northern Neck of Virginia prior to that date but no definite connection has been established.[3] The elder Robert Mitchell married Sarah Smith about whom nothing is known. In 1687, they bought a small plantation which remained in the family for four generations. This 120-acre tract was well developed, with a house, gardens, outbuildings, and orchard, having had several previous owners.[4]

1. Laing MSS, University of Edinburgh Archives, subsequently referred to as UE.

2. J. Motley Booker, "Mitchell Family Bible," *Northern Neck of Virginia Historical Magazine* 14 (December 1964):1280. See John Frederick Dorman and James F. Lewis, "Doctor John Mitchell, F.R.S., Native Virginian," *Virginia Magazine of History and Biography* 76 (October 1968):437.

3. Lancaster County Order Book #2, p. 139, lists Robert Mitchell as being taxed for one tithable in 1683. In 1695, he was one of twelve men "impressed as a Jury" by the County Court "to lay out a patent" of 650 acres of land on the Rappahannock River granted to Edward Mitchell on the 2 May 1650 (Lancaster County Deed Book #7, p. 100; also see Book #4, p. 162, for original grant to Edward Mitchell). Robert had a sister named Mary, who married John Wells. Widowed in 1697, she married Thomas Parfitt (Lancaster County Wills #8, p. 70). Photostats and microfilms of county records are in the Virginia State Library, subsequently referred to as VSL.

4. Matthew Sparks and his wife Anne sold this land to Mitchell and his wife on 14 March (Lancaster County Deed Book #7, p. 5). Sparks had bought it from Robert Pollard two years previously (ibid., p. 4), who had acquired it by marriage c. 1659 to the widow of Vincent Stamford, the original owner (Lancaster County Order Book #3, p. 87), VSL.

Dr. Mitchell's grandfather was both a planter and a merchant in a modest way. At the time of his death in 1702, he was a widower with four children. John and Robert, the two eldest, were to be guardians for George and Sarah, both minors. John inherited the plantation in his father's will but it was to be home for his sister and brothers until they married or were otherwise provided for. The remainder of the estate was to be divided among the four children by the executors: his brother-in-law, Thomas Parfitt, and his nephew, John Wells. It was not large. The inventory included 3,129 pounds of tobacco, a number of cattle and hogs, rather sparse household furnishings and personal belongings, and some merchandise, indicating that he had operated a small store. There were bolts of serge, linen, flannel, and dimity, quires of paper, a parcel of thread, and buttons, etc. It would seem that his son Robert received this merchandise, since he definitely operated a store and his brother John's will gives no indication that he did so.[5]

The younger Robert Mitchell (1684–1748) was just eighteen when his father died. When he was twenty-six he married Mary Chilton Sharpe, widow of John Sharpe. Widows rarely remained single for any length of time in those days. It has been said that they were "so promptly courted and remarried that the new husband often brought the will of the deceased to probate and settled the estate."[6] This was certainly the case with Robert Mitchell. In fact as early as February, 1709/10, he was answering suits against Sharpe's estate, although the will was not recorded until July.[7]

The first marriage of Mitchell's mother to John Sharpe had connected two prominent families of the Northern Neck. The Chiltons had been among the early settlers there. They had come from the English county of Kent in 1654 and they had prospered in Virginia.[8] The Sharpes had patented a large tract of land in the county the following year and they, too, had fared well.[9] Mary's parents were John and Joan Chilton

5. Lancaster County Wills #8, p. 127 and pp. 123–25, VSL. John Wells died two years after his uncle. He appointed his cousin, John Mitchell, an executor and guardian to his two minor children (Lancaster County Wills #8, pp. 107–9, VSL). The inventory of John Mitchell's estate is given in Lancaster County Will Book #10, pp. 68–70, VSL.

6. J. Motley Booker, "Old Wills in the Northern Neck and Essex Counties," *Northern Neck of Virginia Historical Magazine* 14 (December 1964):1319.

7. Lancaster County Order Book #5, pp. 234, 247, 251, 253, 265, 290, VSL.

8. Ann Chilton McDonnell, "Chilton & Shelton, Two Distinct Virginia Families," *William and Mary Quarterly*, 2d ser. 10 (January 1930):57.

9. 4 September 1655, Lancaster County Deed Book #9, pp. 215–16, VSL.

and their home was Currioman, a substantial brick home on Currioman Bay.[10] In addition to her dowry, Mary received a substantial portion of her father's estate when he died in 1708.[11] John Sharpe inherited a large estate from his father, most of which came to Mary upon her husband's death.[12] Evidently Dr. Mitchell's mother was quite wealthy by the standards of the day and his father comfortably so at the time of his son's birth.

Mitchell's mother died while he was still an infant and his father promptly remarried. His stepmother was Susannah, daughter of a prosperous planter, William Payne. There were soon half brothers and sisters to keep John company. They lived in property leased from Anne and Bryan Phillips for thirty pounds sterling and one ear of Indian corn "lawfully demanded" on Christmas Day of each year. There was not only a house and outbuildings but a livery yard and orchard as well. The fifty acres, situated on Moratico Creek, included well-fenced fields and a small forest, but the lease precluded any cutting of oaks or other timber. It is interesting to note that the lease was drawn to be in effect "during the life" of Robert Mitchell and his son William. This provision for the second son seems to suggest that the first son would be sufficiently provided for by his mother's estate.[13]

Robert Mitchell's mercantile activities must certainly have derived from those of his father. They included the operation of a store, with the customary exchange of tobacco and other produce for goods purchased abroad. This, in turn, involved the sale of tobacco abroad and the purchase of goods there. Many of the merchants with whom he dealt were Scots. Scotland had become a strong competitor of England in this mercantile trade. Fifteen merchant companies from Glasgow alone were operating in the Chesapeake Bay as early as 1696. Many of these firms had their own stores in Virginia, with a "tobacco factor"

10. McDonnell, "Chilton & Shelton," *William and Mary Quarterly*, 2d ser. 10 (January 1930):57. Records in Westmoreland County Deeds & Wills #3, VSL, raise some doubt as to whether this plantation belonged to Mary's father or her brother John.

11. Mary inherited his Negro Tony whom her father had assigned to John Sharpe and shared in the remainder of the estate after small bequests were made (Westmoreland County Deeds & Wills #4, p. 39 and pp. 122–23, VSL).

12. Much of the original land grant to his grandfather came to John through his father (also a John) who had died sometime prior to 1704 (Lancaster County Deed Book #9, p. 129, VSL). Mary and her husband lived in White Chapel Parish and his will is recorded in the Lancaster County Will Book #10, pp. 35–36, VSL.

13. Lancaster County Order Book #11, pp. 60–61 and 201–2, VSL.

in charge. Robert Mitchell probably acted in this capacity for one or more of them. He held power of attorney for John Wood in 1716, David Crawfurd in 1717, William Eccles in 1720, and James Crosby in 1726.[14]

However small its beginnings may have been, Robert Mitchell's emporium grew to one of sizeable importance. Young John and his brothers and sisters must have found it a fascinating place. Like a modern department store, it carried everything. There was a variety of textiles, including camblet or camel's hair, printed linen, Scotch plaid and other woolens, cambrics, and even silk. Leather goods for sale included gloves, breeches, shoes, and pumps. There were notions of all sorts: buttons, silk handkerchiefs, horn combs, shoe buckles, needles, thread, knives, razors, and brushes. There were tools of all kinds: bed linen and blankets, stationery and ink powder. Indian corn was sold by the barrel and spiritous liquors included peach and apple brandy as well as rum.[15]

Robert Mitchell's activities and income were further increased in 1722 when he was appointed Tobacco Receiver for Lancaster County. Still later, he served in the same capacity for Richmond County. His name appears often in court records of cases involving tobacco. For three years at least (1727-30) he served as one of the justices of the county court.[16] With increasing prosperity, he purchased additional land and slaves and devoted more time and attention to farming operations. He built up a large stock of cattle, horses, and sheep. He bought farm implements of all sorts. The home, too, exhibited signs of growing affluence. In addition to the usual furnishings, there were a dozen "Rusha" leather chairs, "Delph Ware" dishes, "30 History Books," two dozen pewter dishes, a punch bowl, brass candlesticks, several looking glasses, silver spoons, and tongs. The Mitchell family steadily increased in size. There were ten children by the second marriage, but

14. Theodore Keith, "Scottish Trade with the Plantations before 1707," *Scottish Historical Review* 6 (1908):32-48; Jacob M. Price, "The Rise of Glasgow in the Chesapeake Tobacco Trade, 1707-1775," *William and Mary Quarterly*, 3d ser. 11 (April 1954):179-99; Lancaster County Order Book #11, pp. 65, 76, 159, 307, VSL.

15. See store inventory, Lancaster County Deeds and Wills, 1743-50, pp. 227-28, VSL.

16. Appointed receiver 22 October, Lancaster County Order Book #7, p. 65; some of his cases: ibid., pp. 100, 101, 107, 172, and Lancaster County Deed Book #13, pp. 95, 146, 280, 284, 307, 313, 316, 317, etc. Richmond County Deed Book #10, pp. 315-17. His appearances as justice recorded in Lancaster County Court Order Book #7, first mention, p. 262 (all in VSL).

several of them died in infancy. A number of the later children saw little of their half-brother John since he was no longer at home.[17]

John Mitchell has left us no references to his early education and nothing is known of it. It was certainly a very good one, if one can judge from his later accomplishments. Perhaps he was tutored by a local clergyman or attended some small local private school. He later attended the University of Edinburgh but how early he was sent to Scotland is not clear. Colleges and universities of that day complained, as they do today, of the lack of preparation of their students. Both the College of William and Mary in Virginia and the University of Edinburgh found it necessary to conduct classes in Latin, Greek, and other subjects at the preparatory school level for some of their students and some were admitted at a very early age.[18] It is very probable that Mitchell was sent to Edinburgh in the care of relatives or friends while still in grammar school and that he remained there for quite a period of years. Matriculation records for the university at this period are incomplete, but in 1722 a John Mitchell was recorded as a pupil of William Scott, professor of Greek. A John Mitchell was a student in 1728 of Professor Colin Drummond, who taught Logic and Metaphysics. David Hume had been a student of his too in 1725, at the age of fourteen. John Mitchell who received a master's degree in 1729 was almost certainly the Virginian.[19]

Regardless of his age, Mitchell must have found Edinburgh a strange contrast to rural Tidewater Virginia. It is unlikely that he had seen anything of the hilly parts of Virginia, much less the mountains. The land of Lancaster County, as in other coastal areas, is low and flat, and it has often been said that it would be impossible to find a rock to throw at

17. Inventory of his estate, Lancaster County Deeds and Wills, 1743–50, p. 227, VSL. At least four died in childhood: William (b. 1715), Margaret (b. 1719), George (b. 1720/21), and Catherine (b. 1722/23). The five surviving children were: Sarah (1716/17–1752) who married Thomas Chinn; Robert (1724–58) who married Hannah Ball; Elizabeth (1726–85) who married Moore Fauntleroy; Richard (1728–81) who married Anne ———; Frances (1730/31–?) who married William Sydnor; and Judith (1732/33–1791) who married George Glascock.

18. Alexander Grant, *The Story of the University of Edinburgh*, 2 vols. (London, 1884), 1:267–68.

19. Matriculations, University of Edinburgh, 1704–62, UE. He graduated on 6 June and was described as "Scotus-Americanus." (*A Catalogue of the Graduates of Arts, Divinity, and Law of the University of Edinburgh* [Edinburgh, 1858], p. 202.) Mitchell was the only graduate of that date and was listed as the "139th Class."

a bull. The steep rocky hills of Edinburgh must have seemed forbidding and formidable to a boy a long way from home. A description of the city by a visitor a few years later seems pertinent:

> It stands on a kind of precipice in the middle of a hill, that is very steep both above and below, in the bottom is a great lake; on the summit of a wild spiral rock, that commands the town, stands the castle; it has one fine street paved like *St. James* square, which would be the grandest in *Europe* if a church and an ugly row of houses were not built in the middle of it. The houses are eight or nine story high, and almost every floor is a separate dwelling. The stair cases are very dark and steep, excessively narrow and dirty. I believe so great a number of people are no where else confined in so small a compass, which makes their streets as much crowded every day, as others are at a fair.[20]

Unless he lived with relatives or friends of his family, Mitchell probably followed the common practice of living in the home of a faculty member. Faculty supplemented their meager incomes by taking in student roomers. If he was lucky he might have found a "house master," as a later student did, who "possessed excellent translations of the classics." Some few wealthy students had tutors, but it is unlikely that Mitchell could afford such luxury. Students' meals were fortunately reasonable. For four pence, dinner included broth, roast, potatoes, fish at least three times a week, and all of the beer they could drink before the "cloth was removed."[21]

Mitchell's surviving writing makes little mention of his studies at Edinburgh other than his botany classes with Charles Alston. Nevertheless, it is evident that he received a broad, liberal education and a sound one. He was well grounded in ancient and modern languages and in all branches of natural philosophy, including chemistry and physics. He benefited from instruction in logic, showing a natural aptitude for deduction and logical development of a thesis.

More is known of the faculty under whom he must have studied. While few students took Professor Scott's course in Greek, all premedical students were obliged to obtain proficiency in that language as well as in Latin. Robert Stewart was professor of natural history. When "Jupiter" Carlyle was in his class a few years after Mitchell, he

---

20. "Account of a Journey into Scotland," *Gentleman's Magazine* 36 (May 1766):211.

21. *Edinburgh University: A Sketch of its Life for 300 Years* (Edinburgh, 1884), pp. 41–42.

reported that it "was very ill taught, as he was worn out with age, and never had excelled." As a result, Carlyle spent most of his class time at the billiard table "within fifty yards of the College." It is unlikely that Mitchell had a similar reaction to the course for it included Optics, Newton's Colours and Principia, Dr. David Gregory's Astronomy, mechanics, and the use of microscopes, all of which helped Mitchell in his later years. Laurence Dundas was professor of humanity, William Law taught moral philosophy and Charles Mackie universal history. Mitchell particularly benefited from the fine course in mathematics taught by Colin McLaurin. Carlyle noted that "Mr. M'Laurin was at this time a favourite professor, and no wonder, as he was the clearest and most agreeable lecturer on that abstract science that ever I heard. He made mathematics a fashionable study. . . ." In later years, several colleagues were much impressed by Mitchell's knowledge of the subject and it was to be a useful tool in some of his work unconnected with medicine.[22]

Several of Mitchell's teachers remained his friends in later life. Charles Alston seems to have had a particularly strong influence. He came from the west of Scotland, where his father was a nonpracticing physician of very little means. The Duchess of Hamilton, a relative, took an interest in the son and assisted him in studying, first at the University of Glasgow, and then at Leyden under the great Boerhaave. Upon his return to Edinburgh he became Keeper of the Garden at Holyrood, with the title of "King's botanist." He was not, however, professor of botany at the university until 1738 when George Preston retired from that post. He did conduct classes in botany and Mitchell was his student.[23]

The King's Garden was primarily furnished with "simples," plants used in medical treatments. Many of Alston's lectures were conducted in the gardens where taxonomy was emphasized. The different genera and species were identified and classified and their medical virtues men-

---

22. Grant, *The Story of the University*, 2:317–35; John Hill Burton, ed., *The Autobiography of Dr. Alexander Carlyle of Inverask, 1722–1805* (Edinburgh, 1910), pp. 49 and 37.

23. For more information on Alston (1683–1760) see Richard Pulteney, *Historical and Biographical Sketches of the Progress of Botany in England*, 2 vols. (London, 1790), 2:9–17; William Martin Smallwood and Mabel S. C. Smallwood, *Natural History and the American Mind* (New York, 1941), p. 61. For a detailed history of the garden, see John Macqueen Cowan, "The History of the Royal Botanical Garden, Edinburgh," *Notes from the Royal Botanical Garden* 19 (1933):1–62.

tioned. This might easily have been a dull cataloguing but Alston conveyed his own enthusiasm to his students. Others besides Mitchell remembered him with affection and took pleasure in sending him plants from foreign parts.[24] Although hundreds of plants, having come from Europe and such exotic places as Africa, were unknown to Mitchell, many were the familiar English plants to be found in his stepmother's garden. To his delight, too, there were many trees, shrubs, and plants native to Virginia's woodland.

In winter, Alston taught *materia medica*, in which the preparation and uses of the simples were stressed. He left the chemistry to the apothecaries, but gave instruction in the parts of the plants to be collected, their curing, grinding, mixing, and their use as anodynes, palliatives, scorbutics, specifics, and antidotes. He was interested in the history of the subject and traced its origins from the early Arabs, Greeks and Romans to the current time. Few aspects of plant anatomy and physiology, indeed of botany, were neglected.

The lecture notes of a student who attended Alston's classes soon after Mitchell shed some light on the material covered and on his views on certain aspects of botany with which Mitchell concerned himself a little later.[25] In concluding his review of botanical history, Alston discussed the most recent discoveries concerning the "anatomy of Vegetables," in which he stressed the work of Nehemiah Grew and Marcello Malpighi. In regard to the division of the roots and the source of nutritive juices, he said: "The ingenious and always to be mentioned with Honour Mr. Hales has put this affair in a just light," referring to Stephen Hales's *Vegetable Staticks*, which had just been published in 1727. Noting the movement of sap, he spoke of Thomas Fairchild. A man of little education, Fairchild had still devised several ingenious experiments concerning it. The flower's structure and use were not neglected by Alston, and he again mentioned Fairchild when speaking of the structure of the seed: "I have another reason why Mr. Fairchild's Mule-Pink (this is a particular Flower partaking of the nature of a Carnation and Sweet William both in Colour and shape) should be propagated no other way than by slips. He says that the Species of Mongrell Quadrupeds from whence it derives its name, never produce their own likeness, neither therefore [do the] Vegetables; But I think that the du-

24. Mitchell to Alston, 4 October 1738, Laing MSS, UE.
25. "Alston's Lectures on Materia Medica, 1736," UE.

plicity and multitude of the Petala hinder the Stamina from performing their proper action, and this I take to be the Case in most Double flowers that are seldom propagated by Seed."[26] Whatever Alston considered to be the function of the stamens, he did not accept the idea of sexual reproduction in flowering plants or that Fairchild had produced an interspecific hybrid that was sterile. Mitchell was intrigued by Fairchild's experiment. The more he thought about it the less he could agree with his instructor's interpretation. The puzzle was not forgotten and lay semidormant in his mind for ten years when he found an interesting application for it.

In his treatment of taxonomy, Alston analyzed the contributions of a series of early workers, comparing their systems and noting important advances and weaknesses. He included among others Conrad Gesner, Fabius Columna (Fabio Colonna), Caspar Bauhin, Robert Morison, John Ray, Joseph P. de Tournefort, and his own teacher, Herman Boerhaave. A few of his comments serve to illustrate his approach. Thus, he said of Morison that "His descriptions are exact, his Copper Plates very good ones, and exceedingly accurate, his method is not so convenient as one could wish, he follows Caesalpinius in several things without mentioning him, nay entirely adopts his method without adding much of his own save the Division which he makes of them into Scandentia, Leguminosa, etc. . . . His vanity in extolling himself, and the pleasure he took in Condemning others, tho very deserving men, such as the Bauhins, gave occasion to others who came after him to use him in the same manner." He objected to Ray's use of the cotyledons of the embryo since he said "in some we can't discover even with Glasses, whether the seed has one or more Cotyledons, till it is suffered to germinate. In Tobacco for instance, you can't know in what Class to affix it till the seed has swelled."[27]

Alston believed the system of Tournefort "to be the best extant, tho it is not perfect, neither indeed can we expect a perfect Method, till all the plants on the Earth are discovered. . . ." Again, in referring to an ideal method he commented that it was thought Sherard would propose one but that he died and "tho he left a Convenient Salary and orders to carry it on to Dr. Dillenius, yet it is to be feared, it will not be perfected, tho this Gentleman seems to have a Genius suitable to the

26. Ibid., p. 45.
27. Ibid., pp. 52–56; quotations pp. 55 and 56 respectively.

between 1726 and 1733, in spite of large numbers of students in the classes.[35]

Mitchell found himself one of ninety students in the anatomy class in 1729. Monro's reputation was well known to all of them and many were familiar with his book, *The Anatomy of Human Bones*, published in 1726. Like others before him, Mitchell fell under the spell of Monro's personality. While he was only of average height, Monro possessed such boundless vitality and enthusiasm he seemed to dominate everyone. Yet, with it all, he was both sympathetic and gentle with his students.[36] Like Alston, he infected them with his own deep interest in the study of the human body. Mitchell became skillful in dissection and impressed with the importance of autopsies. Examining cadavers to discover the cause of death was unusual for the time and particularly so in the American colonies where Mitchell would practice. Thanks to Monro, he became a careful and adept pathologist when the opportunity offered. It served him well not only in medical research but in zoological as well.

The year of Mitchell's entry to the medical school saw a new development which must have done much to improve instruction in some areas. This was the opening of a small infirmary of six beds, known as the "little house." It provided patients for clinical studies, something of an innovation for medical schools. Dr. Rutherford, who taught the associated course, explained to his students what his approach would be: "I shall examine every Patient capable of appearing before you, that no circumstance may escape you and proceed in the following manner: 1st, Give you a history of the disease. 2ndly. Enquire into the Cause. 3rdly, Give you my Opinion how it will terminate. 4thly, lay down the indications of cure yt arise, and if any new Symptoms happen acquaint you them, that you may see how I vary my prescriptions. And 5thly, Point out the different Method of Cure." He added, "If at any time you find me deceived in giving my Judgement, you'll be so good as to excuse me, for neither do I pretend to be, nor is that Art of

35. John D. Comrie, *History of Scottish Medicine*, 2 vols. (London, 1932), 1:303; D. B. Horn, *A Short History of the University of Edinburgh* (Edinburgh, 1967), p. 44; *List of the Graduates in Medicine in the University of Edinburgh from MDCCV to MDCCCLXVI* (Edinburgh, 1867).

36. Guthrie, "The Three Alexander Monros," *Journal of the Royal College of Surgeons of Edinburgh* 2 (September 1956):26; Wilson, "The Influence of Edinburgh," *Proceedings of the Institute of Medicine of Chicago* 7 (1929):133.

Physic infallible, what you can in justice expect from me, is some accurate observations and remarks upon Diseases."[37]

For his second year at the medical School, Mitchell lived in the home of Professor George Young according to Monro's record book.[38] It is thought that the "Scholars" were possibly apprentices to the surgeon "Masters" with whom they lived. There are no records indicating that Mitchell remained for a third year and he did not receive a degree from the University of Edinburgh. He may have traveled and studied on the Continent in the last months of 1731, receiving an M.D. from a European university. Numerous men did just that, among them Carolus Linnaeus. In fact, that well-known scientist spent but a week defending his thesis and satisfying degree requirements at Harderwijk. Although no evidence has been found to prove that Mitchell acquired his degree, there is reason to think that he had one. On at least two occasions, when there was small likelihood that one without an M.D. would have been referred to as "Doctor of Physic," he was publicly given that title.

Mitchell returned to Virginia with a broad liberal education and sound medical training. An unusually sensitive and intelligent student, he had acquired knowledge in many fields, and he had all the attributes of a true scholar. His years at the university had trained and disciplined a mind already well endowed with curiosity. He had been thoroughly indoctrinated with the experimental approach to scientific problems. He was to be little influenced by previous *dicta* and concepts. He would in the future rely upon his own observations and apply a trained mind to logical development of his own theories.

37. Horn, *Short History*, p. 56, quoting Notes of Rutherford's Clinical Lectures, which are in the Royal College of Physicians' Library, Edinburgh.

38. Other students at Professor Young's house were Samuel Kay, Joshua Fletcher, James Crawford, William Adam, Michael Carmichael, James Pedan, ——— Frazer, Alex Troup, James Haddo, and a William Mitchell.

II ⚜ Return from Edinburgh

> "*These are a small Specimen of the many unknown Beautifull, curious & useful plants, our Country affords. I had thought of sending you a Catalogue of the rest but for want of a Botanical library & Companions, I have not finished that to my mind, & doubt if ever I shall be able. . . .*"
>
> Mitchell to Alston, 4 October 1738[1]

The return of the young doctor to Tidewater Virginia must have again required a difficult adjustment. It is questionable that he ever felt completely at home there. In his immediate family there had been many changes. Several of the older half brothers and sisters had died, and others had been born during his absence. Only Sarah, now fifteen, survived from the group which he had known. The additions included Robert eight, Elizabeth six, Richard four, and Frances one. Judith was born soon after his return.[2] All were too young to impress a sophisticated young physician of twenty-one but it must have been comforting to have a doctor in the family. No doubt he was welcomed by all of the old friends who gathered each Sunday at little St. Mary's Church: the Paynes, Wells, Balls, Foxes, Chinns, and many others.

There was abundant evidence that his father's fortunes had prospered during Mitchell's absence. The furnishings of the house, the increased farming activity, and the enlargement of the store all gave proof of it. A new plantation had been acquired, two hundred acres in Farnham parish, Richmond County.[3] This adjoined a plantation and mill in Northumberland County which Mr. Mitchell already owned.[4]

For the next two years, Mitchell apparently practiced in Lancaster County, possibly living with his family there. Only one bit of evidence has been found concerning it. Lancaster County court records for 14 March 1733, show that "In Action of Debt between John Mitchell Doctor of Physic pltf. and Thomas Wharton, planter, deft. for twelve

1. Laing MSS, UE.
2. See chap. 1, note 17.
3. John Harcum sold him this land for fifty pounds on 2 March 1725 (Richmond County Court Deeds #8, p. 324, VSL).
4. See his will, Lancaster County Court Deeds & Wills, 1743–50, p. 212, VSL.

hundred & ninety pounds of tobacco for sundry medicines adminis-
tered and sundry visits made to the sd. deft. and his family by the sd
John as in the declaration set forth the sd parties agreed to referr the
trial of the issue joined in the Cause to the Court . . . the Court ordered
that the Court be adjourned til tomorrow morning ten o'clock." The
case was postponed repeatedly and was not settled until the following
February. It seems unlikely that a young physician starting practice
would bring legal action to collect a bill until that bill had been outstanding for some time. This helps to date Mitchell's return as late 1731
or early 1732.[5]

It was not until the fall of 1734 that he finally found an ideal situation
in which to establish a permanent practice. This was the small town of
Urbanna, directly across the Rappahannock River from Lancaster
County. Lying in Middlesex County, Urbanna had been laid out by
Major Robert Beverley on land which he had purchased from Ralph
Wormley. Building had been started in 1680 and a courthouse erected
in 1693, but it was not until the tobacco Inspection Act of 1730, that
prospects for growth began to be realized. Under the Act, Urbanna
became an inspection center with large tobacco warehouses.[6] The
Major's grandson Robert, son of Captain Harry Beverley, inherited
some of this land in Urbanna from his father. He died in May, 1733,
and his wife Anne and cousin, William Beverley, son of the historian,
were named executors. One of the items of the will directed that they
sell all his Urbanna houses and lots "for the most money that can be
gott for them."[7]

This was the property which interested Mitchell. Four of the lots,
numbered 41–44, encompassed a whole block, bounded by a creek on
the north, Caty Lane on the east, Virginia Street on the south, and
Physick Lane on the west. The fifth lot was on the other side of Physick
Lane, adjoining the water.[8] There was a large comfortable house,
barns, stables, various outbuildings, and a delightful prospect across

5. Lancaster County Court Order Book, 1729–43, pp. 82, 87, 89, 92, 95, 98, 100, VSL.

6. Wesley Newton Laing, "Report on a Building at Urbanna, Virginia," prepared
under the general direction of the Ralph Wormely Chapter and a Special Committee
from APVA 1958–60 (photostat typescript, VSL).

7. W. G. Stanard, "Major Robert Beverley and His Descendants," *Virginia Magazine
of History and Biography* 3 (July 1895):383, 388.

8. Survey and plat of Urbanna made 30 May 1747 (copy in VSL), show Mitchell's
lots.

the river. The indenture of sale from the Beverleys to Mitchell was proved at the Middlesex County Court held on November fifth.

It was probably word of this new practice at Urbanna to which mathematics professor Colin McLaurin at Edinburgh referred in a letter to his friend Archibald Campbell, of Knocklevy, Inverara, when he wrote: "Mr. Mitchell has got a good place that will be worth near £500 per annum. I wish you may have good accounts of our American friends."[9] The Scots were well represented in Urbanna. Among Mitchell's closest neighbors were a Mr. McKennie, Alexander Fraser who was one of the witnesses to Mitchell's deed of sale, Thomas Laughlin, and Patrick Cheap, who became one of his closest friends.

Within the next few years, Mitchell added other buildings to those which he had purchased. The first was an apothecary shop, and later a chemical laboratory.[10] Doctors in small towns had to prepare their own prescriptions and often maintained apothecary shops. Over the door of such establishments there usually hung a golden ball, a mortar and pestle, or some similar device traditionally associated with the trade. Passing children must have loved the colorful carboys in the windows. Inside, there was the potent aroma of spices which were also sold. On the prescription counter were displayed brass scales, shiny white tiles for mixing pills, presses, mortars and pestles, and a primitive distilling apparatus. Shelves lined the shop, filled with colorful bottles of all sizes and shapes. These contained the drugs: Tamarind fruit, Cream of Tartar, snakeroot, and dried fern rhizomes. There were emetics, purges, lenitives, sudorifics, and alexipharmics. Some displayed labels of popular patent medicines such as James Powder, which has been called the eighteenth-century aspirin.[11] In Dr. Mitchell's shop one very popular remedy was absent, tar-water. He thoroughly disapproved of this cure-all, suggesting that had the well-known treatise about it been written by "Dean Swift instead of [Bishop] Berkeley, it might have been reckoned a very proper performance for his wit, & a good banter upon the many extravagant publishers of new medicines."[12] He was

9. Phot. 1105, Laing MSS 2:236, UE.

10. *Virginia Gazette*, 21 November 1745.

11. Wyndham B. Blanton, *Medicine in Virginia in the Eighteenth Century* (Richmond, 1931), p. 40.

12. Mitchell to Cadwallader Colden, 10 September 1745, Cadwallader Colden, *Letters and Papers of Cadwallader Colden*, 9 vols. (New York, 1920), 8:326 (subsequently referred to as LPCC).

cautious about accepting reports of remarkable cures due to popular remedies.

To supplement his supply of dried medicinal herbs obtained elsewhere, Mitchell planned to raise many of his own. He had now plenty of land for doing so. He lost no time in enclosing his property with a fence and laying out a physic garden. There was plenty of room for other gardens as well: an herb garden for the kitchen, vegetables for the table, and interesting plants from his botanic studies. He was grateful for all that he had learned from Dr. Alston and was eager to add to this knowledge.

Somewhere along the way Mitchell acquired a wife. No record of the marriage has been discovered. She does not even appear in the family Bible where her husband's birth and death dates are neatly recorded. Her name was Helen and there are occasional references to her but she remains, at this time, a shadowy figure indeed.[13] She and her husband seem to have been well provided with servants, both black and white. There is reference to Jenny, a Negro girl of fifteen, in court records for 1737.[14] Another slave is mentioned in an advertisement for the sale of their house in 1745. Indentured white servants seem to have presented more problems. One, Patrick Flood, was an Irish baker who nonetheless spoke "pretty good English." His romantic Hibernian temperament seems to have led him astray in 1738. In any event, dressed in a cinnamon-colored coat of drugget and new leather breeches, he eloped with one Sarah Carrol on a stolen mare. Sarah was a weaver, tall and slender "with a wry look." Armed with forged passes and discharged indentures, they were believed to have gone south toward Carolina. Whether or not the four gold pistoles which Mitchell offered for their return proved sufficient to blight this romance is unfortunately unknown.[15]

A year later, Mitchell was again offering rewards, this time for the return of two menservants. James Stewart, a Scottish gardener, was "a lusty, short, broad Fellow, with his own Hair, which is of a sandy Colour, and is of about 25 Years of Age; has an honest country Look, and smiles when he speaks, which is pretty broad Scots; and has one

13. The name Helen is mentioned in the deed of sale of the Urbanna property, 8 January 1745/46 (Middlesex County Deed Book, 1740–54, pp. 183–86, VSL).

14. 2 August, Middlesex County Court Orders, 1732–37, p. 85, VSL.

15. *Virginia Gazette*, 17 March 1738.

Leg a little shorter than the other. He had on, when he went away, a very good black Rateen Coat, with close Cuffs and Horse Hair Buttons, a Manx Cloth Jacket and Breeches. . . ." His companion was an Irishman of no particular trade, a fat man with a high color. Mitchell offered three pistoles for the return of Stewart but only two for Campbell. Two were sufficient as a reward for Campbell at least, for he was returned and continued to be a troublemaker.[16] He made complaints to the court about Mitchell in August, 1742. The court dismissed the charges when it met in September.[17]

Young doctors with limited practice were often saved financial embarrassment in those days by appointments to care for the poor of the parish. The fees were not munificent but they did supply a small basic income in tobacco and provided the experience which a young physician needed. In 1735, the vestry of Christ Church, Middlesex, offered this post to Mitchell and he accepted.[18] His financial position is by no means clear. It seems probable that his father had provided the funds for his education, his new home and practice from the estate left by his mother. She seems to have left no will but her husband should have inherited a considerable estate. This belief is supported by the fact that Mitchell appeared in his father's will only as a residuary legatee.

The county which Mitchell had chosen for his practice was a prosperous one. Middlesex had a number of wealthy planters with fine estates. One of the more noteworthy of these was Ralph Wormley. His home was Rosegill, noted among other things, for a very fine library, said to be even better than that of William Byrd. His wife was Sarah, daughter of Edmund Berkeley II, the owner of Barn Elms. The Beverleys lived at Brandon, the Robinsons at Hewick, and the Corbins at Buckingham. The last were extremely wealthy even by Virginia standards. Their home consisted of two large brick buildings, connected by a bridge, having floors and mantels of marble. Colonel William Churchill lived at Bushy Park and the Whitings at Montebello. All of

---

16. Ibid., 23 May 1739.

17. Middlesex County Court Orders, 1740–44, pp. 198 and 201, VSL.

18. G. S. Chamberlayne, *The Vestry Book of Christ Church Parish, Middlesex County, Virginia, 1663–1767* (Richmond, 1927), p. 231. The following payments of tobacco "allow'd pr Acct" were made to Mitchell: 800 pounds on 12 October 1736 (p. 241); 125 pounds on 12 October 1738 (p. 246); 1300 pounds on 8 October 1741 (p. 254); and 75 pounds on 12 October 1744 (p. 261). Actually, Dr. Bird replaced Dr. Mitchell as parish doctor in 1741 (p. 255).

these men played a prominent part as Councillors and Burgesses in the government at Williamsburg. Medical practice should have been lucrative but Mitchell was only one of several doctors who shared it. It is not known which, or how many, of these families were his patients.[19] Sarah Lister, ward of Edmund Berkeley, was one, but her guardian also employed another physician.[20] Patients or not, Mitchell was associated with most of them in one way or another. Richard Corbin is known to have been a particular friend. A Commission of Peace appointed in December, 1738, included Mitchell, Corbin, Wormley, and a Mr. Montague.

While building a medical practice took time, it also gave Mitchell some leisure in which to pursue his other interests. Some of it he devoted to exploring and botanizing in Middlesex and adjoining counties. The familiar Virginia landscape held a new fascination since his botanic studies at Edinburgh. He was eager to find new plants to report to friends there and to satisfy his own curiosity. He brought in many specimens to dry for his *Hortus Siccus*, and others were planted in his garden for further observation. All were studied with care and the more he studied the more he missed Alston and the university library. He had brought some books with him from Scotland, and had access to others, among which were Boerhaave's catalogue of the plants at Leyden as well as that of Herman, Ray's *History of Plants*, Tournefort's *Institutiones Rei Herbariae*, one of Columna's, the first volume of Catesby's *Natural History of Carolina*, Parkinson's *Theatrum Botanicum*, Denis Dodart's *Memoires pour servir a l'Histoire des Plantes*, and Morison's *History of Plants*. Of those books which he used, Ray's with its account of the plants which John Banister had collected in Virginia, was the most useful. There were still many which he could not identify and thought to be new, but he very much needed a fellow botanist with whom to exchange opinions.[21]

Although botanists were indeed scarce in eighteenth-century Virginia, it was not long before this problem was partially solved, as the most able among them was actually not too far away from Urbanna. He was John Clayton (1693–1773), Clerk of Gloucester County Court,

19. Carroll C. Chowning, "Some Colonial Homes of Middlesex County," *William and Mary Quarterly*, 2d ser. 22 (April 1942):145–57.

20. Berkeley Papers, Alderman Library, University of Virginia.

21. Mitchell to Alston, 4 October 1738, Laing MSS, UE.

whom Mitchell either met on a plant-collecting expedition or through mutual friends. Clayton had been born in England and had come to Virginia about 1715. For many years he had been avidly collecting plants, specimens of which he sent to the famous Mark Catesby in England. Clayton's father, the attorney general of the Colony, had met Catesby during his visit to Virginia in 1712 when both men were guests of William Byrd II at Westover. As Catesby remained in Virginia for seven years, there is every likelihood that it was he who first interested Clayton in botany.[22] Catesby left Virginia in 1719 but was later sent out by English patrons to collect in the Carolinas and the Bahama Islands. When he returned to England permanently in 1726, he commenced his life work, the magnificent *History of Carolina*, in which he recorded the birds, fish, insects, animals, and plants of the New World. He illustrated it with large engravings, often handcolored, of sketches which he had made, many of them from life. These delightful illustrations insured the immense success of the work, which was published in sections. The first five of these were completed in 1732 to form the first volume. It was not until 1747 that the second volume and appendix were finally completed. By 1738, and possibly before, Mitchell was finding Catesby's first volume extremely useful. It may have been Clayton's copy that he borrowed or he may well have ordered one for himself by then.[23]

From Clayton, Mitchell heard much about Johann Frederic Gronovius (1690–1762), a Leyden doctor. About 1735, when Catesby found duplicates among Clayton's plant specimens and seeds, he started sending them on to his friend Gronovius, who was another natural history buff. It was not long before Clayton was collecting directly for the Leyden doctor, forwarding them to him through Catesby.[24]

It was just about this time that Gronovius's interest was further stimulated by the arrival in Holland of a young Swedish doctor, Carolus Linnaeus, a name familiar to botanists and nonbotanists today, and sometimes called the "father of modern botany." It was Gronovius

22. For a life of Clayton, see Edmund Berkeley and Dorothy Smith Berkeley, *John Clayton: Pioneer of American Botany* (Chapel Hill, 1963).

23. For a life of Catesby, see George Frederick Frick and Raymond Phineas Stearns, *Mark Catesby: The Colonial Audubon* (Urbana, 1961).

24. Berkeley and Berkeley, *Clayton*, pp. 58–59.

and a Scottish friend, Isaac Lawson, who financed the publication of Linnaeus's *Systema Naturae*. Linnaeus, Gronovius, Lawson, another doctor, two chemists, and a microscopist formed a select group which met each winter Saturday evening. Under Linnaeus's presidency, the members studied botanical, zoological, and mineral specimens, often testing the practicality of his method of classification. Many of the plants used were those sent by Clayton.[25]

Prodded by Gronovius's enthusiasm and encouragement, Clayton was spending every available moment in searching not only his own county, but far and wide, for new plants. He was delighted to find a young man with similar interests, and their meeting was mutually beneficial. Mitchell must have learned much from Clayton's greater experience with local *flora*, and his advices from Catesby, Gronovius, and Linnaeus. He could relate much of what he had learned at Edinburgh and he even turned up some plants that Clayton had missed. The two men must surely have enjoyed discussing the international botanical circle which was then operating in many countries in an informal fashion. Collectors in England and on the Continent were eager for New World discoveries and encouraged the colonists to become collectors. They even financed expeditions by people such as Catesby and, by correspondence, they exchanged a great deal of information and supplied the needed incentive to spur the collectors on.

Mitchell was already familiar with the names of men such as Sir Hans Sloane (1660–1753) in London and Johann Jacob Dillenius (1687–1747) at Oxford, both of whom Alston had mentioned in his lectures. Dillenius, a German botanist, was then Sherardian Professor of Botany at Oxford, and both Clayton and John Bartram in Philadelphia had been sending him plants. Mitchell may not have known of Peter Collinson (1694–1768), a Quaker merchant in London, who perhaps did more than any other man to keep the various members of the botanical circle in touch with each other. His vast correspondence provided a medium for the exchange of information and he was eagerly promoting the introduction of plants from the colonies into England. It was he who distributed the seeds and plants collected by Bartram among those in England who could afford them, and collected from them the funds which remunerated Bartram. He had a number of correspondents in

25. Ibid., pp. 59–62.

Virginia, including John Custis, William Byrd II, John and Isham Randolph, and Clayton.[26]

This network of men all over the Western Hemisphere, working together to uncover nature's secrets, is fascinating. For many the only connection was by correspondence. Few would ever meet. Yet from what Clayton said, it was obvious that many became as close friends with men an ocean apart as with those whom they saw daily. This was particularly important to those isolated members of the circle in the colonies, who felt far removed from the learned world and very much in need of encouragement and support. To know that the august members of scientific societies, such as the Royal Society of London, were interested in their work did much to keep up their spirits and enthusiasm.

When Mitchell made Clayton's acquaintance, the latter was involved in drawing up "A Catalogue of Plants, Fruits and Trees Native to Virginia" for Gronovius, in appreciation for the Dutchman's assistance. When he finally dispatched it to Holland, Gronovius, without the Virginian's knowledge or permission, published it in 1739 under the title of *Flora Virginica*. Clayton was evidently more gratified than offended by the liberty, since he collaborated with Gronovius in preparing a second part of the *Flora* which was published in 1743, and collected material for a projected third part which never appeared. This *Flora Virginica*, and a later edition in 1762, became the first Virginia *flora* and the only one published for two centuries.

Mitchell and Clayton were unfortunately not close neighbors. Depending on the roads which existed at that time, they were fifteen or twenty miles apart, a goodly distance on horseback. Nevertheless, they managed to meet and to visit one another from time to time. When Mitchell found what he considered a new plant, he consulted Clayton. Those which were new duly appeared in the second edition of the *Flora* with proper acknowledgment.

On his collecting trips, Mitchell was ranging as far as time permitted. Over in Lancaster County, he discovered a pondweed, of which Clayton wrote in the *Flora*: "Our friend D. J. Mitchel first collected this specimen in Lancaster County, near the edge of the sea called Chesapeack. It flowers at the end of July."[27] Nearer home in

26. Ibid., pp. 84–85 and 80–84.
27. John Clayton and John Frederic Gronovius, *Flora Virginica* (Leiden, 1762), p. 23.

Middlesex and Essex Counties, Mitchell explored Dragon Swamp, described by a contemporary as "near sixty miles long, and is over-run with briars, thorns and wild beasts, which herd there, because the place being almost inaccessible, the inhabitants cannot come at them, at least not so easily. . . ."[28] There he found an unidentified ivy about which Clayton commented in the *Flora*: "It was first discovered by D. Mitchel in a deserted, bushy marsh (called in English Dragon Swamp) and is now a delicate nursling of his garden."[29] Clayton also credited Mitchell with "The Euonymous with oblong, lanceolate leaves, bearing petioles, a capsule with four receptacles, with compartments, each compressed sharply in the manner of the Fraxinella capsules, was discovered by D. Mitchel" (*Euonymous atropurpureus Jacq.*).[30]

Mitchell soon joined the ranks of those who were sending plants to Dillenius at Oxford. Dillenius was particularly interested in the mosses, but Mitchell sent him both seeds and plants of the higher plants which soon found a place in the Oxford physic garden. In 1737, he sent a shipment of several hundred plants, of which the only one specifically mentioned was *Yucca filamentosa* L. In 1738, he sent a large collection of seeds.[31] The catalogue of plants in the Oxford garden, which Dillenius prepared a few years later, does not credit Mitchell with many of those present.[32] There were, however, a great many Virginia plants, and Dillenius was not noted for crediting his sources. Among these were species of *Euonymus*, *Aralia*, Sumac, Cedar, Arbutus, Red Bud, Virginia Creeper, and others. Among the eleven that Dillenius did attribute to Mitchell was *Ketmia Syres*. This may have been *Hibiscus palustris* L., although someone has added a notation of "snowdrop tree" to Dillenius's notes, which would suggest *Halesia carolina* L. There was a Dogwood from Mitchell which Dillenius noted had bloomed in May–June. There was also a wild cherry and several hawthorns, including a *Crataegus crus-galli* L. or "Cockspur Hawthorn." A "Lotus" was also one of Mitchell's. This was probably what is now known as *Celtis occidentalis* L., the hackberry or nettle tree (Pliny had used the term for

28. *A New and Complete History of the British Empire in America* (London, 1756), pp. 185–86.

29. Clayton and Gronovius, *Flora Virginica*, p. 34.

30. Ibid., p. 33.

31. Mitchell to Alston, 4 October 1738, Laing MSS, UE.

32. Sherard MSS #208, Bodleian Western MSS, Oxford University, subsequently referred to as OU.

a sweet-berried lotus which had been described by Herodotus and others). There was an Acacia, called by Mitchell "Honey Pod," which was *Gleditsia triacanthus* L. or Honey Locust. Two Virginia grapes, one a Fox Grape, came from Mitchell several years later. Collinson had donated a Red Root (*Lachnanthes tinctoria* [Walt.] Ellis) from some of the plants which he had received from Mitchell.

So valuable did Dillenius find his North American moss collections, that he postponed publishing his account of the mosses in 1740 until he could study parcels which he expected from Bartram, Clayton, and Mitchell.[33] He then proceeded to publish his *Historia Muscorum*, in which there are few accreditations. Mitchell's name does not appear at all but in Dillenius's herbarium two of his mosses have survived the years.[34] In February, 1742/43, Dillenius gave Collinson a copy of his book to be forwarded to Mitchell. He did not send it directly, but shipped it in care of John Custis, to whom he was writing. He suggested that he read it and commented that "It is a surpriseing Curious Work who both Collected the Materials and Drew them very Curiously on paper & then Engraved them all himself. Please to give Dr. Mitchell Notice of it, that He may Send for It as oppertunity offers."[35]

Dillenius was not the only recipient of plants from Mitchell. On 4 October 1738, he sent a shipment of 42 plants to Dr. Alston at Edinburgh, with an accompanying letter.[36] It was his first shipment to Alston and was probably inspired by news of his appointment as Professor of Botany in March of that year, although Mitchell made no reference to it. Alston seems to have been a somewhat formidable personality and even while sending him what must have been a very welcome gift, Mitchell is somewhat apologetic. He explained that he was

33. Collinson to Bartram, 10 June 1740, William Darlington, ed., *Memorials of John Bartram and Humphry Marshall* (Philadelphia, 1849), p. 135.

34. #476, *Authouros laevis*, L., "Represented only by the plant from Virginia e Dr. Mitchell . . ." (C. G. Druce and S. H. Vines, *An Account of the Dillenian Collections in the Herbarium of the University of Oxford* [Oxford, 1907], p. 217) and *Mnium reclinatum*: "In Virginia paludosis legit J. Mitchell, Dill." (J. Mitchell collected [it] in the swamps of Virginia) in James Edward Smith, "Remarks on the Generic Character of Mosses, and Particularly of the Genus *Mnium*," *Transactions of the Linnean Society of London*, 7 (1804): 262.

35. Collinson to Custis, 6 February, Earl G. Swem, *Brothers of the Spade: Correspondence of Peter Collinson of London, and of John Custis, of Williamsburg, Virginia, 1734–1746* (Barre, Massachusetts, 1957), p. 85.

36. Laing MSS, UE.

taking the liberty of sending them as he knew that they had not been in the gardens when he was a student. He begged that Alston would correct any mistakes which he had made in assigning them to genera and species. It was an interesting collection. There were two which Mitchell considered to be species of *Sassafras*. The first, evidently *Sassafras albidum* (Nutt.) Nees, he referred to as the *Sassafras* "of the shops, who are unacquainted with the three best parts of this most salutiferous tree viz. the bark of the root, the berries & their expressed oil, with wch. they much abound." His second appears to have been our Spicebush, *Lindera Benzoin* (L.) Blume, a well-known specific for the treatment of colic, according to Mitchell. A Dogwood (*Cornus florida* L.) was included because its bark was often used as a substitute for Jesuits' bark or quinine. He had observed cures with it in some difficult cases. His contemporary, William Byrd II, had made good use of it in treating malaria when his party was surveying the North Carolina-Virginia line.[37] In addition to these, the box contained plants of Sweet Gum, Black Gum, Redbud, Black Walnut, Hickory, Blood Root, Lupin, Chinquapin, and a number of others. He offered to send any particular plants that Alston might wish since this was but a small sample of those available. He had hoped to send a catalogue of all of the plants but "for want of a Botanical library & Companion" he had not completed it and had begun to doubt that he ever would.

There were several plants that Mitchell believed to have good possibilities as drug plants but which he was reluctant to discuss with Alston until he had more opportunity to make observations of their effectiveness. He requested Alston's advice concerning the preferred method of testing a new plant for medicinal properties. He knew that a chemical analysis was a very desirable starting point but he was not then equipped to undertake one. For that reason he was enclosing a sample of the popular Rattle snake-root (*Polygala senega* L.) hoping that some chemist at the university would make an analysis for him. He then demonstrated his caution in such matters by adding that it was:

37. "Several of our men had Intermitting feavers, but were soon restor'd to their Health again by proper Remedies. Our chief Medicine was Dogwood Bark, which we used, instead of that of Peru, with good Success. Indeed, it was given in larger Quanty, but then to make the Patients amends, they swallowed much fewer Doses." William Byrd, *Histories of the Dividing Line Betwixt Virginia and North Carolina*, with introductions by William K. Boyd and Percy G. Adams (New York, 1967), p. 148.

a medicine generally used by our Patients; to the no small detriment of some of them; for altho it's virtues seem to be great, yet they are unknown. I have known it vomit, purge violently, sweat, as violently, prove diuretic, & an-others have no sensible operation; according to the Regimen, constitution, distemper (for it's applyed in all) of the Patient, & dose of the medicine, which is undetermined. I have been credibly informed of two persons, cured of an Anasaria [dropsy], threatning an Ascites [hydroperitoneum], by the sole use of this medicine; which it carried off by Urine. I have known severall that have taken it, in the first attack of the gout, of wt some have imagined they were relieved thereby; but most (of whom I have seen some) have com-plained that in a little time after the use of it, they have found it attack them with much more violence, & in allmost all the joints of their body at once; which would leave them, on the disuse of the medicine & return on its' use. as for the distemper its first discoverer applyed it to, I believe few can judge from his inaccurate observations, what it was; nor does he seem to write as if he knew it himself. . . .

Mitchell's last bitter comment referred to the recent publication, *Essay on the Pleurisy*, by Dr. John Tennent of Williamsburg. Tennent had become almost a fanatic in his advocacy of snakeroot as a remedy for pleurisy. He had secured endorsements from Byrd and Sir Hans Sloane, even traveling to England in his promotion of the cause. The Burgesses had rewarded him with £100 upon his return to Virginia in 1738.[38]

Mitchell concluded his commentary on the snakeroot by noting that "we have a particular Peripneumonia Notha frequently epidemic among the labourers of this Countrey; the Pathognomic of which is a sudden debility, occasioned (as appears by the opening dead bodies) by an obstruction of the lungs that are puffed up, as it were by the wind, with a livid grumous blood like half coagulated milk; the history of which distemper is particular; in which this root seems to promise some good effect." If this were the present-day virus or primary atypi-cal pneumonia, snakeroot probably did help in its treatment as it is still used today in bronchitis as an expectorant.

For over five years Mitchell, as an educated and mature man, had observed his native land. He had committed his random thoughts on the various aspects of nature and medicine to scattered notes in a series of journals. Just prior to 1738, he began a correspondence with that

38. Raymond Phineas Stearns, *Science in the British Colonies of America* (Urbana, 1970), pp. 289–90.

fascinating character, Peter Collinson, which inspired him to carry his scientific activities further. Collinson seems to have initiated the correspondence but it may have been suggested by any one of several mutual friends. Clayton or William Byrd would be possibilities but the most likely was Byrd's brother-in-law, John Custis of Williamsburg. Custis was an avid gardener who frankly considered his garden to be the finest in Virginia. He had started a correspondence with Collinson in 1734 when his friends, Sir John Randolph and Isham Randolph, told him that Collinson was anxious to obtain some Virginia Bluebells (*Mertensia virginica* [L.], Pers.) and he had obliged by sending both seeds and roots.[39] No matter how Mitchell's correspondence with Collinson began, it became a very much valued and important one to him, as he very freely admitted. To Mitchell he was, as he was to so many others, both guide and goad. He became tutor to the Virginian's postgraduate studies in natural history. Encouraged, Mitchell began to study his observations, formulate his thoughts and opinions, and reach for answers to problems. Some of his ideas resulted in articles on varying subjects and a few eventually found their way into print.

39. Custis to Collinson, 1734, Swem, *Brothers of the Spade*, p. 23.

III ❧ Botanical Harvest

> "Whatever I have written *on plants is at* your request and exhortation *and you* are yearly a spur and incitement to one that is lazy in botanical matters. . . ."
>
> Mitchell to Collinson, 11 March 1741[1]

In the course of collecting and studying Virginia plants, Mitchell found himself frustrated time and again in his attempts to identify and classify them. Like most collectors, he was delighted to find what he believed to be unknown plants, but when he attempted to place them according to any of the existing systems with which he was familiar, he found it very difficult to do so. He became increasingly disillusioned with them and remembered the criticisms that Alston had made of them in his classes. Gradually he began to evolve what seemed to him a sound basis for a practical method, one involving both scientific deduction and logical reasoning, both of which he believed to be lacking from existing systems. Eventually, in 1738, his ideas crystallized sufficiently to enable him to compose a summary of them. As an introduction he wrote:

The first principle and very foundation of botany and zoology seems to be the interpretation of genera, the study of all described species, combining those which agree in a great many natural characteristics and special attributes, and separating those which differ in the same. It is not yet well-understood, in spite of the hard work of so many men, and there is no general agreement among those who are concerned with it, as to which plants or which animals belong to which genus, much less which, or even how many, attributes of the appropriate genus are required to establish a natural pattern. It would seem to me to follow from this—that no certain and proven principles preponderate, nor any proofs known from these, nor even any method of experiment from which (as in all other natural sciences) they are bound by logic to deduce and demonstrate its principles—that just as it is true of holy writ, it is necessary to accept some things not fully understood . . . no matter how carefully and repeatedly we define genera, they none-the-less are satisfied to assemble together by genus plants which differ in some measure from

---

1. Herbert Thatcher, "Dr. Mitchell, M.D., F.R.S., of Virginia," *Virginia Magazine of History and Biography* 40 (January 1932):102.

the given generic description, and vice-versa, which is well-known by all who prefer to deduce science from nature rather than from books.[2]

In reviewing the various systems of classification which had been used, Mitchell came to the conclusion that there were but two bases "from which they derive the indices of generic agreement." The first was conformity in many attributes and the second only in the structure of the reproductive organs. In objection to the first, he felt that "in establishing a method of plant (classification), in resolving it and making it simple, one does not by any means drily undertake an investigation of the many attributes and a selection of one which conforms in most of the greatest characteristics as evidence; and consequently the promoters of this system, when it comes to establishing the generic character which (or how many) attributes are necessary to establish . . . the genus . . . come to a standstill, and are divided into different opinions." They distrust their judgment so much that, with superficial botanical knowledge, they all, like so many automatons, "join the same plants together; they are, however, unable to teach others their science or to propose any firm and definite principles."[3]

The most knowledgeable botanists, Mitchell thought, had turned to the second method, grouping on a basis of the reproductive structures. He thought that this, too, had suffered from many of the defects of the first. Although there are a large number of reproductive parts "never is it explained or established which might be the necessary parts, or even the most essential, for determining this generic relationship or difference." Consequently, there was a plethora of systems "in which each person is his own Law," and great confusion arises "from the diversity of these principles and systems . . . since they increase rather than decrease in producing new ones. Indeed, most botanists, with a certain illicit caprice, and more by unrestrained disapproval than by sound laws, overthrow the discoveries of our ancestors, change the names, classes, families, genera and species . . . and surrender rules from a plundered science to establish their own opinion, and, what is worse,

2. D. D. Jo. Mitchell, "Dissertatio Brevis de Principiis Botanicorum et Zoologorum deque novo stabilende naturae rerum congruo cum Appendice Aliquot Generum plantarum recens conditorum . . ." *Acta Physico-Medica Academae Caesarae . . . Ephemerides* 8 (1748):88.

3. Ibid., 189–90.

they contend that all of the rules of their system are better than the laws of nature."[4]

Since there is great diversity in reproductive structures, many plants were arbitrarily placed in the same genus which showed little relationship to each other. This artificial system, having no natural basis, made no allowance for such discrepancies. The Palm, Mitchell thought, to be a flagrant example. Such systems produced very strange bedfellows when their overall characteristics and appearance were considered. External appearance alone might give a better clue to true relationship.[5]

Mitchell believed that only a system based on natural laws could have any long-range validity. He recognized that practical aspects would make such a system difficult and he was not anxious to be critical of others, but his quarrel was that these systems did not work either. He believed that by a careful study of nature true laws of relationship would become apparent. When these were known, all botanists could cooperate in establishing rules to follow.[6]

He was not being entirely theoretical. He had a method to propose which would be truly natural. How practical it was is another matter. In arriving at his proposal he recognized that, in plants as well as in animals, nothing was more important in nature than methods of reproduction, although the "structure or shape of the parts is often inconstant and variable." For that reason, if "the application of these" is examined, a relationship can be established:

Animals had first suggested this consideration to me and I shall provide an example: in these indeed we see a great many different cohabitations for impregnating themselves reciprocally: I am convinced the most part of these belong to the same genus, however much authors are divided on the different directions of nature's law, the most studious accept from the practice of nature herself: thus, I say the horse and the ass by their very nature belong to the same genus of animals of which the most decided proof is the mule, a product of both. . . .

Such characteristics as length of ears, tail, and mane Mitchell believed to be specific rather than generic. Thus, by hybridization, animals demonstrate a generic relationship. Zoologists had been quite as dilatory as botanists in recognizing this obvious clue. They had largely ne-

4. Ibid., 190–91.
5. Ibid., 191–92.
6. Ibid., 193–94.

glected the experimental approach which this would make possible.[7]

Lacking such experiments, it was necessary to study those known to have occurred largely by chance. Mitchell viewed many such reports with skepticism but considered them. He avoided basing any definite conclusion on most of them because he did not think that the accounts could be trusted. Thus, he mentioned the Kumrah, offspring of a cross between an ass and a cow. This had first been reported by Caesar's Carthaginians long ago and more recently by Dr. Shaw in the account of his African journey. Mitchell wished that Shaw "had sensibly described the particular nature of the animal and the arrangement of birth." Other examples mentioned included the Leopard or Lion-panther, the Camel-panther, the Lynx-panther, the Wolf-dog, the Dog-wolf, the Ram-she-goat "provided there may be such, Dog-cat, Baboon-man, and similar other mules, hybrids and wonders here and there mentioned by authors; however, I greatly doubt the existence of so very many productions against the laws of nature . . . or at least in a constant and non-artificial production."[8]

If, in a number of cases, certain animals of different types consistently produced offspring, they would then be considered as belonging to the same genus, even though the offspring might differ considerably from either parent. Many observations and many experiments would be necessary to establish all of the genera. If this were not enough to keep the zoologists busy, Mitchell suggested some related studies. Would it be possible to study in detail the sperm "in whatever uterus" and the ensuing process of gestation up until birth? Should not the varying forms and actions of the reproductive organs be studied? Should not there be comparative studies of gestation periods and numbers of off-spring? He marveled over the case of the mule, where the sperm in the uterus of a different species developed into an offspring so different from the ass: "when a female of the same genus introduces such a meta-morphosis of the ass's seed, does it not seem credible, a great future alteration in heterogenous females. . . ."[9]

Animal species, in Mitchell's view, would be those "truly different ones which bear abundant and prolific offspring, or are vigorous to propagate a species, a species to differ little, to diversify only by acci-

7. Ibid., 194–95.
8. Ibid., 195–96.
9. Ibid., 196–98.

dent." To illustrate his point he quoted John Ray, who claimed that all dogs belong to the same species "they mingling together in generation, & the breed of such mixtures being prolifick." He disagreed with Ray in believing that deer in Virginia were the same species as those in England which Ray had questioned.[10]

Mitchell then turned his attention to the plant kingdom, for which he laid down three postulates which he considered to have been established by experimental studies of the last twenty-five years. The first of these was that plants, like animals, have male and female reproductive organs for generation of offspring. He cited in support of that view the experiments of James Logan, of Philadelphia, as reported in his article, "Some Experiments Concerning the Impregnation of the Seeds of Plants," in the Royal Society's *Transactions* for 1736.[11] Logan was not the first to recognize sexuality in plants but he was probably the first to demonstrate it experimentally. Logan had used the Indian corn, about which he wrote:

In each corner of my Garden . . . I planted a Hill of that Corn, and watching the Plants when they grew up to a proper Height, and were pushing out both the Tassels above, and the Ears below; from one of those Hills, I cut off the whole Tassels, on others I carefully open'd the Ends of the Ears, and from some of them I cut or pinc'd off all the silken filaments; from others I took about half, from others one fourth and three fourths etc. with some Variety, noting the Heads, and the Quantity taken from each: Other heads again I tied up at their Ends, just before the Silk was putting out, with fine Muslin, but the Fuzziest or most Nappy I could find, to prevent the Passage of the *Farina*; but that would obstruct neither Sun, Air or Rain. I fastened it also very loosely, as not to give the least Check to Vegetation.

The Consequence of all which was this, that of the five or six Ears on the first Hill, from which I had taken all the Tassels, from whence proceeds the *Farina*, there was only one that had so much as a single Grain in it, and that in about four hundred and eight Cells, had but twenty or twenty one Grains, the Heads, or Ears, as they stood on the Plant, look'd as well to the Eye as any other. . . .

In the Ears of the other Hills, from which I had taken all of the Silk, and in those that I had cover'd with Muslin, there was not so much as one mature grown Grain, nor other than as I have mentioned in the first: But in all the

---

10. Ibid., 198–200.
11. Ibid., 192–95.

others, in which I had left Part, and taken Part of the Silk, there was in each the exact Proportion of full Grains. . . .

This beautiful experiment has been cited often and deserves to be. Mitchell was in complete agreement with Logan concerning the sexual process in plants although, curiously enough, his old professor, Alston, was still unconvinced twenty years later.[12] Furthermore, Logan had demonstrated precisely the experimental approach which Mitchell thought should be applied to taxonomy.

Mitchell's second postulate was that plants which are of the same species mutually fertilize and produce abundant fertile offspring. He believed that this had been clearly established by the observations of Philip Miller, author of the well-known *Gardener's Dictionary*, who had reported his observations of cross-fertilization in cabbages and other plants. Thirdly, Mitchell postulated that plants which are of different species may still cross-fertilize but that their hybrid offspring will be sterile. By way of illustration he cited the experiments of Thomas Fairchild mentioned by Alston in his *materia medica* lectures. They had first been described by Richard Bradley in 1717.[13] Fairchild had successfully crossed the Carnation with the Sweet William. The resulting hybrid had "its flowers double like the Carnation—the size of a Pink—but clusters like the Sweet William . . ." but was sterile.[14]

Thus, Mitchell continued, since Nature is consistent in all things, if different species of a genus produce sterile hybrids when crossed, then, logically, plants which produce either monsters or no offspring at all when crossed must belong to different genera. If this view is accepted, then an experimental basis is provided for determining the generic relationships of plants. Taxonomists need only master the comparatively simple technique of artificially pollinating the flowers of the plants which they wish tested, and then study carefully the results. If

12. In vol. 25 (1755):465–66, of the *Gentleman's Magazine* there was an article by Alston describing his experiments with violets, hemp, spinach, and mercury which he was convinced disproved the bisexuality of plants.

13. Mitchell, "Dissertatio Brevis . . . ," pp. 200–201. Pulteney described Bradley as "a popular writer on Gardening and Agriculture" who made no really new discoveries of his own but whose collection of others' work was important. He published a series, in decades, called *Succulent Plants* between 1716 and 1727 (2:129–32).

14. Collinson to Bartram, 22 July 1740, Darlington, *Memorials*, p. 36. This was a cross between *Dianthus caryophyllus* and *D. barbatus* (Conway Zirkle, "Plant Hybridization and Plant Breeding in Eighteenth-Century American Agriculture," *Agricultural History* 43 [January 1969]:29).

abundant and fertile offspring are produced, then the plants are of the same species; if sterile offspring resulted, then the plants were of different species but the same genus; if no offspring were produced, or if monsters were formed, then the plants belonged to different genera. While an experimental basis was provided for the determination of genera, a further method would be needed for the establishing of families, tribes, orders, and classes.[15]

This essay established Mitchell as the first North American to write on taxonomic principles. He anticipated Clements's call for an "experimental taxonomy" by one hundred and sixty odd years. It is unfortunate that Heiser overlooked both of these points in his recent short history of taxonomy.[16] As Zirkle so correctly pointed out, Mitchell understood the true significance of hybridization, and "he made a most logical attempt to place taxonomy on a genetic basis. If his suggestion had been followed it is possible that today we should have neither 'splitters' nor 'lumpers.' At least the species concept would be precise and classification would be on an objective basis." We would not have had to wait until the 1920s for the beginnings of the "new taxonomy."[17]

To Collinson, Mitchell dispatched his taxonomic treatise and descriptions of thirty new genera, writing him that these were "the *first fruits of my botanical labours*, and [*I*] *send you 560 specimens of somewhat rare plants* as a gift, to be passed on to your botanists for the furthering in any way of the *divine science*. . . ." This letter was dated 11 March 1741 and is the only surviving evidence of a correspondence between Collinson and Mitchell which began much earlier.[18] Collinson was delighted with Mitchell's fine collection of plant specimens, as well he should have been. One in particular fascinated him. This was the Cucumber Tree, *Magnolia acuminata* L. Mitchell had obtained the specimen from a tree in a pasture on Nicholas Smith's plantation in Essex County, which had attracted a great deal of attention. A tree of the mountains, it was certainly a long way from home in Essex County.[19]

15. Mitchell, "Dissertatio Brevis . . . ," pp. 201-2.

16. Charles B. Heiser, Jr., "Taxonomy" in Joseph Ewan, ed., *A Short History of Botany in the United States* (New York, 1969), pp. 110-15.

17. Conway Zirkle, *The Beginnings of Plant Hybridization* (Philadelphia, 1935), p. 140.

18. Thatcher, "Dr. Mitchell," *Virginia Magazine of History and Biography* 40 (April 1932):101.

19. Bartram to Mitchell, 3 June 1744, Darlington, *Memorials*, p. 364. and Collinson to Custis, 10 March 1743/44, ibid., p. 171.

Travelers went out of their way to see it and unsuccessful attempts to propagate it had been made by Byrd, Clayton, Custis, and Mitchell.[20]

Some of the plants included in Mitchell's new genera had been known for some years but he was convinced that they had either been poorly described or placed in a wrong genus. As an instance of this, he objected to Gronovius' treatment of our Trailing Arbutus in his editing of Clayton's *Flora Virginica*:

So, for example, the most expert botanist, Dr. Gronovius, referred our Memaecylum to the [genus] Arbutus (F. Virg. p. 49) and reconciled [it] by no means unreasonably, following his system; but the Arbutus is a tree, the other so very low as to be trampled underfoot, a small ground-clinging plant, a thing which nevertheless I know some do not consider of much worth; according to Boerhaave, the Arbutus' flower is bell-shaped, spherical and urn-shaped, the Memaecylum, at the same time, is funnel-shaped, long, divided into large slender lobes evenly spread out; the fleshy fruit of the former is berry-like, the latter delights in a dry, fragmented capsule, as I assume the calyx and the involucre [whorl of bracts supporting the flower], in all of which it is easy to differentiate without rejecting nature, although I admit the strong affinity of the genera.[21]

Mitchell emphasized that he preferred to consider the entire plant when determining the genus, although he sometimes found it necessary to use the sexual characters as the main determinant. He preferred to use sexual characters primarily for determining species within a genus. He was somewhat concerned about the propriety of including poisonous species in the same genera with wholesome ones. His main point of emphasis was that criteria for genera should arise *"rather* from the *laws of nature* than from the *opinion of the botanists."*

Collinson was so much impressed with the new genera that he could not resist sending the list on to Linnaeus. The latter inquired concerning the etymology of some of Mitchell's names, particularly that of *Elymus.*[22] When Collinson passed on the inquiry to Mitchell, he replied that he was astonished that Linnaeus would object to it. Linnaeus had criticized Burman "for not knowing or remembering the ancient names; vide *Crit. Bot.* p. 117." Mitchell chose *Elymus* because it was the

20. Collinson to Custis, 2 April 1744, Swem, *Brothers of the Spade*, p. 88.

21. "Letter to the Botanical Reader," Mitchell, "Dissertatio Brevis . . . ," p. 204.

22. Collinson to Linnaeus, 18 January 1743/44, James Edward Smith, *A Selection of the Correspondence of Linnaeus and other Naturalists*, 2 vols. (London, 1821), 1:9, subsequently referred to as CLO.

name that Dioscorides gave *Panicum*. He was not above a little dig himself and remarked that Linnaeus had placed *Diodia* in his fourteenth class when it actually belonged in the fourth.[23] Both Clayton and Mitchell were quite familiar with Linnaeus's system of classification introduced in his *Systema Naturae* in 1735 and elaborated in his *Genera Plantarum* two years later.

Collinson suggested to Mitchell that he be permitted to undertake the immediate publication of his papers but Mitchell delayed him. He wanted to add to what he had sent before publishing any of it. Three years later, on 18 January 1743/44, Collinson wrote to Linnaeus that he hoped "in a year's time you will see his Essays in Botany (In Lattin) printed. I have the First part finished but he intends to add another so the printing of the first is Defer'd."[24] It was still another four years before Mitchell's papers were published.

Mitchell had sent Collinson descriptions of thirty genera.[25] Five of these involved new names or descriptions for existing genera, but twenty-five he believed to be new. He realized that he might well be mistaken about this, and asked Collinson: "If indeed there are any other genera lately determined, and they have not yet been duly seen by me to be in them, I beg you will ascribe to *my abode being off from books and learning* rather than to my carelessness."[26] Mitchell's concern on this point was well founded. Sprague has recently studied his genera and concluded that in 1748 when they were finally published, of the 25 which he believed to be new, 10 actually were, 12 were congeneric with genera already published, and 3 have never been definitely identified.[27] It is unfortunate that Mitchell's genera were not published sooner. Among his genera published by others during the interim, was *Malachodendron*, which Linnaeus converted to *Stewartia*, honoring John Stuart, Earl of Bute, with whom Mitchell by an odd combination of circumstances later became closely associated. *Stewartia malachodendron* today retains Mitchell's generic name as the specific one.

Of those genera which were still new when they were finally pub-

23. Collinson to Linnaeus, 1 September 1745, ibid., 1:13.

24. Ibid., 1:9.

25. It had been hoped to include Mitchell's new plant genera as an appendix to the biography but unfortunately that has not been possible.

26. Mitchell, "Dissertatio Brevis . . . ," p. 205.

27. Thatcher, "Dr. Mitchell," *Virginia Magazine of History and Biography* 40 (April 1932):270.

lished, all but one were included in Linnaeus's *Species Plantarum*, and are thus today attributed to Linnaeus rather than Mitchell. Ironically, only *Penstemon* is credited to Mitchell and that because Linnaeus mistakenly thought it to be a *Chelone* and therefore failed to include it in the *Species Plantarum*.[28] Among those which he did include was our Partridge Berry which he gave the name *Mitchella repens*.

28. Linnaeus to Haller, 13 September 1748, CLO 2:429.

IV ❧ Possums, People, and Pines

"Nor must I pass over the things which both of us have in our minds (owing especially to your support and encouragement) as to the elucidating other parts of the Natural History of Virginia. *. . . ."*

Mitchell to Collinson, 11 March 1741[1]

Mitchell was by no means limiting his investigations to botanical matters. It was almost certainly Collinson who interested him in studies of the most unique animal to be found in North America. Prior to the discovery of this country, Europeans knew only those mammals that we presently call placental mammals, who nourish their embryos internally by a placenta until birth, at which time they are completely formed, even if somewhat helpless. They knew nothing of the egg-laying mammals, the Duckbilled Platypus and the Spiny Anteater, or of the marsupial mammals whose young are brought forth in a very undeveloped state and complete their development in a pouch or marsupium. Their astonishment when they encountered the American o'possum can well be imagined. The quotation from a 1693 letter which follows will serve to illustrate their reaction. The writer was Colonel John Walker of King and Queen County, Virginia, and he was addressing John Evelyn in England. The letter had been suggested by Daniel Parke II, father-in-law of both William Byrd II and John Custis. Parke had asked Walker to send Evelyn some Sassafras oil, and Walker had done so. He accompanied the jars of oil with a letter in which he discussed other curiosities of the New World, one of which was an animal

about the bigness of a raccoone eared like a batt tailed like a Ratt which hath in it a false belley hared on all sides, with dugs in it, out of which duggs come a substance like unto the stones or pride of a sow pigg the biggness of a very small pae, att the biggness of a kidney beane full shape and life hanging att

1. Thatcher, "Dr. Mitchell," *Virginia Magazine of History and Biography* 40 (January 1932):103.

the tett by the mouth to the number of nine some less, pull them of and you teare the teat or mouth, they grow in theire, att the bigness of mise they be haired att the bigness of old mise they fall from the teat and kepe sucking, runing in and out of the false belley till they are biger then the bigist ratt and then left to proide for them selves, their tails always hang out of the false belley like soe many snakes it is a creature that doth hide all day and seeke for food att night which is our green Corne wild fruits, tame and wild foule as the fox it is an extreordinary fatt Creature god rosted the tail poyson in other creatures wheir the parts are all leane this all fatt wee scald them and rost them as a pigg. I told part of this to docter tyson of bethlehem, but I belive he thought it incredable but it is a reall truth I have proved it severall times and sent one to mr. Jno. Watts att Chelsey, the skin with 7 yongue ones nott haired att the tetts they are male and female and in genter as other Creaturs.[2]

Watts was the Curator of the Apothecaries' Garden at Chelsea. Dr. Edward Tyson, to whom Colonel Walker referred, later dissected a female possum that William Byrd II sent to the Royal Society of London in 1697. The society had been presented with one still earlier. Dr. Clopton Havers had given a report of a dissection in 1690, but his account was never published.[3] Tyson's report appeared in the *Philosophical Transactions* of the society in 1698, complete with illustrations. Tyson had also received accounts of the dissection of a male animal by the surgeon William Cowper (later Earl Cowper, Keeper of the Great Seal), but curiosity about the animal continued.[4]

Among Collinson's curious collection of influential friends was Sir Charles Wager, First Lord of the Admiralty, whose officers frequently sent him curiosities which they had encountered in their travels. In 1736, Lady Wager sent a male possum to Collinson and he, in turn, forwarded it to Sir Hans Sloane, then president of the Royal Society. He suggested that Sloane remove the animal from the jar in which he had sent it and keep it in the kitchen until warmer weather.[5] It did not help much, because the possum died. Collinson, as usual, determined to continue the investigation in spite of problems, and wrote to John Custis for help. Custis complied by sending a live female with six

2. #1338, Christ Church College, OU.

3. Stearns, *Science in the British Colonies*, pp. 245–46.

4. Ibid., p. 281.

5. Collinson to Sloane, n.d., Sloane MSS 4058, f. 169, British Museum, subsequently referred to as BM.

young and instructions concerning food and care, but to no avail. All were dead upon arrival. As Custis pointed out, possums in capitivity are not especially attractive, and it had doubtless been neglected aboard ship.[6]

Still determined to get full information about the possum, Collinson tried another tack. In January 1738/39, he wrote to Custis: "I should think that with you a Male & Female might be procur'd and kept in a suitable place paled in with high pales and be so Situate as to be Near Dayly Observation & Inspection and soone after Copulation be Dayly Examined by some person Skilled in surgery and anatomy and if necessary be Desected and Examined, to see if there was any Ducts or Vessels Lead from the Uterus to the Teats, for it is highly probable they First received their Formation and Vivification in the Womb and in their Minutest State by proper ducts be conveyed to the Teat but all this is conjecture it may amaze and confound us, but can't satisfie us. . . ."[7]

Whether Custis or Collinson enlisted Mitchell in the project is not known but he was just the man to take it on. He obtained both male and female possums and made careful dissections of them, sending an account of his findings to Collinson. It was duly presented to the Royal Society and read at a meeting on 10 February 1742/43.[8] Collinson had also made reference to the possum in his letters to John Bartram and Bartram had expressed his contempt for the animal. He was sternly taken to task by Collinson for such an unscientific attitude:

This contemptible creature—in thy eyes—has been remarkably distinguished from other animals, in the wonderful provision contrived for the preservation of its young (as if a creature of great consequence); and another wonder attending it, is, how the young comes so very small to the teat. This, none has yet been able to ascertain, but by conjecture; and it has puzzled all our anatomists to find the apparatus requisite to carry on this delicate operation. Doctor MITCHELL, at Urbana, in Virginia, has employed some of his leisure time in examining the internal structure of this wonderful creature; and I doubt not, but in time, will clear up the doubtful points, as their Generating is Different from most animals so there is reason to believe the other particularities that attends this Creature have some foundation in Nature.[9]

6. Collinson to Custis, 25 January 1738/39, Swem, *Brothers of the Spade*, p. 59.
7. Ibid.
8. Journal Book XVIII, pp. 32–33, Royal Society of London, subsequently referred to as RSL.
9. 16 May 1742, Darlington, *Memorials*, p. 156.

Bartram may or may not have felt properly ashamed of himself after that eloquent discourse. Mitchell, however, was definitely making the proper scientific impression at the English-speaking world's most prestigious scientific society. He was much gratified to learn of the enthusiastic reception given his work. Martin Folkes, who had succeeded Sir Hans Sloane as president of the Royal Society, suggested that two of their medical members, Dr. Edward Milward and Dr. James Parsons, should send Mitchell a list of queries which the society would like him to investigate further. This was accordingly done and Mitchell obtained a pair of possums which he kept in his house for the next two years for intensive study, no doubt to the despair of his wife. Finally, in 1745, he made a detailed and meticulous report of all of his observations.[10] It has been said that "There are few, if any, comparable papers in American zoological literature prior to 1750."[11] In fact, Sir Peter Chalmers, (recently secretary of the Zoological Society of London) wrote to Thatcher: "Without doubt it was a substantial and valuable addition to the knowledge of his time. There are a few points on which he is not quite confirmed by modern knowledge, but he was far in advance of his time."[12]

Having given a detailed report on his anatomical observations of the o'possum, Mitchell added some interesting theory to relate its unique manner of bearing its young to some other unique habits of the animal. He noted that the possum moves very slowly and, if cornered, "lies down as if dead . . . and may be tumbled and tossed about, without once offering to stir." If not cornered, instead of playing possum it will make its way to a tree and hang by its tail. It will also hang by its tail when picking fruit. "Now," Mitchell wrote, "as this inverted pendulous posture of this quadruped seems peculiar to it, so the structure of its parts seems to be made with a design, and as well contrived to suit it. For were the young bred in the womb within the abdomen as in other animals, their compression on the abdominal viscera, when

10. At the Library of Congress (subsequently known as LC), there is a photostat of the letter of Drs. Edward Milward and James Parsons to the Royal Society, Ac3456, Miscellaneous Personal Correspondence. There is also one of Mitchell's report, dated 8 July 1745, and Thatcher published it in his article on Mitchell, *Virginia Magazine of History and Biography* 40 (October 1932):338–46.

11. Hornberger, "The Scientific Ideas," *Huntington Library Quarterly* 10 (January 1946–47):285.

12. "John Mitchell," *Virginia Magazine of History and Biography* 41 (January 1933):60.

the *uterus* comes to be fully distended would either occasion many disasters . . . or would deprive it of this, its greatest preservation." All of which must have sounded very convincing to people unfamiliar with the kangaroo!

Even in discussing the compression of an animal's viscera, Mitchell could not forget his duties as a doctor. He warned his readers on the dangers of pressure on viscera or heart, during gestation or, in fact, at any time. He inveighed against the fashion of "buttoning and lacing tight; by sitting to read and write in a reclining position with pressure upon the *Precordia*, and by lying down with our heads low, when the stomach is distended with meats or drink, but above all with wine." Neither could he forget his religious duties and he ended his dissertation with the comment, "How manifold are thy works, O Lord. In wisdom hast thou made them all."

Mitchell's botanical and zoological studies failed to fully occupy his restless mind and he turned his attention to still another area. He learned that the Academy at Bordeaux had offered its annual prize for the best paper presented on the causes of different pigmentation in people and he felt fully competent to undertake one. He approached the problem in his usual methodical and thorough manner, so much so that he let the deadline for submission of papers pass and, when his paper was complete, it was too late to submit it to the academy. Instead, he sent it to Collinson, saying that his medical duties left him little time for such studies. Despite his apologies he suggested "If you think it deserves so great an Honour, pray communicate it to the Royal Society; and if it merits their particular Regard, I submit it to be printed in your learned and curious Memoirs." His optimism was well founded, for the society devoted four successive meetings in May and June of 1744 to consideration of it, and did publish it in the *Philosophical Transactions* for that year.[13] This was Mitchell's first publication and one can imagine his gratification.

In his approach to the question posed by the Bordeaux Academy, Mitchell borrowed Sir Isaac Newton's method in examining the causes of color. His dissertation thus began with seven "Propositions," each of which he discussed at some length. These were:

13. The Society's Journal Book XIX records the readings on pp. 243, 249, 256, 274–77. Mitchell's letter to Collinson was written on 12 April 1743 and is printed on p. 102 of his essay in the *Philosophical Transactions* 43 (June–December 1744):102–50.

I. The Colour of white People proceeds from the Colour which the Epidermis transmits; that is, from the Colour of the Parts under the Epidermis, rather than from any Colour of its own.

II. The Skins of Negroes are of a thicker Substance, and denser Texture, than those of white People, and transmit no Colour thro' them.

III. The Part of the Skin which appears black in Negroes, is the Corpus reticulare Cutis, and external Lamella of the Epidermis: and all other Parts are of the same Colour in Them with those of white People, except the Fibres which pass between those two Parts.

IV. The Colour of Negroes does not proceed from any black Humour, or fluid Parts contained in their Skins; for there is none such in any Part of their Bodies, more than in white People.

V. The Epidermis, especially its external Lamella, is divided into two Parts, by its Pores and Scales, two hundred times less than the particles of Bodies, on which their Colours depend.

VI. To determine and explain the proximate Cause of the Colour of Negroes, Indians, white People, &c. from the foregoing Propositions.

VII. The Influence of the Sun, in hot Countries, and the Ways of Life of the Inhabitants in them, are the remote Causes of the Colour of Negroes, Indians &c.; And the Ways of Living, in Use among most Nations of white People, make their Colours whiter, than they were originally, or would be naturally.

While Mitchell cited various authorities in supporting his propositions, he had one tremendous advantage over most others writing upon this subject. He was able to draw upon his own observations, dissections, and experiments. He referred to his study of the composition of Negro skin: its thickness, and reaction to blistering and scarring. He could present facts rather than theories on certain points. Perhaps his most significant proposition was number four. In this he categorically denied the validity of the claim of Marcello Malpighi, the great seventeenth-century Italian anatomist, that the black color of Negroes is caused by a juice or fluid of a black color lying beneath the epidermis.

The paper was concluded by Mitchell with a series of Corollaries which he "rationally deduced from the foregoing Propositions." There were eight of these, some rather lengthy. The last of them, Corollary VII, is the most interesting:

From what has been said about the Cause of the Colour of black and white People we may justly conclude, that they might very naturally be both descended from one and the same Parents, as we are better assured from Scripture, that they are; which may remove the Scruples of some nice Philosophers on this Matter, who cannot or will not believe even the Scriptures, unless it be so far as they can be made agreeable to their Philosophy: For the different Colours of People have been demonstrated to be only the necessary Effects, and natural Consequences, of their respective Climes, and Ways of Life; as we may further learn from Experience, that they are the most suitable for the Preservation of Health, and the Ease and Convenience of Mankind in these Climes, and Ways of Living: So that the black Colour of the Negroes of *Africa*, instead of being a Curse denounced on them, on account of their Forefather *Ham*, as some have idly imagined, is rather a Blessing, rendering their lives, in that intemperate Region, more tolerable, and less painful: Whereas, on the other hand, the white People, who look on themselves as the primitive Race of Men, from a certain Superiority of Worth, either supposed or assumed, seem to have the least Pretensions to it of any, either from History or Philosophy; for they seem to have degenerated more from the primitive and original Complexion of Mankind, in Noah and his Sons, than even the Indians and Negroes; and that to the worst Extreme, the most delicate, tender and sickly. — For there is no Doubt, but that Noah and his Sons were of a Complexion suitable to the Climate where they resided, as well as all the rest of Mankind; which is the Colour of the southern Tartars of *Asia*, or northern *Chinese*, at this Day perhaps, which is a dark swarthy, a Medium betwixt Black and White: From which primitive Colour the *Europeans* degenerated as much on one hand, as the *Africans* did on the other; the *Asiatics* (unless, perhaps, where mixed with the whiter *Europeans*) with most of the *Americans*, retaining the primitive and original Complexion. — The grand Obstacle to the Belief of this Relation between white and black People is, that, on comparing them together, their Colours seem to be so opposite and contrary, that it seems impossible that one should ever have been descended from the other. But, besides the Falsity of this supposed direct Contrariety of their Colours, they being only different, altho' extreme, Degrees of the same Sort of Colour, as we have above proved; besides this, I say, that is not a right state of the Question; we do not affirm, that either Blacks or Whites were originally descended from one another, but that both were descended from People of an intermediate tawny Colour; whose Posterity became more and more tawny, i.e. black, in the southern Regions, and less so, or white, in the northern Climes: Whilst those who remained in the middle Regions, where the first Men resided, continued of their primitive tawny Complexions; which we see confirmed by Matter of Fact, in all the different People in the World.[14]

14. Ibid., pp. 145–47.

In remarking on this paper, R. P. Stearns has said: "Mitchell's arguments are, of course, outmoded. He knew nothing about cell structure, pigmentation, genes, Mendel's law, or Darwinism. But his logic was impressive. . . ." Fifty years after Mitchell wrote his paper, there were those who were influenced by it.[15] Dr. Samuel Stanhope Smith, president of Princeton College, used it as the basis for one of his own, *An Essay on the Causes of the Variety of Complexion and Figure in the Human Species* (Philadelphia, 1787).[16]

Mitchell soon became involved in still another study directly or indirectly inspired by Peter Collinson. Among the varied productions of the New World which were of great interest to Europeans were the many species of trees, especially our evergreens. Wealthy English and Scottish noblemen collected them as curiosities for their gardens and at least one, the Duke of Argyll, carried on extensive forestation practices. In 1735, Judge Paul Dudley, of Massachusetts, sent a lengthy paper on New England evergreens which occupied two meetings of the Royal Society in the following April.[17] This seems to have stimulated Collinson to begin an evergreen collection, as well as to distribute them among his friends. Soon afterwards, he wrote to John Bartram: "I believe it will be acceptable to all thy friends, to make a general collection of all the Pines, and Firs, your part affords. I am apt to think the Jerseys may afford all the Pines and Firs mentioned by Dudley. . . . We are very poorly furnished with this tribe."[18]

Collinson became so persistent in his requests for Pine seed that he eventually irritated the usually placid Bartram. He protested that he could not be "in three or four hundred distant places in three or four days time," and hence could not procure the great quantity and variety which Collinson wanted.[19] In 1742, Collinson wrote: "I observe thou mentions three sorts of three-leaved Pines, and they are thus distinguished: *First*, the Great three-leaved Pine; *Second*, the three-leafed Pine whose cones keep shut for one, two or three years; *Third*, the Bastard three-leafed Pine. As our knowledge of these noble trees is very slender, Lord Petre, as well as myself, desires, when opportunity offers,

---

15. *Science in the British Colonies*, pp. 546–47.

16. Blanton, *Medicine in Virginia in the Eighteenth Century*, p. 139.

17. Collinson to Bartram, 7 June 1736, Darlington, *Memorials*, p. 79; Stearns, *Science in the British Colonies*, p. 471.

18. Collinson to Bartram, 26 February 1736/37, Darlington, *Memorials*, p. 90.

19. Bartram to Collinson, 10 December 1745, ibid., p. 174.

that thou will gather fair specimens of each sort, with their ripe cones on them—each distinguished by its name. . . ."[20] Collinson was becoming so well informed about Pines that he planned a publication on the subject, or so Mark Catesby understood. He omitted any consideration of Pines from his *Natural History of Carolina* because Collinson had a "large Fund for a complete History of this useful Tree."[21] Catesby's optimism was ill-founded, as no important publication on Pines was published by Collinson. He did publish two rather superficial articles in the *Gentleman's Magazine* in 1755.[22]

Mitchell undertook a careful study of the Pines of Virginia, which was written but never published. The surviving copy of his paper is undated, but it was written in 1744 or 1745. From Collinson's poorly organized and very brief account of southern Pines, it is apparent that he never saw Mitchell's paper. It was given to Bartram in 1744 and may have been intended only for him.[23] Virginia Pines, according to Mitchell, were of only two species, one three-leaved and the other two-leaved, although he recognized some common variants of these. He was definitely what present day taxonomists call a "lumper," and he was well aware of it for he wrote: "These different varieties are often taken for distinct species; which might be easily multiplied; but the most remarkable that I have met with are the two following: which seem different in some respects, but will be reckoned the same species by a Botanist who is careful to distinguish accidental varieties from distinct species; which was not the care or humour of Botanists in former days." He would thoroughly disapprove of our "splitters" today who recognize six species which can be identified among the variants which Mitchell described. His three-leaved species included four common variants:

1. "The fox-tail or old field pine." This is still known by the same common names and is recognized as the distinct species *Pinus echinata* Mill. Al-

20. Collinson to Bartram, 16 May, ibid., pp. 154–55.

21. Frick and Stearns, *Catesby*, p. 76.

22. The first article dealt with the White or Weymouth Pine and in it Collinson quoted at length from Dr. Douglass's book on New Hampshire (25:503–4). The second article lists other varieties of New England Pines as well as mentioning Jersey, southern and even Ohio ones. He touched on tar and turpentine production (ibid., pp. 550–51).

23. Bartram to Colden, 25 January 1744/45, Gratz Collection, Case 7, Box 21, Historical Society of Pennsylvania, subsequently referred to as HSP. Mitchell's paper did

though it was first described by John Banister, it was confused with the Weymouth Pine, or White Pine, *Pinus strobus* L., a five-leaved Pine which it does not at all resemble. Miller, in his *Gardener's Dictionary*, clarified the matter and retained Banister's reference to its spiny cones in his specific name of *echinata*.[24]

2. "Large Swamp Pine." This seems to be our Pond Pine or Marsh Pine, *Pinus serotina* Michx.

3. "Highland Pine." Our Pitch Pine, *Pinus rigida* Mill.

4. "White or Long-bearded Pine." This was our Long-Leaf Pine, *Pinus australis* Michx. The eighteenth-century appellation "white" referred to the wood. Mitchell stated that trees twenty feet in circumference and over one hundred feet tall were not rare in Tidewater Virginia, "especially if surrounded by other trees, making one of the tallest trees in our woods except the Poplar & Cypress." He added that it often provided eighty feet clear of limbs for ship masts.

His two-leaved species were:

1. "The Light-wood Pine," our Loblolly Pine, *Pinus taeda* L. A tree was successfully raised in London by George London, Bishop Compton's gardener, from seeds or a seedling sent over by Banister. Both Banister and Plukenet supposedly referred to this as "The Frankincense Tree," according to Ray,[25] but Mitchell disagreed. He thought that Banister meant our Long-leaved Pine, *Pinus australis* Michx. In discussing the turpentine from this tree, he wrote that it "turns hard & brittle when dryed long enough in the sun or when got in hot summer months, resembling the thus officium or frankinsense tree; altho that name is now hardly known in Virginia, & never was as far as I can learn, but to those skilled in Botany. This frankinsense is white intermixed with red lumps, & veins & resembles the common sort in flavour for which it may be safely Substituted. . . ." Mitchell explained the name of Light-wood Pine also: "When this tree grows old the wood turns hard and full of resin, & will burn like a torch. This wood is called Lightwood by our planters, which signifies a torch pine or Teda; & it is used for the same purposes instead of candles by the poor people."

---

not survive but it had been copied by Bartram and preserved as part of his papers at the HSP for over two hundred years.

24. Joseph Ewan and Nesta Ewan, *John Banister and His Natural History of Virginia, 1678–1692* (Urbana, 1970), p. 231.

25. Ibid., pp. 230–31.

2. "Old field Pine," our *Pinus Virginiana* Mill. This is known today as the Virginia Scrub Pine, Poverty Pine, Jersey Pine, and perhaps also by some as the Old Field Pine.

Mitchell accounted for the variations which he recognized as common in the two species which he described, as arising from differences in soils, light, moisture, and crowding of individual trees.

He was interested in the reproduction of the Pines and made some comments on their life cycle. He observed the very small ovulate, or female, cones in their first year and mistakenly thought that they were not pollinated until the second year. He was much impressed by the amount of pollen produced and some common misinterpretation of it:

After great rains & high winds in the spring of the year, which are commonly attended with sharp thunder & lightning there is frequently to be observed a yellow dust of a pretty strong smell sometimes floating on the surface of the pudles of rain water which is taken notice of by Mr. Claton in his account of Virginia.[26] This our common people generaly recon to be brimstone proceeding from the thunder & they will tell you that the air smells strong of brimstone at such times. It does indeed so much resemble flowers of sulphur that I have seen many intelligent people take it for some such thing; but this dust exactly resembles the farina foecundans of the pines, & I never remember to have seen it in any weather, but when the Pines are in blossom or nigh to where they grow in plenty from whence proceeds great quantities of this yellow farina. Those then who have a mind to try Mr. Miller's experiment of fecundating their flower gardens &c with the farina of plants might get plenty of this. This perhaps might be the more serviceable in our countrey where dung is apt to burn & parch the roots of many tender europian plants that grow in our hot & parched soil & clime.

Mitchell's essay on Pines is an interesting contrast to his earlier botanical treatises, which were purely theoretical and descriptive. In this,

26. "A letter from Mr. John Clayton . . . Giving an Account of Several Observables in Virginia, and in His Voyage Thither, More Particularly Concerning the Air," *Philosophical Transactions* 17 (1693):787. The "Mr. Claton" (1657–1725) to whom Mitchell referred was a distant kinsman of his friend, the botanist in Gloucester. He was also named John and was a scientifically inclined clergyman who had lived in Virginia for two years, 1684–86, while minister of the James City Parish. There he spent as much time observing the country and its people as he did ministering to his parishioners. He knew and compared notes with another minister of similar inclinations, the Reverend John Banister. When Clayton returned to England he wrote several accounts of his observations for Robert Boyle, Nehemiah Grew, and the Royal Society. The latter published some of these essays in 1693 and 1694.

he included not only taxonomic factors, but ecological and physiological as well. He also dealt with the highly practical aspects of medicinal and commercial aspects of these trees. He has been accused by some critics of being solely concerned with the practical aspects of botany, but this was certainly not the case. As the son of a merchant-planter, he was, of course, conscious of practical aspects of any study which he made, but this was never his sole concern. In the case of the pines, he mentioned the use of the trees for a variety of purposes including everything from fence rails to ship building. He indicated which kinds were most used for turpentine, rosin, pitch, and tar. He compared them from the point of view of durability when used for various purposes.

Mitchell considered the Loblolly Pine to be the most useful of all the Pines which he knew. He thought that there should be plantations of them in among other kinds of trees. They would soon overtop the other trees but, unlike Oaks and Hickories, they produced better timber when crowded a bit. He thought that they had acquired an undeserved reputation for short life in ships and houses because too many of them had been harvested from open land. He found that they grew well on a variety of soils: sandy, dry, moist, etc. When aged, the lumber becomes so hard as to be difficult to cut and, for this reason, it was excellent not only for planking but also for shingles, posts, sills, and scantling. A friend had told him that when he broke up an old ship some of whose timbers had rotted, the Loblolly used in it was perfectly sound but Oak timbers had decayed.

Being a doctor, Mitchell was particularly interested in the medicinal uses of pine products, especially turpentine. He described that obtained from the Longleaf Pine as "somewhat thicker than honey, white, clear & transparent at first." He found it

more adhesive, agglutinating and strengthening than the common turpentine in the shops which makes it rather more serviceable to cleanse & strengthen the kidneys, womb & lungs, in seminal weakness, Gonorrheas & gleets or pains in the loins, in the fluor albus, & moist coughs and Catarrhs: for which purposes it is so often used by our people with good effect; externally it more powerfully Supporates, it is likewise common among our good women to mix this turpentine [with] the yok of an egg like the common digestive, to dress most sorts of wounds & ulcers with; but what is commonly got is too thick for that purpose, for this digestive soon turns hard & dry; but this turpentine disolved in the decocted oil of sassfras berries more or less as occasion requires, makes a most excelent balsam for most kind of wounds & ulcers espetially of the nervous and tendinous parts, which might be had in great plenty without cost at every door almost in Virginia.

It was proper that Mitchell should have been impressed by the medical possibilities of turpentine. We make more use of it and its derivatives today than perhaps the general public is aware. Some of these uses are as a counterirritant in liniments, in dressings for deep-seated infections, as an antiseptic in the treatment of certain skin diseases, as a disinfectant, an expectorant, and a diuretic. It is also the source of the well-known Terpin Hydrate extensively used with Codeine in the treatment of bronchitis and related ailments.

The method of collecting turpentine from the tree also concerned Mitchell. It was customary to make cuts in the bark and to collect the sap which ran down the bark of the tree. This obviously collected trash and debris. He suggested boring a deep hole in the tree and stripping off the bark from the collecting area. The sap which flowed down the tree should "be strained through a basket, like the terebintha communis officium" (Venice Turpentine, which is still collected this way). Our present "cup and gutter system" of collecting is something of a modification of Mitchell's idea, except that instead of drilling a hole, a large area of bark is removed and a series of V-shaped incisions are made, leading into a central collecting spot, where metal gutters direct the oleoresin into a bucket.

He experimented with the turpentine obtained from the Loblolly Pine. He found it much thicker than most turpentines in this country, more like the Chian turpentine obtained from the Terebinth tree (*Pistacia terebinthus*) of the Mediterranean region. When it remained on the tree during the summer it turned as hard and brittle as the Gum Thus or Olibanum (Frankincense obtained from trees of the genus *Boswellia*), sold in lumps in the apothecary shops. When he had dried it still further, he found it easy to powder and sieve in preparing it for medicinal use.

The common method of preparing pitch and tar was described by Mitchell in some detail. People living along the Virginia-Carolina border seemed to make a specialty of producing it at this time. They collected Pine knots and, in some cases, drilled into the trunks of small trees to the heart, which made the stumps below turn hard and suitable to use for tar. These materials were split and stacked in a pyramid which was covered with turf to shut out oxygen. This was fired and persuaded to burn with a minimum of air. The trick was to get a fire hot enough to melt the tars without burning them. He noted that American tar was not popular with sailors and he made some suggestions for its improvement.

V ❧ New Friends with Scientific Interests

". . . that one Society be formed of virtuosi or ingenious men residing in the several Colonies, to be called The American Philosophical Society who are to maintain a constant correspondence."

Benjamin Franklin's Proposal[1]

Dr. Mitchell's practice grew over the years and much of his time was spent on the road between his patients' plantations. On these long rides he reviewed his cases, considered ways in which the New World diseases differed from those which he had studied in Edinburgh, questioned his own treatments, and debated new methods. Over the years, he made a habit of noting down these thoughts and ideas, writing later: "My views then were to inform myself as well as to qualify myself to inform others (if any desired such information, which very few, too few, among us so much as do of the nature & Cure of our other popular Maladies . . .) as well as of the nature of effects of our Climate, minerals, vegetables & animals &c. . . ."[2] Eventually, he hoped to compile a Natural and Medical History of his country.

To his medical records, he added many notes on an apparently new disease which appeared in epidemic form in Virginia in 1737, and again in 1741 and 1742. He has left us a detailed account of it since he knew no one had ever given descriptions of any autopsies performed on victims of this disease.[3] The doctors were baffled by its strange character. It was extremely contagious and its mortality very high. The onset was characterized by sudden and severe pain in the head, usually just above the eyes, with short remissions. This caused dizziness and a general feeling of malaise, sometimes accompanied by nausea. Fever followed within a few hours and pain was often present, in both the back and the region over the heart, which became excruciating as death

1. *Proposal for Promoting Useful Knowledge among the British Plantations in America,* quoted by Brooke Hindle, *The Pursuit of Science in Revolutionary America, 1735–1789* (Chapel Hill, 1956), p. 69.
2. Mitchell to Benjamin Franklin, 12 September 1745, LPCC 3:152.
3. Ibid.

approached.[4] On the fourth day, a juandice appeared. This day like-wise marked the crisis: prognostications indicated death on the sixth day or recovery on the seventh. If there were relapses, they were apt to occur on the eleventh or fourteenth day.[5]

Sometimes whole families were decimated and almost always several succumbed to the disease.[6] In one family of slaves, fourteen died before one recovered.[7] It may well have been that the treatment was as responsible for the deaths as was the disease itself. At that time, the majority of the medical profession attributed ill-health to an imbalance of the morbid humors or fluids: blood, phlegm, yellow and black bile. To restore a proper balance, "cleansing" was achieved through a series of evacuations. This involved drugs to implement perspiration, diaphoretics, emetics, and purgatives, all of which would rid the body of impurities. To this was added phlebotomy, the taking of blood, also called venesection. While Mitchell was of this general school, he was also a firm believer in moderation. He looked with little approval upon the enthusiastic employment of such drastic practices in toto, with little regard to the individual patient or to the type of disease.[8] His treatment, which seems extreme today, seemed mild then. Perhaps because of this, many of his patients survived, particularly those "under puberty."[9]

At the first evidence of the disease, when the patient complained of headache, Mitchell found it advisable to draw off six to eight ounces of blood before the fever started. To those patients who did not sweat as a result of this treatment, he gave a dose of ipecacuanha, which produced the desired effect. He found this treatment quite successful. In fact, it apparently saved all fifteen in one family that he treated. He noted that "wherever it was duly complied with, the good effects of it were evident." Although most venesection was done in winter, the blood appeared extremely thin for that time of year.[10] This was true of the thirty or forty cases that Mitchell had heard of. On the other hand,

---

4. *The American and Philosophical Register* (subsequently referred to as APR) 4 (1814): 183.

5. Ibid., pp. 194–95.

6. Ibid., p. 195.

7. Mitchell to Cadwallader Colden, 10 September 1745, LPCC 8:324–25.

8. APR 4:197–98, 200–203.

9. Ibid., p. 203.

10. Ibid., pp. 195–96.

the arterial blood was far different. Upon cooling, it developed a "purulent yellow skin . . . the crassamentum [dregs] was very cohesive, thick and blackish at bottom."[11] Mitchell preferred not to use emetics unless it was necessary, although his colleagues employed them enthusiastically. He wryly commented that it might be said of them "what Celsus said of bleeding in an apoplexy, 'They either kill or cure.' "[12]

His treatment fell into four parts. Since the inflammation of the viscera was the prime effect of the illness, "large evacuations" were necessary. This would indicate "plentiful bleedings," in the "benign inflammatory fevers," Mitchell said, but he felt the converse to be true in those cases because as the "red globules of blood" were already "in too small a proportion." Many phlebotomies resulted in a very slow pulse. Therefore, to drain off the serum, he felt that induced perspiration was the answer. Even this first part of his treatment should be approached with some care. Second, he prescribed "mild relaxing chologogue apozems . . . to keep up a constant diarrhoea, rather than speedy purgation." These were cathartic decoctions used to eliminate the choler or yellow bile. In this manner, the viscera's "feculent corruptible contents are discharged before they corrupt and produce any ill effects." This also resulted in beneficial sweats. Mitchell came to this treatment from observing nature as he had in his taxonomic theories. He learned, too, that those who had not had this gentle evacuation, often suffered relapses. Sweating should only be induced at the very start of the disease, certainly not during fever, although lenitives (mild drugs) were possible during remissions. He continued, "None but the mildest diluting laxatives are ever proper."[13]

The third part of Mitchell's treatment was to counteract the peculiar characteristic of the illness which resulted in the accumulation of the blood in the "liver, spleen, pancreas, omentum, messentery and lungs." To accomplish this, he found a mixture of "some alkaline absorbent or warming alexipharmic" fairly satisfactory. He was still searching for better remedies and studied every article he could find. It has not until the 1742 epidemic that he read in the Edinburgh *Medical Essays* of the successful treatment of smallpox with Peruvian bark (*Cinchona*). This was confirmed by one of his correspondents who had used it in three

11. Ibid., p. 188.
12. Ibid., p. 197.
13. Ibid., pp. 198–204.

cases in Minorca. He was Dr. John Fothergill (1712–81) of London, who had completed his medical training at the University of Edinburgh in 1736. He had spent two years at St. Thomas's Hospital and studied on the Continent as well. He had just begun practice in London in 1740. It is unlikely that Mitchell and Fothergill met in Scotland. It is more probable that either Collinson, a fellow Quaker, or members of the Edinburgh faculty suggested that the two men correspond. Having used *Cinchona* in only one instance, Mitchell was not able to judge its effect properly, but was most hopeful. In some cases, there was a prolonged debility after the crisis. It was in these he thought the bark would be especially beneficial. When he had conversed with those who had taken part in the recent expedition to Cartagena with Lieutenant Governor Gooch, he learned that many of the soldiers and sailors, suffering from the supposedly same fever, had been treated successfully with the bark.[14]

With the appearance of the icterus (jaundice), Mitchell found diaphoretics incapable of relieving the patient. He therefore prescribed mild purges although at times he substituted warm opiates. He emphasized again that all circumstances should be considered in each individual case, before prescribing. No "general method of cure" could be stated in this disease.[15]

Virginia doctors were extremely concerned over the severity of the epidemic. Mitchell talked with many of them, comparing symptoms and treatment. It was not until 13 February 1741/42 that he was asked to perform an autopsy on one of the fever victims, a twelve- or thirteen-year-old girl. The child had been dead for several days, but the body was preserved so that Mitchell could perform an autopsy as other members of the family had also died. Phlebotomy was the only treatment which she had received as no one had suspected that she had this malignant fever. She succumbed on the sixth or seventh day. Mitchell found some icterus in the body fat, the liver and lungs were affected, as were the stomach and duodenum.[16]

Richard Chichester, a wealthy Westmoreland planter, with an estate in England, sent for Mitchell the following day. He wanted an autopsy performed on one of his slaves, "an elderly woman past forty." He and

14. Ibid., pp. 204–11.
15. Ibid., pp. 211–15.
16. Ibid., pp. 186–87.

several others watched as the doctor went about his grisly task. Mitchell found the fat to be much more yellow than that of the child. The omentum (a fold of peritoneum which supports the viscera) appeared to have disintegrated entirely. The liver was "turgid and plump" and normal on one side but black on the other side and "mortified and corrupted" close to the gallbladder. The latter was a dark yellow, filled with "a black ropy coagulated atri-bilis," (black bile). Blood clots also appeared in lungs and stomach. Mitchell's account of his dissection was detailed and meticulous.[17] Of it, Blanton has said: "His descriptions are remarkably exact, noting the jaundiced mucous membranes and serous coats, the color and consistency of the liver, the thickness of the bile, the dark contents of the stomach, the emphysema of the lungs with their hemorrhagic areas and the relatively normal appearance of the other organs of the body. He showed familiarity with the writings of Hippocrates, Galen, Celsus, and Sanctorius."[18] Mitchell discovered that his findings were similar to those made in two autopsies performed in 1737. A similar confirmation came from another in September, 1742, although the origin of the fever was different from that of the preceding winter.[19]

It was not until three days after Mitchell had performed the autopsy on Chichester's slave that he felt certain of the identification of this dread disease. When the blood from a phlebotomy of another patient was carefully studied and the serum revealed a pronounced yellow color he felt there could no longer be any doubt that this was yellow fever. He had suspected this ever since he had read with great interest Dr. Henry Warren's 1732 letter to Dr. Mead which had been published in 1740 as *A Treatise concerning the Malignant Fever in Barbadoes and the Neighboring Islands.*[20]

With the identity of the fever tentatively established, Mitchell thought some of his Scottish medical friends might be interested in an account of it. He decided to send a short paper to Edinburgh for publication in the *Medical Essays.* He set a scribe to copying the details of his two autopsies and other extracts from his notes which he thought

17. Ibid., pp. 183–86.
18. Blanton, *Medicine in Virginia in the Eighteenth Century,* p. 138.
19. APR 4:187.
20. Ibid., pp. 188 and 182.

should be new and of particular interest relating to treatment. He made no effort to be too detailed since he knew they were all quite familiar with Warren's book and he was not writing for the general public. Since he was addressing it to Alexander Monro I, he felt any such explanation "might be . . . impertinent." Upon receiving Mitchell's essay, some of his friends wanted to print it immediately as a pamphlet since the *Medical Essays* had been discontinued. Monro and Dr. Clarke, however, thought it would be lost among the dozens of such publications printed yearly. They felt it was of definite value and importance and thought that Mitchell should amplify his subject. He did not act upon their suggestion, being very busy at the time and not too well.[21] Monro sent a copy of Mitchell's paper to Collinson in London. The latter made a note of this on the back of Mitchell's dissertation on skin color, now in the Royal Society archives.[22]

By the spring of 1744, Mitchell had been back in Virginia over eleven years. His practice was still increasing and kept him extremely busy. Although he had managed to survive the three fever epidemics, he suffered continuous bouts of malaria which left him with little energy and even less *joie de vivre*. It was while recuperating from these that he found time for his essays and correspondence. In May, he wrote to John Bartram in Philadelphia. The two men had never met although the Quaker had made an extended trip to Virginia in the fall of 1738. He had come by way of Fredericksburg, then down the Rappahannock River, crossing to Williamsburg by way of Gloucester County where he had hoped to visit John Clayton. He was disappointed not to find Clayton at home. They were probably already acquainted through correspondence, so he was not too surprised to find that the botanist had gone to the mountains on a collecting trip.[23]

He had better luck in the capital where he visited Custis for two nights and a day. Collinson had forewarned Custis that Bartram might call upon him, "a down right plain Country Man." He need not have bothered to do so, for Custis wrote him that his visitor was "the most taking facetious man I have ever met with and never was so much de-

21. Mitchell to Colden, 10 September 1745, LPCC 8:324–25, and Mitchell to Franklin, 12 September 1745, LPCC 3:152–53.

22. 14 June 1744, Letters and Papers of the Royal Society of London, no. 8.

23. Berkeley and Berkeley, *Clayton*, p. 77.

lighted with A stranger in all my life.''[24] The liking was mutual, and Bartram wrote Custis upon his return home: "Now, dear friend, I can't forget thy kind entertainment; and it is with great satisfaction and pleasure that I think upon the agreeable hours I spent in thy conversation, as well as thy kind expressions at parting. . . ."[25] Custis conveyed his enthusiasm for his new friend to Mitchell who had already heard about him from Collinson.

In June, Mitchell received a reply from Philadelphia. Bartram was delighted to begin a correspondence with the Virginia doctor. In order to insure a continuance he wrote at length describing his 1738 trip and his return through the Valley of Virginia. He told of his many travels through the Jerseys and north to the Catskills. He listed many things of interest there: birch bark on which one could not only write, but print and draw; a fifteen foot *Sorbus*; and many varieties of evergreens. His most recent venture had taken him to Onondago in the previous fall. He had gone with the interpreter, Conrad Weiser, to the peace conference between the Six Indian Nations and the governments of Virginia, Pennsylvania, and Maryland. Mitchell had already had reports of this conference and the Treaty of Lancaster which resulted, from William Beverley, one of the Virginia representatives.[26]

It is distinctly possible that the surviving copy of this letter, which was kept by Bartram, is incomplete. It makes no mention of a scientific matter with which he was very much concerned at this time, and this seems out of character for Bartram. This was the formation of a scientific society in Philadelphia, somewhat along the lines of the Royal Society of London. Bartram had long wished for the exchange of ideas which such a society would provide. He had mentioned it to Collinson in a letter in 1739, and the Londoner replied: "As to the Society that thee hints at, had you a set of learned, well-qualified members to set out with it might draw your neighbors to correspond with you. . . ."[27] Four years later, in 1743, Benjamin Franklin had published *A Proposal for Promoting Useful Knowledge among the British Plantations in America*, establishing the American Philosophical Society. The active members

24. Collinson to Custis, 24 December 1737, Swem, *Brothers of the Spade*, p. 50, and Custis to Collinson, n.d. but possibly 12 August 1739, ibid., p. 61.

25. 19 November 1739, Darlington, *Memorials*, p. 312.

26. Bartram to Mitchell, 3 June 1744, Bartram Papers, 1:27, HSP.

27. 10 July 1739, Darlington, *Memorials*, p. 132.

were naturally Philadelphians, but a few in other colonies were soon asked to become corresponding members.[28]

One of the first to be invited as a corresponding member was Dr. Cadwallader Colden (1688–1776), who had actually suggested the formation of such a society some years previously. An alumnus of the University of Edinburgh, he had studied medicine in London before emigrating to this country. He settled first at Philadelphia, but, in 1717, he removed to New York, where he abandoned medicine to become surveyor general of that province. He achieved a sound literary reputation with his *History of the Five Nations*, in addition to recognition as an Indian authority. He retired to his country estate, Coldengham, in 1739, and devoted his time to a variety of studies including both botany and history, and wrote numerous papers on both botanical and medical subjects. His current interest at the time the Philosophical Society was founded was in the realm of physics.[29] He had the time to indulge in a wide correspondence on scientific matters in this country and abroad.

On April 29, 1744, Bartram wrote to Colden:

our Philosophical Society increaseth finely. I think we had 7 members initiated last meeting of which thee was one by unanimous consent as for those three thee mentions they are persons of little curiosity & I believe was never acquainted with our proposals or not till very lately; indeed James Logan was acquainted with it as a compliment but I tould Benjamin that I believed he would not incourage it; & we should have been as well pleased with his name at the top of our List, as his person in our meetings. however we resolved that his not favouring the design should not hinder our attempt & if he would not go along with us we should Jog along without him.

Ye next fifth day night we are to have another meeting where Doctor spence will accompany us. he exhibits Philosophical lextures now at Philadelphia & approves of our design: offers to take our proposals with him to the West indies with A favourable account of our proceedings.[30]

Colden was delighted with the invitation and informed Collinson that he and several other gentlemen in the neighboring colonies had been asked to join.[31] Invitations went to two Virginians, probably on

28. Hindle, *Pursuit of Science*, pp. 68–69.

29. Ibid., p. 59. For an excellent account of Colden's life, see Stearns, *Science in the British Colonies*, pp. 559–75.

30. Gratz Collection, Case 7, Box 2, HSP.

31. June 1744, LPCC 3:60.

Bartram's recommendation. One of these was John Clayton, who kept his Dutch friend, J. F. Gronovius, informed about the society. Gronovius wrote to Linnaeus that the Philadelphia society, founded to promote natural history, included "the most distinguished members," Clayton, Colden, Mitchell, Bartram, and others.[32] Exactly when Mitchell received his invitation is not clear, but it was prior to the late summer of 1744.

He was very gratified by his membership and often yearned to attend meetings, where such interesting persons as Dr. Adam Spencer (Bartram's "Doctor spence") lectured. He was haunted by thoughts of Philadelphia with its large coterie of curious scientists. So it was that when the first damp days of fall presaged his annual bout of malaria, he determined to avoid his old enemy by traveling north to the Quaker City. He packed his clothes and the treatise on Virginia Pines which he thought Bartram might enjoy. He also took along a copy of the yellow fever notes which he had sent to Monro, thinking that "it might make a fit piece for the records of the Philosophic Society."[33]

In contrast to Williamsburg, Philadelphia was a huge and bustling city with a busy harbor. The streets were wide and straight, many of them paved. Houses were mainly of brick or stone, several stories in height. Cypress shakes were used for the roofs. Mitchell was astonished at the number and beauty of the churches. Both the impressive Town Hall and the Court House boasted towers and bells.[34] The excitement of the city made Mitchell nostalgic for Edinburgh.

He lost little time in calling on John Bartram whose farm was three miles from town. There, in 1731, the Quaker had constructed a two-story house of stone with his own hands. Pleasing in its proportions, it was enhanced by the great variety of trees and shrubs which Bartram had collected in his travels. Inside, white walls set off the simple furniture and from the back windows there was a charming view of the Schuylkill River.

The warmth of Bartram's greeting was all that Mitchell had been led to expect by Custis. He found his host above average in height, much more vigorous and strong at forty-five than he was himself,

32. 17 April 1745, Linnean Correspondence (subsequently referred to as LCLS), 5:484, Linnean Society of London.

33. Mitchell to Colden, 10 September 1745, LPCC 8:325.

34. *Peter Kalm's Travels in North America*, ed. Adolph B. Benson, 2 vols. (New York, 1937), 1:18–20, 25–26.

although twelve years younger. Bartram's long face was deeply tanned from the summer's sun and what lines there were had resulted from humor rather than from aggravation. His genial disposition and kindliness were implicit in every word.

Only too glad to have his work interrupted, he took Mitchell for a long tramp about the farm. Their peregrinations, however, were not to admire the sleek cattle, the fields of ripening grain, nor yet the young orchards. They were to visit Bartram's gardens, if they could be called by such a name. He had the rarest of plants often completely run over by common weeds and the most unusual shrub hidden in the deepest brush, but he never forgot where his treasures were hidden.[35] The Virginian was captivated by the number and variety of plants. He was particularly interested in those which Bartram had brought back from the Catskills, those from Lake Ontario which he had visited with Conrad Weiser, and those from other northern areas. Some resembled their southern counterparts, while others had no relationship.

As they crossed one meadow, Mitchell spotted an unusual species of oak and looked around for some acorns.[36] Coming upon Horse-balm, named in honor of their London friend, Mitchell said that neither he nor Clayton had ever found any *Collinsonia*. He quickly gathered in some seeds and a specimen for his herbarium.[37] Bartram added that Conrad Weiser had once cured an Indian of a rattlesnake bite with a decoction made from it.[38] When Bartram pointed out a handsome specimen of the climbing Bittersweet (*Celastrus scandens* L.), Mitchell said that Collinson had wanted some of its seed for a long time.[39] Bartram gathered up two or three handfuls of the berries for Collinson and Mitchell collected some too, which he later sent to Dillenius.[40] Never had a day passed quite so rapidly for the two men. Bartram had enjoyed himself as much as the Virginian. He was delighted by Mitchell's enthusiasm and interest but even more by his botanical knowledge. He

35. For a detailed and lively description of Bartram's garden, see Dr. Alexander Garden to Colden, 4 November 1754, LPCC 4:471–73.

36. Collinson to Bartram, 5 March 1750/51, Darlington, *Memorials*, p. 183. Darlington thought this might have been *Quercus heterophylla* Mx., known as "the Bartram oak," a hybrid of *Q. Phellos* L. (the Willow Oak) and *Q. rubra* L.

37. Bartram to Colden, 10 November 1744, LPCC 3:189.

38. *Kalm's Travels*, 1:106.

39. Bartram to Collinson, December 1744, Darlington, *Memorials*, p. 173.

40. Dillenius's list of plants in the Oxford garden, Sherard MSS #208, Bodleian Western MSS, OU.

had not previously had the opportunity to converse on botanical matters with a southerner who had been specifically trained in botany at a university.

Realizing with a start that the sun was rapidly setting, Mitchell prepared to leave. Bartram insisted so vehemently that he spend the night, that Mitchell was delighted to accept. Meals were served at a long table bountifully supplied. There he met the kindly Mrs. Bartram, the six children, and the hired hands as well. Had he come a few years later, he would have found the Negroes also eating with the family for, by the mid-sixties, Bartram, like other Friends, had freed his slaves and was paying them a yearly wage.[41]

The evening was spent in the study in conversation with his host. They had so many things about which to talk. Bartram told of his long years of friendship with Collinson and of the wasps' nests which he had just sent to him.[42] They agreed upon their great debt to the Londoner. Not only had he been of assistance to both of them but, even more welcome, he had been instrumental in introducing them to many new friends in this country and abroad. They spoke of Sir Hans Sloane, of Mark Catesby, of Dr. John Fothergill, and of John Jacob Dillenius. They compared notes on the various mosses which they had sent to Dillenius at Oxford and on the botany professor's book in which they both appeared.

Bartram questioned Mitchell about Clayton whom he had never met, but with whom he corresponded. He told him how extremely useful he had found the *Flora Virginica*. Gronovius had sent him a copy, he said, "whereby I have been informed what kind of plants my brother Claton hath described and how far to ye northward he hath navigated. . . ."[43] Mitchell told him about his own taxonomic theories and the plant descriptions which he had forwarded to Collinson to be printed. He promised to send his new friend a copy of the book as soon as it was published. This delighted Bartram and he assured Mitchell that it would be of the greatest help to him.[44]

From Clayton, conversation turned rather naturally to Cadwallader

41. Darlington, *Memorials*, p. 47.
42. Collinson exhibited these and gave an account of them to the members of the Royal Society the following April (Journal Book XVIII, pp. 400–401).
43. Bartram to Collinson, n.d. but c. 1740–41. Bartram Papers, HSP.
44. Bartram to Colden, 2 November 1744, LPCC 3:78–79.

Colden with whom Bartram corresponded on Collinson's suggestion. On his trip north in the fall of 1741, he had missed seeing Colden, but the following year he had met him. He told Mitchell, as he had Collinson, that Colden was "one of the most facetious, agreeable gentlemen" that he had ever met and as he later reported to the New Yorker: "I could not help mentioning my friend Colden to him & set thy abilities & Character in such a clear light before him which together with some specimens of thy performance so inflamed ye doctors mind (that tho his Constitution is miserably racked) he said that if he was sure he could see thee at York he would venture so far for ye sake of A little of thy Company."[45] Mitchell told Bartram that he was not the only one who had spoken of Colden to him. For several years now, his praises had been sung by his next door neighbor in Urbanna, Patrick Cheap, who had known him well. In fact, Colden's son, Alexander, was Cheap's godson. It is surprising that this had not led to correspondence with Colden.[46]

While discussing the new Philadelphia society, Bartram was astonished to learn that Mitchell knew no one in Philadelphia. He immediately offered to introduce him to Benjamin Franklin. The following day, 13 September, he accompanied Mitchell to town to call upon "friend Benjamin." They found him about to write to Colden but far from loathe to turn to conversation instead.[47] Franklin's home contained his printing shop as well. In addition to his business, he sold a great variety of goods: stationery, pencils and slates, books, ink, maps, compasses, patent medicines, coffee, even cheese, fish, and sack. It was not precisely a quiet place for a visit, but Franklin often took guests to a nearby tavern for conversation.[48] Mitchell found Bartram's friend most congenial for he had that same boundless curiosity and far-reaching interests which he had himself and a delightful sense of humor as well.[49]

45. Bartram to Colden, 25 October 1744, LPCC 3:79.
46. Mitchell to Colden, 10 September 1745, LPCC 8:314, and Colden to Mitchell, 7 November 1745, LPCC 8:338.
47. Franklin to Colden, 13 September 1744, *The Papers of Benjamin Franklin*, ed. Leonard W. Labaree (New Haven, 1960–), 2:415.
48. Carl van Doren, *Benjamin Franklin* (New York, 1938), pp. 125–28.
49. Evidence of this can be seen in the epitaph that he designed for himself: "The body of Benjamin Franklin, printer (like the cover of an old book its Contents torn and

Franklin told Mitchell of the Library Company which he and his friends had started in 1731. Those who became members had paid forty shillings with an annual premium of ten. This money was used for the purchase of books which the subscribers could borrow. Nonmembers were eligible to borrow books, but paid a rental fee. Collinson had persuaded the Library Company to allow Bartram to borrow books without charge. This was a delight to him as their collection of scientific books soon became one of the finest in the country.[50] This scientific interest resulted in many gifts of scientific equipment: an air pump, globes, and even a telescope. There were natural history displays as well.[51] Franklin was to say later: "this was the mother of all the North American subscription libraries, now so numerous. . . . These libraries have improved the general conversation of the Americans, made the common tradesmen and farmers as intelligent as most gentlemen from other countries, and perhaps have contributed in some degree to the stand so generally made throughout the colonies in defence of their privileges."[52]

His guests had to view Franklin's "open stove," which heated more efficiently and with less wood than the conventional one. He told the Virginian that his engineer friend, Lewis Evans, had made the drawings for his invention. It was made of Pennsylvania cast iron, of several sizes. The stove was raised slightly from the floor so that air could enter. Models differed in the number and arrangement of the dampers. On top, one could heat chocolate or boil a kettle for tea. Franklin also showed Mitchell the pamphlet, *An Account of the New Invented Pennsylvanian Fire-places*, which he had just published.[53]

They discussed the new society and all its hopes and aspirations. Mitchell took out his paper on yellow fever, which he had thought might be suitable for publication in the records or transactions which Franklin had proposed. He was disappointed to learn that these had been given up, at least for the time being, but thought that perhaps Dr. Colden might like to read his treatise. Franklin was certain that the

---

stript of its lettering and gilding) lies here food for worms: yet the work itself shall not be lost, but will (as he believed) appear once more in a new and more beautiful edition, corrected and amended by THE AUTHOR!"

50. Stearns, *Science in the British Colonies*, pp. 586–87.
51. Hindle, *The Pursuit of Science*, p. 65.
52. Benjamin Franklin, *Autobiography* (New York, 1955), pp. 87–88.
53. *Kalm's Travels*, 2:652–54.

New York doctor would be interested and promised to get Lewis Evans to make a copy of it.[54]

Talk turned to the summer's meeting with the Indians at Lancaster and Mitchell found that Franklin was as disturbed as Virginians were over the gradual encroachment into English territory by the French. It was especially dangerous now that France and England were at war. Franklin knew that Pennsylvania would indeed have trouble raising the militia that England had recently authorized, since the provincial government was controlled by the Quakers. Strangely enough, there were some among the Friends who approved of "defensive war." One of these was James Logan. Both Bartram and Franklin had been among his protegés and the printer offered to take Mitchell to call upon Logan the following day. As added bait, Franklin said he could then show him Colden's "Fluxions," which he had forwarded to Logan for an opinion. Mitchell needed no bait for he had long been familiar with Logan as a botanist.[55]

Stenton, Logan's home, was four miles from the city in the area of Germantown. Although Mitchell could not but have realized that Logan was well-to-do from his friends' remarks, he probably was little prepared to find a Quaker whose wealth dwarfed that of most Virginia planters. Logan, a Scot, had come to Pennsylvania as William Penn's secretary in 1699, but soon became secretary of the province and clerk of the council. Holding important governmental offices through the years, he eventually became president of the council. His tremendous fortune was derived from Indian trade and investments in land.[56] In 1728, he had purchased five hundred acres and built his home from bricks made of the fine clay on the place. They were Flemish bond "with black headers." The house was of noble proportions, fifty-five feet wide and forty-two deep. It was two stories, with a dormered hip roof. Around the lawn, pines, hemlocks, and oaks had been planted, some of which are still living today. The seventy-year-old Logan was crippled and semiparalyzed but still very impressive and of "aristocratic bearing."[57]

54. Franklin to Colden, 25 October 1744, LPCC 3:77–78, and Franklin to Colden, 28 November 1745, ibid., 182.

55. Franklin to Colden, 13 September 1744, *Papers of Franklin*, 2:415.

56. There is an excellent sketch of Logan in Stearns, *Science in the British Colonies*, pp. 535–39.

57. Descriptions of Stenton are given in Harold Donaldson Eberlin and Cortland

Stenton was as impressive inside as out. There was the luxury of a fireplace in the brick-paved hall. It was white paneled to the ceiling as were the two parlors on either side. The one on the left had "shell-coved china cupboards" on each side of the fireplace, which was most unusual. It was faced with blue-veined marble, inside which was a single row of Delft tiles. The one in the opposite parlor was similar but of pink. There was an ingenious trapdoor opening into an underground tunnel to the barns.

Their host led Mitchell and Franklin upstairs to his huge library that stretched across the whole front of the house. A contemporary wrote it "was customary with him, to any Persons of Account. He had really a very fine Collection of Books, both Ancient and Modern, he seem'd to Regrate that none of his Sons knew how to use them, and that he design'd them as a Legacy to the City when he Died."[58] The library was so immense that it required two fireplaces to heat it, but it was the superb collection of books which fascinated Mitchell. He had never seen anything like it as it was the finest library in the Colonies. It was especially strong in scientific works of all types, from Newton to Linnaeus. There were journals as well. Among them were the *Philosophical Transactions* of the Royal Society of London, which Peter Collinson sent to Logan regularly.[59] Though Mitchell had considered Logan a botanist, he found that the Quaker was a student of mathematical optics as well. He had written two books on the subject which had been published in Leyden. Mitchell had some mathematical facility so he and Logan enjoyed the discussion of Newton and similar subjects. Botanical conversation occupied much of the time as well as a visit to the orangery.

When Franklin and Mitchell returned to the city that Friday, 14 September, the doctor repaired to a coffeehouse. The trip had proved chilly for one accustomed to Virginia's hot early fall. There he found a number of doctors, including Dr. Phineas Bond and a most congenial physician from Annapolis, Dr. Alexander Hamilton (1712–56). They were both surprised to learn that Hamilton's father had been principal

---

Van Dyke Hubbard, *Portrait of a Colonial City, Philadelphia, 1670–1838* (Philadelphia, 1939), pp. 184–85, and Robert Shackleton, *The Book of Philadelphia* (Philadelphia, 1918), p. 291.

58. R. Alonzo Brock, ed., "Journal of William Black," *Pennsylvania Magazine of History and Biography* 1 (1877):407.

59. Collinson to Bartram, 26 January 1738/39, Darlington, *Memorials*, p. 124.

of the University of Edinburgh while Mitchell had been a student. Hamilton had first studied pharmacy with David Knox, then medicine, at the university where he received his degree in 1737. His older brother being a minister in Maryland, Hamilton emigrated to that colony to practice. Coincidence also played a part in the two men's state of health, for Hamilton had suffered from "fevers and bloody spitting," which convinced him that he was developing consumption. For that reason, he had traveled to Philadelphia like Mitchell, in the hope of improving his health.[60] The Virginian should have found Hamilton an amusing conversationalist. A contemporary later described the Annapolis physician as "a man of strict honor and integrity, of a friendly benevolent disposition and a most cheerful facetious companion amongst his friends, whom he never failed to delight with the effusions of his wit, humor and drollery in which acquirements he had no equal. . . . Altho' his jokes are occasionally somewhat indelicate, and he frequently chants the pleasures of the bowl, no man exceeded him in temperance and purity of morals."[61]

After Mitchell and Hamilton had compared their state of health, the talk must have turned to reminiscences of Edinburgh and mutual friends there. Hamilton was also a botanical enthusiast. Like Mitchell, he was fluent in Latin and had a useful knowledge of the French language. He had delivered a letter from Dr. Thomas Moffatt of Newport to Dr. Adam Spencer, who was also relaxing at the coffeehouse.[62] Perhaps it was he who introduced Mitchell to Spencer, although the Virginian may well have met him before. Spencer, too, was an alumnus of Edinburgh, and had come to this country in 1743, well recommended as "an experienced Physician and Man-Midwife" by eminent London physicians such as Dr. Richard Mead. However, Spencer was so fascinated by the whole realm of science that he had abandoned his practice to devote his time to lecturing on the subject. His talks were enlivened by colorful demonstrations which ranged from proof of Newton's theories of light and color to the circulation of the blood.[63]

Spencer's lectures in Philadelphia were advertised in Franklin's paper

60. Carl Bridenbaugh, ed., *Gentleman's Progress: The Itinerarium of Dr. Alexander Hamilton* (Chapel Hill, 1948), xii–xiii; Albert Bushnell Hart, ed.. *Hamilton's Itinerarium Being a Narrative of a Journey* (St. Louis, 1907), p. xii.

61. Upton Scott of Annapolis furnished this description, ibid., pp. xxv–xxvi.

62. Ibid., pp. 232–33.

63. *Papers of Franklin*, 2:450–51n

and subscriptions could be bought at the postmaster's office. Franklin had met Spencer the previous year in Boston where the latter had shown him some of his electrical experiments. After lecturing in New York, where he had met Colden, the doctor had come to Philadelphia the previous spring. His first course was oversubscribed in spite of a stiff admission fee. Even a second series in May failed to supply the demand and he offered one at the very end of July. To those who had attended either of his previous courses, he tendered tickets at half-price.[64] It is possible that Mitchell may have attended at least one of his lectures that September.

Many of the subjects which Spencer discussed in his morning talks at the state house were those familiar to Mitchell at least through books. Even some of the actual experiments would have been known to him from his university courses: magnetism, gravity, and vacuums. One subject was certainly new: electricity. It must have come up in their conversation even if Mitchell did not attend the lectures. In these, Spencer demonstrated electricity's property of attraction and repulsion which had been known for many years, but his most dramatic experiment was the suspension of a lad by ropes from the ceiling. Standing at a short distance away, Spencer rubbed a glass tube which caused sparks to fly to the boy's face and hands. Not until two years later was the invention of the Leyden jar to make possible a true study of electricity but the subject was already becoming very popular.[65] Mitchell was as fascinated with it as his contemporaries although it was not until fifteen years later that he published an account of a small experiment.

For three weeks Mitchell indulged himself in Philadelphia's stimulating atmosphere. He spent several nights with Bartram and still they knew that many topics that they meant to discuss had been forgotten. He remembered to give Bartram his piece on the Pines and left it with him so that he could copy it.[66] Over a year later, Colden wrote to Bartram that he would like to see it. Bartram suggested that Lewis Evans might make a copy for Colden since he was under obligation to him. This was agreeable, so the botanist delivered his copy of the treatise to Evans for transcribing. Mitchell had requested that the original be

64. I. Bernard Cohen, "Benjamin Franklin and the Mysterious 'Dr. Spence,'" *Journal of the Franklin Institute* 235 (January 1943):4–6.

65. Ibid., pp. 6–13.

66. Bartram to Gronovius, 6 December 1745, Darlington, *Memorials*, p. 353.

returned to him.[67] In the two hundred years since that time, the original has disappeared but Bartram's copy, with his own inimitable spelling, still survives in the archives of the Historical Society of Pennsylvania, where it was recently identified.

Through Bartram and Franklin, Mitchell met a great many Philadelphians. Among them was a former apprentice of Dr. Hamilton, Dr. Thomas Bond (1712–84), who had studied medicine abroad as well. Epidemiology was one of Bond's special concerns and he was much interested in Mitchell's experience with yellow fever. As many of the other doctors were also interested, Mitchell asked Franklin to let those who wished read his manuscript.[68]

In spite of his obvious ill health, Mitchell's personality and knowledge made a deep impression on those whom he met. Bartram wrote to Colden later that Mitchell "is an excellent Phisitian & Botanist & hath dipped in ye Mathematicks which inclined A Gentleman in Town well known to us to say to me that our doctors were but novices to him, but another person more volatil & more extravagantly expressed his value for him tould me they had not ye Millionth part of his knowledge. . . ."[69]

67. Bartram to Colden, November 1745, LPCC 3:180.
68. Mitchell to Franklin, 12 September 1745, LPCC 3:152; Mitchell to Bartram, 2 June 1747, Darlington, *Memorials*, p. 365.
69. 25 October 1744, LPCC 3:79.

VI ✎ Last Days in Virginia

> *"I think this world is pestered with this Itch of many to appear in print, which makes many so little regarded that do."*
>
> Mitchell to Franklin, 12 September 1745[1]

On 25 October, Franklin wrote a letter to Colden in which he said, "Enclosed I send you a Piece of Dr. Mitchels' (of Virginia) which I caus'd to be transcrib'd while he was here. He desires your Sentiments of it and to be favour'd with any other Observations you have made on the same Distemper (the Yellow Fever). When you have perus'd it, please to return it."[2] Colden read the paper with great interest but rather hurriedly as he was about to leave home on a trip. Not liking to have a copy of it made without permission and unwilling to retain it for too long, he returned it to Franklin without having the leisure in which to study it as he would have preferred. It was while traveling that he had a few hours free one evening. He used them to record some rough notes of his reactions and thoughts on Mitchell's essay. He left them with his son, still a lad, to copy and send on to Franklin, who forwarded them to Virginia.[3]

Mitchell was delighted with Colden's comments and remarked upon them in a letter to Franklin sometime in March.[4] He emphasized the peculiar characteristics of the disease which he had observed: the inflammation of stomach or liver and adjacent areas, and the jaundice. From these symptoms, diaphoresis or sweating was indicated as treatment. When the disease occurred in winter, as it often did, this was difficult to achieve. It was for this reason that he recommended purging as a substitute, although he agreed completely with Dr. Colden that great discretion should be employed in its use. In answer to Colden's question whether any patients recovered without sweats, he admitted that in some cases they did. Colden had theorized that exposure to cold might cause the relapses. Mitchell was inclined to think that too little

1. LPCC 3:154.
2. LPCC 3:77–78.
3. Colden to Mitchell, 8 June 1745, APR 4:378.
4. March 1745 (?), ibid., pp. 383–87.

care in convalescence and an improper diet were the most likely culprits.

When Franklin passed on these remarks to Colden, the latter addressed Mitchell directly, hoping for a regular correspondence with the Virginian.[5] He admitted that he had not practiced medicine for years and had never seen a case of yellow fever, so Mitchell must realize that his thoughts on the subject were purely speculative. He inclined to the view that the "velocity" of such a fever should be regulated "by giving vent to the fiery particles by a *free perspiration*," using diluents. Dr. Berkeley's tar-water was said to be quite successful in such a capacity. Colden did not add that he had just completed a pamphlet on tar-water.[6]

Colden's letter, which had been written the eighth of June, did not reach Mitchell until early September, 1745. He had spent a miserable summer. When he forwarded his paper on the possum to the Royal Society in July, he said that his "very bad and even dangerous state of health" prevented a better account.[7] To Franklin, in September, he went into more detail:

My health is so impaired by this summer & fall, that I am not able to follow my own necessary calling. Since the last of June, I have been afflicted with a Diarrhea several times, a slow hectic [fluctuating but recurrent fever, as in consumption], with spitting of Blood, & troublesome Piles: I had no sooner got over these, (When our weather began to break in ye fall, wt Rains & Easterly winds) than I was seized with an Intermittent fever, the origin & source of all my disorders.—with this I was afflicted, when I received yours, & as I kept the house, I have been more prolix in what I have wrote, having nothing else to amuse me, which is the reason, why I have said so little in so many words; which I hope Dr. Colden & you will excuse.[8]

Mitchell's letter to Colden on 10 September was indeed lengthy, the longest of any of his which have survived.[9] He had been so delighted to hear from Colden directly that he took much time and care in his reply.

5. Colden to Mitchell, 8 June 1745, APR 4:378–81.

6. Ibid., p. 382; *An Abstract from Dr. Berkeley's Treatise on Tar-Water with Some Reflexions Thereon, Adapted to Diseases Frequent in America* (New York, 1745).

7. Mitchell to Drs. Milward and Parsons, 8 July 1745, Thatcher, "Dr. Mitchell," *Virginia Magazine of History and Biography* 40 (October 1932):346.

8. Mitchell to Franklin, 12 September 1745, LPCC 3:151.

9. LPCC 8:314–28.

He was embarrassed that Franklin had sent his rough notes on Colden's remarks to him, particularly since he had not even kept a copy of them. He could not agree with Colden's proposal of relying completely on diluents. It "is only *Lionem subere excipere* (as the Latins say) to throw at a lyon with corks instead of stones." Mitchell considered purges, used with discretion, an absolute necessity and said so for a number of pages, including a short discussion of Rattlesnake root employed in this manner. Likewise, in a postscript, he gave an account of purging in three specific cases. He had no experience with tar-water, but took a dim view of Bishop Berkeley's treatise on the subject.

He could not close without a discussion of the possible origin of yellow fever. He had made a study of available evidence which proved that at four different times, the fever was imported by ship from England "after a long & tedious voyage." In Philadelphia, doctors had told him that it had been imported there twice in a similar manner, "once by the Palatines, & once from Bristol." Some Philadelphia physicians believed that it had been produced from the air, but Mitchell remarked that air might propagate but not originate the contagion. He thought it probably proceeded from animal putrefaction.

As for combating its spread, Virginians daily employed a combination of salt, smoke, and vinegar with which to fumigate. They had likewise found steaming with sulphur to be effective. He thought it advisable that such methods be used aboard ship. Vinegar should be boiled continuously and a regular smoking with sulphur instituted. Air holes or some sort of ventilation should be incorporated between decks where the sick lay. Since such methods to prevent the spread in town and country were impossible, isolation was the only hope. He would like to hear Colden's opinion of the history of yaws, since he was such an Indian authority.

In the same post, Mitchell received a letter from Franklin, who invited him for a visit which Mitchell had to decline.[10] He had planned to go to northern Virginia at this time to avoid malaria but was so unwell that he had not even been able to do that. Franklin wanted to publish the yellow fever paper in his proposed monthly, *American Philosophical Miscellany*. Mitchell expressed his appreciation for the suggestion: "I was highly delighted to see so good an opportunity any one might have to oblige the publick, & to promote the arts of Sciences, as your Press

10. Mitchell to Franklin, 12 September 1745, LPCC 3:151-54.

affords; better than I expected to have found in our new world. I look upon myself obliged, thro' gratitude to you, as well as the justice due to your laudable industry & improvements in that way, to encourage your press as much as I can. The Debt likewise which we all owe to the publick, would make me do what I could to discharge it." However, Mitchell had to refuse: not only was his health poor but the essay was not ready for that type of publication. Colden had also urged its publication but Mitchell had only considered the proposed American Philosophical Society's *Transactions* as a possible vehicle. He felt that it would need extensive rewriting before publishing elsewhere.

It was from Dr. Spencer that he learned that all thought of the publication had been abandoned.[11] Spencer had come to Virginia sometime before mid-September, 1745, and was busy making preparations for a series of lectures. Not until 9 January was he able to announce them in the *Virginia Gazette*: "Doctor Spencer begins a Course of EXPERIMENTAL PHILOSOPHY, on *Wednesday* next, at Four o'Clock in the Afternoon, and to be continued on such Days, and at such Hours as shall be agreed upon by the Majority of the Auditors at the first Lecture. N.B. Catalogues of the Experiments may be had *gratis*, at his House in *Williamsburg*, where the Course is to be performed." It was pleasant for Mitchell to have Spencer so nearby and he passed on Colden's regards which were sent in his next letter.

The letter that Mitchell wrote to Colden on 10 September he sent in Franklin's care, telling the latter that he was quite welcome to read it. He was enthusiastic about corresponding on yellow fever with anyone interested, he wrote Franklin, "But you must excuse my not publishing any thing yet a while. I think this world is pestered with this Itch of many to appear in print, which makes many so little regarded that do. Authors ought to be Masters not only of the particular subject, but of the whole art, they undertake to instruct the world in, & when they are—*Nonum prematur in annum*, saies Horace."[12]

Colden was quite ready to continue the yellow fever discussion. In November, he wrote to Mitchell, sending his letter through Franklin for his perusal.[13] He asked Mitchell if any acids had been used in the treatment. He recounted the history of New York's two yellow fever

11. Mitchell to Colden, 10 September 1745, LPCC 8:323.
12. Mitchell to Franklin, 12 September 1745, LPCC 3:154.
13. 7 November 1745, LPCC 8:328–38.

epidemics and the concomitant etiology, with a precise description of the harbor. He described the filth around the wharves and the marshy areas upon which many houses had been built. The Royal Battery, acting as a barrier, had slowed the healthful current which carried away much of the debris. In the 1743 epidemic, cases were concentrated in the harbor area and surrounding residential blocks, which caused him to conclude that the unhealthy atmosphere propagated if it did not originate the disease. Colden had incorporated his ideas in a short pamphlet, which was reprinted in the New York *Postboy* and in Philadelphia by Franklin.[14] As a result, the New York magistrates set about clearing up the harbor area. The poorer people complained so bitterly over the project that the magistrates were not reelected and the plan was dropped. What little they accomplished may have contributed to a healthy year in 1744. Unfortunately, 1745 again produced the fever. This time it was confined almost completely to the wharves where no prophylactic measures had been taken. New York physicians were so secretive due to monetary considerations that Colden was unable to learn anything in regard to their treatment of patients. The two cases in June which he had heard about had had a mild rash and resembled *Febris Miliaris*. Colden's letter seems rather confused with descriptions of several types of fevers.[15]

As for the yaws, Colden thought that they probably originated in Africa, while the French Pox (syphilis) came from America. He then turned to tar-water's amazing qualities. He told of one of his close friends, Mr. Alexander, who was convinced that it cured him. The last paragraph Colden devoted to a discussion of his latest enthusiasm, *Action in Matter*. As a postscript, he added that Mrs. Colden hoped that Mitchell would tell Patrick Cheap that she wished she could make a bowl of punch "for us as she had formerly done." Colden was unaware that Cheap had died the previous December.[16]

14. Unsigned articles in *New-York Weekly Postboy*, 26 December 1743–9 January 1744. Franklin reprinted them in the *Pennsylvania Gazette*, 11 January–2 February 1744, according to Saul Jarcho, "Cadwallader Colden as a Student of Infectious Disease," *Bulletin of the History of Medicine* 29 (March–April 1955):113, note 31.

15. Jarcho said that epidemics where malaria was followed by typhoid confused the doctors for well over a hundred years. In fact, he thought that cases of yellow fever may well have added to the confusion (ibid., p. 102).

16. Cheap died sometime prior to 4 December 1744 (Middlesex Court Orders, 1740–44, pp. 267–68, VSL). The previous June, Mitchell had sued Cheap, who was administrator for James Compton's estate. When neither party appeared for the court's decision

Although Mitchell's known correspondence does not again discuss yellow fever at length, his essay on it and the resulting correspondence with Colden and Franklin were not lost to the medical world. Not long before Franklin's death in 1790, the well-known Philadelphia physician, Benjamin Rush, borrowed the copy which he had made of the essay.[17] Securing permission, Rush copied long extracts from it which he presented before a meeting of the College of Physicians. Three years later, Philadelphia's historic yellow fever epidemic broke out. It spread so rapidly and the fatalities were so great that the city's doctors were frantic. Rush was no exception:

Baffled in every attempt to stop the ravages of this fever, I anticipated all the numerous and complicated distresses in our city, which pestilential diseases have so often produced in other countries. The fever had a malignity, and an obstinacy which I had never before observed in any disease, and it spread with a rapidity and mortality, far beyond what it did in the year 1762. Heaven alone bore witness to the anguish of my soul in this awful situation. But I did not abandon a hope that the disease might yet be cured. I had long believed that good was commensurate with evil, and that there does not exist a disease for which the goodness of Providence has not provided a remedy. Under the impression of this belief, I applied my self with fresh ardour to the investigation of the disease before me. I ransacked my library, and pored over every book that treated of the yellow fever. The result of my researches for a while was fruitless. The accounts of the symptoms and cure of the disease by the authors I consulted, were contradictory, and none of them appeared altogether applicable to the prevailing epidemic. Before I desisted from the inquiry to which I had devoted myself, I recollected that I had among some old papers, a manuscript account of the yellow fever as it prevailed in Virginia in the year 1741, which had been put into my hands by Dr. Franklin, a short time before his death. I read it formerly, and made extracts from it into my lectures upon that disorder. I now read it a second time. I paused upon every sentence; even words in some places arrested and fixed my attention. In reading the history of the method of cure, I was much struck with the following passages.[18]

---

on 7 August, the suit was dismissed (ibid., pp. 255, 258). Mitchell was plaintiff in another suit that year, in which he sued the estate of Dr. Francis Nicholson for two pounds, three shillings on 4 September. An amicable settlement was agreed upon and the case dismissed (ibid., p. 262).

17. Rush to Samuel P. Griffits, Secretary of the College of Physicians, 24 March 1790, *Letters of Benjamin Rush*, ed. L. H. Butterfield, 2 vols. (Princeton, 1951), 2, note on p. 700.

18. Benjamin Rush, M.D., *An Account of the Bilious Remitting Yellow Fever as It Appeared in the City of Philadelphia in the Year 1793* (Philadelphia, 1794), pp. 196–97.

Here Rush quoted Mitchell at length upon purging: "Dr. Mitchell in a moment dissipated my ignorance and fears upon this subject. I adopted his theory, and practice, and resolved to follow them."[19] Rush incorporated this and other aspects of Mitchell's treatment along with those recommended by his old master, Dr. John Redman, and others.[20] Unlike Mitchell, he favored phlebotomy. In a paper on *An Inquiry into the Proximate Cause of Fever*, Rush quoted Mitchell's essay. He referred to it again in a series of lectures on medical practice printed in 1811.[21] In speaking of keeping the air pure in hospitals, he mentioned that Mitchell had recommended washing the walls. He thought that this would be even more efficacious if lye or salt of tartar were added to the water. Seven years earlier, Rush had sent his extracts from Mitchell's paper to Dr. John Redman Coxe for publication in the *Medical Museum*.[22] His manuscript copy "perished" in the printing office. At Dr. Coxe's death in 1808, his daughter sent Rush a copy of the article together with some of Mitchell's and Colden's subsequent correspondence on the subject. Rush forwarded them to Dr. David Hosack for publication in *The American Medical and Philosophical Register*.[23] Today, the College of Physicians in Philadelphia has two manuscript copies, one given them in 1909 by Dr. S. Weir Mitchell which appeared in a copybook of Dr. John Redman Coxe and another by the family of Mr. John Cadwalader in 1934.[24]

For many years, Mitchell was considered one of the earliest authorities on yellow fever and he was often quoted.[25] As recently as 1931,

19. Ibid., p. 199.
20. Rush to John R. B. Rodgers, 3 October 1793, *Letters of Rush*, 2:698.
21. Printed in Philadelphia, 1796, p. 139; *Sixteen Introductory Lectures, to Courses of Lectures Upon the Institutes and Practice of Medicine, with a Syllabus of the Latter to Which Are Added Two Lectures Upon the Pleasures of the Senses and of the Mind, with an Inquiry into Their Proximate Cause.* Delivered in the University of Pennsylvania. By Benjamin Rush (Philadelphia, 1811).
22. Rush's letter to Dr. Coxe, 31 July 1804, was printed at the beginning of the extracts from Mitchell's essay in the *Medical Museum*, 1, #1.
23. Rush to Hosack, 15 August 1810, *Letters of Rush*, 2:1057.
24. Francis R. Packard, "The Manuscript of Dr. John Mitchell's Account of the Yellow Fever in Virginia in 1741–42, written in 1748," *Proceedings of the Charaka Club* 9 (1938):45–46.
25. Examples of this: August Hirsch, *Handbook of Geographical and Historical Pathology*, trans. C. C. Creighton (London, 1883–86) and R. LaRoche, *Yellow Fever Considered in Its Historical, Pathological, Etiological and Therapeutical Relations*, 2 vols. (Philadelphia, 1855).

Dr. Wyndham B. Blanton remarked that Mitchell exhibited "a mind thoroughly imbued with the spirit of scientific investigations" and that his paper "was a classic among early American medical essays."[26] Nevertheless, as early as 1855, La Roche entertained doubts as to the exact nature of the disease which Mitchell had described, when he was discussing uncertainty in diagnosis of epidemics.[27] At one point, he referred to it as the "so called yellow fever."[28] A century later, Dr. Saul Jarcho gave a paper before the American Association of the History of Medicine entitled "John Mitchell, Benjamin Rush, and Yellow Fever."[29] Jarcho pointed out that six of the seven specific cases occurred during the late winter and early spring when it is impossible for the vector (the mosquito, *Aedes Aegypti*) to transmit the disease. Only one case occurred in September, a normal time for yellow fever. In regard to this, Mitchell stated that the contagion had come from a different place. In 1962, Dr. Gordon W. Jones came to a conclusion similar to Dr. Jarcho's in an article, "Doctor John Mitchell's Yellow Fever Epidemics."[30] In a talk before a *Symposium on American Contributions to the History of Tropical Medicine* in 1967, Dr. John B. Blake agreed with Dr. Jarcho.[31]

There are differing opinions as to the exact nature of these Virginia epidemics. Dr. Jones considers that it may have been typhus or relapsing fever since slaves were especially susceptible and many children had mild cases. One argument in opposition to this theory is that jaundice is seldom symptomatic of these diseases, certainly not to the extent which Mitchell described. Dr. Jarcho quoted Manson-Bahr: "Severe yellow fever may be confused with remittent subtertian malaria, Weil's disease, infective hepatitis, relapsing fever, and blackwater fever. The difficulties of clinical diagnosis are often great, especially early in an epidemic." Although Jarcho considers any hypothesis shaky, he favors the theory that Mitchell's epidemics were infectious hepatitis, since it tends to reach epidemic proportions seasonally. Both doctors were impressed by Mitchell's account which Jones found full of com-

26. Blanton, *Medicine in Virginia in the Eighteenth Century*, p. 54.
27. LaRoche, *Yellow Fever*, 2:416.
28. Ibid., 1:176.
29. *Bulletin of the History of Medicine* 31 (1957):132–36.
30. *Virginia Magazine of History and Biography* 70 (January 1962):43–48.
31. "Yellow Fever in Eighteenth Century America," *Bulletin of the New York Academy of Medicine*, 2d ser. 44 (June 1968):673–86.

mon sense. Jarcho considered it "an essay which contains elements of originality and is a vigorous closely reasoned effort."[32]

From a prolonged study of the various documents exchanged by Mitchell and Colden, it seems more probable that this was Weil's Disease, as it is so similar to yellow fever in symptoms, although they are milder. The pathological findings which Mitchell described closely follow those in Weil's disease as do the symptoms and progress of the illness. Infective hepatitis, while displaying jaundice, is not considered a particularly serious disease and has a low mortality rate. It can also be chronic and from Mitchell's description there seems to be no indication of this in the Virginia epidemics. Relapsing fever is recurrent, with jaundice present only occasionally. Only one epidemic has been reported in this country (1869), but it is endemic in parts of Eastern Europe, with mild epidemics very rarely in "China, India, and North and West Africa."[33] As for typhus, Mitchell himself was quite definite on the subject:

There are many kinds of Pestilential fevers mentioned by authors. The Petechial, Hungarian, Camp & Gaol fevers, with the Pestilential fever from Asia & Africa. Of these ours most resembles the Camp & Gaol fevers in its origin, but not in its appearances & Cure. In these it entirely agrees with the Hungarian fever, (as it was called in Germany in the time of the Holy War), according to the accounts several good writers have given of it. I have seen this & the Gaol fever at the same time, & found them different in circumstances. The greatest difference is in the apparatus of humors in primis viis (Bile, viscid crudities &c.) in our Americans, which chiefly cause the Icterus, & its name among us. In these it agrees with the Hungarian Pestilence . . . as well as in all other symptoms, Causes, & Cure &c. whence I pronouce ym the same disease. J.M.

Of this we have good accounts by ye German writers in ye 16th & 17th Centuries, when this Disease surprised Europe as much as ours has done America, & proved more fatal, lasting 30 years. vid. Jordan, Conradin, Cober, Langius, Crato, Rulendiis, Lennertus, &c.[34]

32. "Cadwallader Colden," *Bulletin of the History of Medicine* 29 (March–April 1955): 104.

33. Russell L. Cecil, ed., *A Text-Book of Medicine by American Authors* (Philadelphia & London, 1934), pp. 432–33.

34. Mitchell to Colden, 10 September 1745, LPCC 8:327–28. Even descriptions of Hungarian fever seem to differ greatly. Pringle wrote that it was contagious and mortal, running a course of 14–20 days. He said it was first described in 1566 when it appeared among the Hungarian soldiers. He quoted Sennertus who said it was made worse by a

The etiology of Weil's Disease fits in well with Mitchell's conviction that the source of the epidemics was ships from England. Weil's Disease is caused by a spirochete (*Leptospira icterohaemorrhagiae*) often present in rats. It is now thought that victims receive the infection from food or water contaminated by the urine of infected rats. It would easily explain whole families succumbing, as Mitchell described, and the apparent inconsistency in its spread.[35]

Whatever the disease may have been, Mitchell's writing on the subject was clearly provocative for many years to come. Jarcho has said "It is well recognized that a given disease such as yellow fever is an abstract concept derived from the primary data, i.e., from clinical and laboratory observations. These abstract concepts necessarily evolve. In the middle of the eighteenth century the abstract concept of yellow fever was incompletely and imperfectly separable from the concept of other febrile diseases in which jaundice occurs. Mature differentiation did not develop until the isolation of the causative virus . . . in 1928. Further evolution occurred in the 1930's. . . . The work of Mitchell and Rush thus represents a crude early stage in a long process."[36]

When commenting on his own health to Franklin in September, Mitchell said that he was no longer able to practice medicine. In fact, since the beginning of the month, he was so weakened as to be unable even to keep his "Journals of observation," in which he recorded notes for an eventual Natural History.[37] To Colden he remarked sadly, "But at the best I find, this is living to no purpose, & only enduring life without the greatest enjoyments of it, and besides availes but little to me, to lay down my pursuits of this kind, for the recovery of my lost health."[38] Bartram wrote to Gronovius that if Mitchell "don't remove soon from Virginia, he can't continue long in the land of the living."[39] As his own physician, Mitchell realized that it would be exceedingly

---

bad climate and was apt to appear in swampy areas. In fact, one doctor told him of an epidemic where the place was swarming with "aquatic insects." Yet Pringle said the same fever appeared in Denmark, but remarked on the petechial spots which were an accompaniment there (John Pringle, *Observations on the Diseases of the Army* [London, 1768], pp. 188–90).

35. Cecil, *A Text-Book*, pp. 438–39.
36. Jarcho, "John Mitchell," *Bulletin of the History of Medicine* 31 (1957):136.
37. 12 September 1745, LPCC 3:151–54.
38 10 September 1745, LPCC 8:314.
39. 6 December 1745, Darlington, *Memorials*, p. 353

dangerous for him to remain in Virginia any longer. In order just to survive, he must remove to a different area as soon as possible and he had chosen England. He wrote to Franklin that he would write again before he left, which was not likely before spring. He was uncertain what he would do in London as it would depend upon the state of his health at that time. He gave no reasons for his choice of England but it is probable that he thought better medical attention would be available there.

Mitchell's house was listed for sale in November, including both the apothecary shop and chemical laboratory.[40] All furniture, as well as books, would be sold. His library was a well-rounded one, "both ancient and modern." It specialized in medicine, surgery, botany, and natural history but there were volumes of philosophy, too. There were recent journals such as the *Philosophical Transactions* of the Royal Society of London and the Edinburgh *Essays*. Four languages were represented: English, French, Latin, and Greek. Mitchell was willing to sell them most reasonably, at the price which they would bring in England which was far below current Virginia prices. Evidently his plan was to immediately replace them when he reached London. Dr. Gordon W. Jones has studied the writing which Mitchell did in Virginia and has identified many of the books which he is fairly certain were part of his library.[41] He reached this conclusion through Mitchell's references and included only those in which he actually gave the page number, indication that he had the book before him. Using the same yardstick, other books may be added to the list from various writing which was not available to Dr. Jones. It is evident that Mitchell was an omnivorous reader.

The Mitchells did not sell their house immediately. As the doctor was attempting to settle his accounts, it was just as well that there was some delay. In order to deal with those debts uncollected before his departure, he drew up a power of attorney for his father, which was witnessed by his half brothers, Robert, Jr., and Richard, Isaac White, and Joseph Ball on 7 January.[42] The following day, papers were signed concluding the sale of Mitchell's property to Dr. Alexander Reade of

40. 21 November 1745, *Virginia Gazette*.

41. "The Library of Doctor John Mitchell of Urbanna," *Virginia Magazine of History and Biography* 76 (October 1968):441–43.

42. Deeds & Wills, Lancaster County, pp. 145–46, VSL.

Gloucester County.[43] Little is known of Reade, except that he was comfortably off and was also to serve as parish doctor.[44] When he died in 1760, he left a large estate, having already presented his sons with the Urbanna property by deed of gift.[45] His estate included houses in Bedfordshire, England. The inventory of his property listed one hundred and twelve books, many of which could have been Mitchell's originally. However, Reade did not purchase Mitchell's library in January. It was advertised for sale again in April, when he might have been the purchaser.[46]

Sixty pounds were paid to seal the contract for sale of the property and other unspecified "goods and valuable Causes and Considerations" were given to complete it. Richard Mitchell, Alexander Frazier, and Francis Tomkies were among the witnesses to the indenture. Mrs. Mitchell was so ill on the day of the sale that she was unable to go to the courthouse. Two Justices of the Court, James Reid and Christopher Curtis, went to the Mitchells' home to take her deposition agreeing to the sale.[47]

Considering the state of Mrs. Mitchell's health, it is unlikely that the Mitchells took passage for England for several weeks. Although they had sold most of their belongings, there were still personal things to be packed. To these, Mitchell added the voluminous medical and natural history notes which he had made over the years. Carefully, he packed his herbarium, consisting of over one thousand specimens, and various seeds which he treasured.[48] As was customary when travelers went to England, friends sent parcels in their care, knowing they would not be neglected. John Clayton made up one to be forwarded to Gronovius at Leyden.[49] Several parcels from Bartram to Gronovius arrived from Philadelphia. Even Dr. Colden sent some for both Gronovius and Linnaeus.[50]

43. Middlesex County Deed Book, 1740–54, pp. 183–86, VSL.

44. Blanton, *Medicine in Virginia in the Eighteenth Century*, pp. 102–6 and 380.

45. Deed of gift dated 21 November 1759, Middlesex County Deed Book, 1754–67, pt. 1, p. 242, VSL. His will was dated less than three weeks later, on 11 December (Middlesex County Wills, 1675–1798, pt. 2, p. 292, VSL).

46. 17 April 1746, *Virginia Gazette*.

47. Middlesex County Deed Book, 1740–54, pp. 186–87, VSL.

48. Mitchell to Linnaeus, 10 August 1748, CLO 2:445–46.

49. J. F. Gronovius to Linnaeus, 6 January 1747, LCLS.

50. Linnaeus to Haller, 23 August 1746, CLO 2:391.

Saying good-bye to family and friends, without knowing when they would again see them, if ever, was very difficult for the Mitchells. It was hard, too, for him to leave this fascinating and exasperating country which he had only begun to investigate. There were so many things which he wanted to know in botany, zoology, agriculture, and medicine. He had never had an opportunity to explore and analyze the medicinal springs as he and Collinson had planned. Since boyhood, he had been thrilled with the tales of those who had traveled inland. He had read the journal of Batts and Fallam, recording their adventures in western Virginia as early as 1671. From Clayton, he had learned of the lands to the west, the Great Valley of Virginia and even the lands beyond. From Spotswood and other Knights of the Golden Horseshoe, he heard of the lands beyond the Blue Ridge. Whenever he had met surveyors, he questioned them closely. Not long before Mitchell sailed, John Peter Salley and a companion had returned to Virginia with the most stirring account of the west up to that time. In 1742, they and four others had made their way to the Mississippi River. They proceeded down this great body of water until captured by the French not far from New Orleans. Salley and one other escaped. Mitchell had been fascinated by Salley's tales and left Virginia with a gnawing frustration that he had seen so little of his native country. He hoped to return home eventually if his health permitted.

When Helen and John Mitchell finally boarded ship, it lay in Hampton Roads for some time. A troop ship with soldiers "designed for Carthagena" and New York forts put into the harbor, anchoring alongside the Mitchells' ship. The stench from the ship was quite unbearable. Going up on deck to investigate, Mitchell could readily see the cause. Most of the soldiers were visibly very ill from some contagious disease of which several had died. From what he could observe, Mitchell suspected yellow fever.[51]

51. Mitchell to Colden, 25 March 1749, Theodore Hornberger, ed., "A Letter from John Mitchell to Cadwallader Colden," *Huntington Library Quarterly* 10 (1946–47): 412–13.

VII ❧ New Friends and Old Correspondents in London

". . . friendly & Phil: meetings. . . ."

Da Costa to James Sherwood, 1748[1]

With such an inauspicious beginning to their voyage and the fact that England was at war, the Mitchells should not have been too surprised by its tragic ending. As they approached land in early May, the "Tiger," a privateer from St. Malo, commanded by Captain Pallier, seized their ship.[2] The passengers were safely landed in France but all of their possessions were taken. With horror, Mitchell saw his years of study, represented in his notes, disappear along with his herbarium specimens and all of the parcels which he was to deliver to Gronovius and Linnaeus. Only some letters to Duhamel and Jussieu were forwarded.[3] Like refugees, the Mitchells finally reached London at the end of the month.[4] It required many weeks for Mitchell, who was still ailing, to recover. By mid-July, he was feeling considerably improved. It was not long before he realized that his health was certainly better than it would have been in Virginia in midsummer. Even Collinson commented on his great improvement.[5] Eventually, his herbarium was returned from France via Hamburg and Rotterdam. Between the ravages of the sea water and the rough handling of the pirates, there was "scarcely a perfect flower left."[6] His observations may have been returned at the same time, although Mitchell made no mention that they had been.

After the quiet of Urbanna, London was noisy and overcrowded

1. 17 May, B.M. Add. MSS 28,542, f. 198.
2. J. F. Gronovius to Bartram, 2 June 1746, Darlington, *Memorials*, p. 356.
3. J. F. Gronovius to Linnaeus, 12 May 1747, LCLS.
4. Franklin to Colden, 16 October 1746, *Papers of Franklin*, 3:92.
5. In a postscript to Gronovius (2 June letter to Bartram, Darlington, *Memorials*, p. 356).
6. Mitchell to Linnaeus, 10 August 1748, CLO 2:446.

and yet exciting. Whether or not either John or Helen Mitchell had been there previously is unknown. No matter how tiny, each house had a small garden filled with trees and flowers, all of the hardier sort which could survive the coal smoke of London. This ever-present pollution was extremely annoying, particularly in the winter when even the snow was dark from it. Many of the streets were unpaved and often muddy. Now, in midsummer, when a dry spell sent dust rising in clouds from the roads, an occasional cart would pass, watering it down. In order to retain even a semblance of cleanliness within the houses, women wore wooden pattens over their ordinary shoes and men were meticulous about scraping off mud or dust before entering the front door. Everywhere, old men and women sat ready to clean shoes for a halfpenny each.[7]

The Mitchells were probably surprised by the prevalence of wigs. Everyone wore them, not just the ladies and gentlemen. Farm servants, "clod-hoppers," and laborers invested a guinea for even mediocre ones. As soon as little boys donned breeches, they were likely to put on a peruke, "sometimes not much smaller than himself." There were many amenities most welcome to the Mitchells. One of these was a speedier and more reliable postal service. It was often a half-mile to the Post-house, so well before it was due to leave, men ringing bells offered to post your mail for a penny a letter.[8] Within two miles of the city, between Fulham and Chester, lay hundreds of gardens, mostly market gardens. Here and there were large brick houses of the gentlefolk. At Vauxhall, across the Thames from Westminster, there were the popular pleasure-gardens frequented by the young in the evenings. Formal allées planted with lime and elm trees made a pleasant place to stroll. Concerts in the large hall commenced as twilight fell, with refreshments served during the interval. Beyond Chelsea lay Ranelagh House where the elderly as well as the young gathered to hear the concerts.[9] There were many similar places of entertainment in addition to the numerous theaters so the Mitchells found that there was a surfeit of amusement when they desired it. The streets themselves provided entertainment with the continual parade of peddlers and their cries. Bas-

7. *Kalm's Account of His Visit to England on His Way to America in 1748*, ed. Joseph Lucas (London, 1892), pp. 85, 37, 12–13.

8. Ibid., pp. 52–53, 63.

9. Ibid., pp. 35, 64, 94–95.

kets on their heads and often bells in their hands, they hawked an astonishing variety of goods: oranges, peaches, strawberries, fish, flowers, eggs, mussels, stockings, periwinkles, chestnuts, Tunbridge ware, and even birch brooms.

Dr. Mitchell's first known address in London was Catherine Street. His mail was directed in care of an apothecary.[10] Catherine Street is no longer in existence. It ran from Covent Garden into the Strand, diagonally across from Somerset House. The eastern side of the street was lined with handsome houses, most of which belonged to prosperous tradesmen. Years before, Pepys had visited the Fleece there and Dr. Samuel Johnson enjoyed the hospitality of another Catherine Street tavern about this time. Six years earlier, James Hall had been executed at the end of the street on a September day.[11]

Mitchell surprisingly soon found numerous congenial friends. A warm English welcome was extended by Peter Collinson. He was short and very pleasantly rounded, called corpulent by his less flattering friends, and modestly attired in the plain garb of the Quakers. "Capable of feeling for distress, and ready to relieve and sympathize . . . he enjoyed in general, perfect health, and great equality of spirits."[12] A friend once said of him: "He was a remarkable instance, that he who is never idle need never be in a hurry."[13] Collinson's mercantile office would have been more than enough to occupy an average man. His worldwide correspondence was voluminous enough to keep a clerk busy but he employed no amanuensis. His circle of friends embraced all strata of British society and he could always find time to do them favors. Yet, with such a life, he was not too busy to welcome the Mitchells.

Collinson was very pleased to meet at last one of his New World correspondents. He had had little hope of seeing any of them face to face, and here was a man who could give him firsthand accounts of Custis and Clayton, Bartram, Franklin, Logan, and many others, and who could answer his many questions about Virginia and Pennsylvania.

10. James Sherwood to da Costa, 17 May 1748, B.M. Add. MSS 28,542, f. 199.

11. E. B. Chacellor, *The Annals of the Strand* (London, 1912), p. 60; Charles Gordon, *Oldtime Aldwych, Kingsway and Neighborhood* (London, 1903), p. 181.

12. John Nichols, *Literary Anecdotes of the Eighteenth Century*, 9 vols. (London, 1812), 5:312.

13. "Genuine Anecdotes of the Life of the Late Peter Collinson, F.R.S.," *Annual Register* (1770):57.

Here, too, was a man whose personality charmed Collinson as it had the Philadelphians. Mitchell, for his part, was equally attracted by Collinson's delightful character and the two men enjoyed many visits with each other.

The Londoner introduced Mitchell to his many friends. He took him out to Mill-hill, near Enfield, where he had his botanical garden. It was beautifully laid out to receive the first rays of the morning sun. Collinson explained that he found that the quadrilateral shape was more practical than the circular. The Duke of Richmond's round one had suffered much from the wind. While not large, Collinson's garden was perhaps unequaled in England for the great variety and rarity of his trees and shrubs.[14] Friends sent them from the Continent. Through sea captains and merchant friends he was able to gradually acquire plants from Africa, India, and even China. Mitchell was excited by all these strange and unusual plants. He was interested, too, in seeing how well many of those from Virginia and Pennsylvania had adapted to the English climate. He recognized Clayton's gifts of *Halesia*, Fringe Trees and a *Stewartia*, which Mitchell called *Malachodendron*.[15] Collinson showed him some of Bartram's offerings: pink and yellow Lady-slippers, Skunkweed, *Martagon Canadense*, upright Honeysuckle (Wild Azalea), Mountain Laurel, and Rhododendrons.[16] The Virginia variety of the last was unable to survive in England. Collinson pointed out *Meadia* (Shooting Star), which Bartram had just sent.[17] It was by no means a new introduction as it had once flourished in Bishop Compton's garden under the name of American Cowslip, but it had been lost.[18] Mitchell was delighted to find that many of the seeds which he had sent to Collinson had germinated into husky plants and trees.

The beds were outlined in a most curious manner as described by a visitor two years later:

For the border or the outer edge of the flower-beds, Mr. Collinson had set knuckle-bones, of horse or ox-legs, such as the boys with us in Sweden and Finland use to make their so-called "*ice-legs*," with which they run upon the

14. *Kalm's Account*, pp. 66–68.
15. Collinson to Colden, 25 February 1764, LPCC 6:290.
16. Mark Catesby, *The Natural History of Carolina, Florida and the Bahama Islands*, 2 vols. (London, 1729–47), 2:72–73, 71, 98; 1:57, 17.
17. Ibid., 1, Appendix, p. 1.
18. Ewan and Ewan, *Banister*, p. 175.

ice. The transversal end, was set down in the ground, and the round curled end stood upwards. All were the same length, and quite close to one another, which performed the same service in hindering the earth from slipping down from the beds, as if there had been boards set round them. This use of horse-leg bones in kitchen-gardens I have seen before at several places just outside *Moscow*, in Russia.

Collinson's ingenuity was also apparent in the skillful clipping of an elm tree and a chestnut to form the roofs of a summer house.[19] There were many gardening secrets which he shared with his friends. He had discovered how to "plant" mistletoe: "The berry is squeezed open, and laid on the smooth places on the bark, of some tree, when it very quickly fastens itself. But if they are laid in the rimes or cracks, of the bark of a tree, they will fasten on to it with difficulty." Cranberry seeds he placed in a pot with no bottom opening, covered it with moss and set it in the shade. Swamp and bog plants responded equally well to this method of germination.[20]

Undoubtedly, one of Mitchell's first questions for Collinson was regarding the status of his essays on botany. As soon as Collinson had received the concluding part from Mitchell in 1745, he had written his Nuremberg, Germany, apothecary friend, Jean Ambrose Beurer for his advice on their publication. His letter to Beurer was quite frank concerning his own fellow countrymen:

As the English in General are too Lazey & Indolent to make themselves Masters of the Lattin Tongue—for that Reason Lattin Books are Little Read & so very Little Encouragement to print any—I have Several very Curious Tracts from a Learned Physician in Virginia in Lattin pray advise mee in what place I can send them to be printed so as they may come to the knowledge & Reading of all the Learned World—1st Tract—is Intituled; Dissertatio brevis de principiis Botanicorum et Zoologorum deque novo Stabiliendo Naturae rerum congruo.
2d Tract—Nova Genera Plantarum
3d Tract—Vires Plantarum
These 3 tracts contain observations treated with great Judgment & Learning & no doubt will be very acceptable to the Botanist & the Physitian—
If these was printed in the Acta Germanica or any other publick Transactions or Memoirs of Literature, or one Book by themselves I submitt to your Docr.

19. *Kalm's Account*, pp. 67, 87.
20. Ibid., pp. 67–68

Trew—if you will be so good to undertake the Trouble of ushering them into the World I will send them next Spring with what Natural Rarities I can gett together for I am greatly in your Debt.[21]

The doctor Trew to whom Collinson referred was Christopher Jakob Trew (1695–1769). A graduate of the University of Altdorf, he had made a scientific trip through Switzerland, Germany, France, Holland, and Danzig in 1717. Upon his return, he had studied medicine at Nuremberg and become a highly successful doctor with a wealthy practice in that town. He was well-known also as a botanist and bibliophile and was one of the first to recognize the artistic genius of Georg Ehret. He commissioned him to make a series of paintings around 1730 and continued as a "lifelong patron and friend" of the man who was to become perhaps the most outstanding botanical illustrator of the century. Even after Ehret settled permanently in England in 1737, their relationship continued.[22]

Through Ehret and a series of gifts to the Royal Society, Trew was known to many in England. The books and periodicals with which Trew graced the society were not without purpose, for Beurer had written Collinson that Trew desired to be elected a foreign Fellow. In February of 1744/45, Collinson had assured his apothecary friend that he would do all in his power to see that Trew was elected. He did not consider that this would be difficult since Trew had formerly sent the society so many publications even if he had not done so well by them recently.[23] Now, in his letter to Beurer concerning Mitchell's papers, Collinson exhibited his expertise as a canny merchant and trader. He expressed concern over the loss of Trew's letters to the society but would present his gift which had arrived. In a subsequent letter in January, 1745/46, he wrote that he would not forget to enclose Mitchell's papers in a box the coming spring, since Beurer had agreed to submit them to Trew. Collinson wrote that he knew how much pleasure they would provide him, Trew, and other learned men. He casually added that Trew would certainly be elected to the Royal Society.[24]

21. 25 November 1745, University Library Erlangen, Trew Papers, subsequently referred to as ENU. The authors are grateful for permission to quote from this and other letters.
22. Wilfred Blunt, *The Art of Botanical Illustration* (London, 1950), pp. 144, 149–50.
23. Collinson to Beurer, 7 February, ENU.
24. Probably written 21 January, ENU.

Although the papers themselves were sent to Beurer, Collinson prepared the ground by writing directly to Trew as well. He accompanied his letter with presents of rare and unusual lilies and narcissi, in which he knew Dr. Trew was greatly interested. The list included a "Red Flowering Narcissus from China," which had been obtained by Mr. Blackburn at Oxford. There was a reddish-purple and white narcissus from Cape Coast Castle in Guinea. This had been sent to Sir Charles Wager, whose stoves Collinson managed while the admiral was at sea. There were lilies from Jamaica, St. Christophers, the Bahamas, and Barbadoes. Collinson's list gave descriptions and references. There were some about which he was doubtful and asked Trew's advice on their identification. As a mere afterthought, he added as a postscript to his letter: "I Recommend Docr. Mitchells Tracts to yr. protection, & Patronage   Beg the Favour you will give them Title pages. You may Insert the Dedication to Sr Hans Sloane, or Leave it quite out, as you like best,—This Docr. Mitchell Desired Mee to Tell you. Mr. Beurer will Deliver the Tracts to you."[25]

This dedicatory letter, intended by Mitchell to accompany the third tract, caused much later confusion, for the letter was printed only with the republication of the first two dissertations some twenty years later, and has long been assumed to have been written in connection with those papers. Thatcher, on this assumption, considered it to have been written in 1738 and others have accepted his view.[26] Careful reading of the letter, however, makes it plain that it was addressed to Sloane with an entirely different paper: Mitchell wrote: "Once I had decided, on the *advice and exhortation of my friends*, to publish this slight work of mine, I was not long in doubt under whose patronage I should do so. . . . But indeed, it was not without good grounds that I wished to offer you, and you alone, these efforts of mine, such as they are, because you are almost the only one that has investigated and skilfully dealt with their subject: *the medicinal plants of America*." It was this letter, however, which led to the discovery that there had definitely been a third paper, the "Vires Plantarum," a treatise on medicinal plants.

When still nothing had been heard regarding publication by the following February (1746/47), Collinson again wrote to Trew on the ninth: "I hope Docr. Mitchells papers are printed in yr. Com. Littm.

25. 30 March 1745/46, ENU.
26. "Dr. Mitchell," *Virginia Magazine of History and Biography* 40 (April 1932):97.

He is now in London and would be glad to see Them. He has as many others Curious by him the Favour of a Line will Greatly Oblige. . . ." At Mitchell's instigation and contrary to his customary practice of only an annual letter, Collinson wrote to Trew again on the eighteenth: "Docr. Mitchell is now in London—He Desires his complements to you & sends the Inclosed to be added to his Nov. Gen.—But if they are not approved to be printed—He begs the favour His papers may be returned for he has no coppy of them."[27] Although Mitchell and Collinson were eager for action by Trew, there were further delays.

Equally hospitable to Mitchell was another correspondent, Dr. John Fothergill. With the common background of their Edinburgh training and a mutual love of plants there was much to talk of. Mitchell may have been a trifle startled when he first saw Fothergill for he often affected unusual attire. He would appear almost completely in white: "a white medical wig, with rows of small curls descending one under another from near the crown to his shoulders; a coat, waistcoat and breeches of nearly white superfine cloth; the coat without any collar, large cuffs. . . ." He was of average height, slender and delicate in his build.[28] By November, 1746, Mitchell and Fothergill were on a completely informal basis. When the latter discovered that he had to go out one afternoon after he had invited Mitchell and Mendes da Costa to visit him at his home at #2 White Hart Court, he dashed off a casual line to da Costa: "Dr. Mitchel I hope will excuse, and I beg the same favour of thy self. If tomorrow is a leisure day with you both, I shall be glad of your company, as soon after dinner as is suitable."[29]

Da Costa (1719–91) was the son of a Jewish merchant of London. A brilliant man and one of many interests, he led a stormy and controversial career, but never a boring one. Eight months after the visit to Fothergill, he wrote to Collinson from "the bottom of a Coalpit at Swannick, Derbyshire, 35 feet deep . . ." sending his regards to the Mitchells and the Catesbys.[30] He was one of a group of congenial men, including Mitchell, who met fairly regularly for impromptu discussions. In March, 1747/48, he went to the Continent with the commissary department of the army, of which his brother-in-law, Abraham

27. 9 and 18 February 1746/47, ENU.
28. R. Hingston Fox, *Dr. John Fothergill and His Friends* (London, 1919), pp. 384–85.
29. 4 November 1746, B.M. Add. MSS 28,537, f. 122.
30. 17 July 1747, B.M. Add. MSS 28,536, f. 57.

Prado, was in charge. From there he wrote to Catesby on 17 May, that he had seen Gronovius in Leyden. He asked him to tell Mitchell that he would write to him very soon "about the collection of Switzerland plants" which he had sent to London. If Catesby wanted to see them "young" Sherwood, Mitchell, or several others could make arrangements.[31] In the same post, he wrote to Sherwood: "I design in the following manner to keep up my Correspondence with you gentlemen of our friendly & Phil: meetings by writing alternately to you, Dr. Parsons & Mortimer Mr. Catesby Dr. Mitchell, etc. of what occurs worthy of notice. . . ."[32] When he wrote to Fothergill in September, he said that he hoped that he would share his letter with Mitchell when he saw him as he did not have sufficient time to write to both of them individually. "Tell Mr. Collinson & Dr. Mitchell that I have got the seeds of those 2 Switzerland Pines they desired, wch my friend has also sent me, & a Quantity of it but till my return to England, wch I hope will be about St. Andrew's Day Nothing can be determined whether I have got the right sort or not."[33]

From John Clayton, Mitchell had heard so much about Mark Catesby (1683–1749) that he felt as if he were already an old friend. He had used Catesby's book as a valuable reference work for many years and the two men may have corresponded. It certainly took them little time in which to reach an agreeable state of intimacy. Although almost twice Mitchell's age and in ill health, Catesby still displayed his insatiable curiosity and enthusiasm. Da Costa later described him as "tall, meagre, hard favoured, and sullen look, and was extremely grave and sedate, and of a silent disposition; but when he contracted a friendship was communicative, and affable."[34] Catesby and Mitchell shared a quiet, teasing type of humor and a keen sense of the ridiculous.

When Catesby had first returned to England permanently, he needed the leisure in which to write up his collections. Both William Sherard and Collinson came to his financial assistance but he augmented this income by working in Thomas Fairchild's nursery at Hoxton. Fairchild was the man who had performed the experiments in cross-pollination

31. Ibid., f. 35.
32. B.M. Add. MSS 28,542, f. 198.
33. 30 September 1748, from Brabant, B.M. Add. MSS 28,537, f. 123.
34. Mendez da Costa, "Notices and Anecdotes of Literati, Collectors, Etc. from a MS by the Late Mendez da Costa, and Collected Between 1747 and 1788," *Gentleman's Magazine* 82, pt. 1 (1812):206

to which Mitchell had referred in his essay. In this manner, Catesby was enabled to study the American plants there and their adaptation to the English climate. By the mid-forties, when Mitchell made his acquaintance, he was living in London in a poor section of Old Street behind St. Luke's Church. Nevertheless, he was loathe to relinquish gardening completely and often visited the well-known Christopher Gray's nursery at Fulham across the Thames.[35]

He was completing work on the *Appendix* to his *Natural History* and consulted Mitchell about various plants. One of these was the *Hamamelis* or Witch Hazel, which Mitchell had designated a new genus, *Trilopus*. Clayton had sent Catesby his specimen which, to everyone's astonishment, had arrived in England in full bloom at Christmas. Catesby included Mitchell's note of reply to his questions in regard to the plant in his *Appendix*:

SIR

This is a new genus of Plants, which I have likewise had an opportunity of describing from the live Plant, which I call *Trilopus*, on account of the triple husk of the fruit, so remarkable, but not described in its character. The inner *Putamen* of the nut is of a hard horny substance, double, inclosing each seed, opening at top, and divided by a valve of the middle husk, which is of a leathern substance, inclosing the whole nut, opening cross-wise at the top. The outer husk resembles the cup of an acorn inclosing half the nut. The petals are, as it were, double at the base; a small petaliform *Nectarium* of the length of the Perianthum, being affixed to the base of each petal.

JOHN MITCHELL[36]

The *Stewartia*, which Clayton had sent in 1742, was another plant which the two men discussed. Catesby showed Mitchell the plant which the latter identified as the one to which he had given the name *Malachodendron*, as a new genus. The older man then brought out a copy of the *Acta Suecica* for 1741 in which it had been described by Linnaeus, from whom he had requested it for use in the *Appendix*. Mitchell was astounded by the errors in it and demonstrated the mistakes in his own specimen. Mitchell's indignation is apparent in his letter to Catesby which also appeared in the *Appendix*, as he referred to the article which

35. Frick and Stearns, *Catesby*, pp. 36–37, 46.
36. Catesby, *Carolina*, 1, Appendix, p. 21.

. . . is so faulty, that it will not even determine the proper class of this Plant in any system of *Botany*, instead of establishing the true *genus*. It is there referred to the class of *Polyandria Monogynia*, Linnaei, whereas it properly belongs to the class of *Monadelphia Polyandria*, in which it makes a new tribe of *malvaceous* Plants, under which it is properly included in all systems of Botany: for the petals are connected at the base, and drop off united together which (according to *Ray* and *Tournefort*) makes the flower *monopetalous*. The stamina are connected in a ring at their base, and are inserted to the base of the petal. There are five styles, as I showed you in a specimen I have. The fruit is a dry capsula with five sharp angles, five cells and five valves, which open at the top, and are not crowned with the calix, which remains on their base. The seeds are single in each cell, of an oblong, oval, triangular shape.[37]

This plant description is one of the three which Frick and Stearns consider adequate in the whole of Catesby's work. Another was by Dr. Gronovius.[38]

At this time Catesby was working on his *Hortus-Britanno Americanus* which Frick and Stearns describe as more than just a catalogue for Christopher Gray.[39] Here again, he benefited from conversation with Mitchell on the puzzling aspect of the variety of Oaks. They both agreed that the amazing number of shapes in leaves on the same trees could hardly be believed by those who had seen only dried specimens. The Black Oak was an example of this, Catesby said. Some leaves may be a foot wide while others are but three inches and quite differently shaped. The subject of hybrids intrigued Catesby as much as it did Mitchell: "Notwithstanding this great variety of appearances of American Oaks, above the number of eleven or twelve species were not apparent to me, till by the indefatigable searches of Dr. MITCHEL, four or five more by him have been discovered in the remote and unfrequented parts of our colonies. Why may not the variety of leaves in this and some other trees, as well as some kinds of herbaceous plants, proceed from the like cause, on impregnating other trees of the same genus, which by deviating from the uniform course of nature produce in like manner a spurious breed?"[40] Many hybrid Oaks are recognized today.

37. Ibid., p. 13. This letter was reprinted in the *Gentleman's Magazine* 23 (October 1753):472.
38. Frick and Stearns, *Catesby*, p. 67.
39. Ibid., p. 68.
40. *Hortus Europae Americanus, or a Collection of 85 Curious Trees and Shrubs, the Pro-*

Conversations between Mitchell and Catesby were not limited to botanic matters. When there was discussion of the popular theory that birds hibernated in the winter, Catesby was certain, from personal observation, that they migrated. In a paper on the subject, "Of Birds of Passage," given before the Royal Society on 5 March 1746/47, he mentioned their discussion:

> Since the Discovery of *America* there have been introduced from *Europe* several Sorts of Grain, which were never known in that Part of the World, and which not before some Length of Time, were found out, and coveted by some of these migratory Birds. No Wonder this Grain should not be immediately known to Birds of distant Regions; for above a half a Century from the Time of cultivating Wheat, Rice, and Barley, in *Virginia* and *Carolina*, before those Grains were found out and frequented by these foreign Birds, of which one has but lately made its first Appearance in *Virginia* as my ingenious Friend Dr. *Mitchel* informs me, that he being in his Garden a Bird flew over his Head which appeared with uncommon Lustre, and surprised him the more, not having seen the like Bird before. Mentioning this to some of his Neighbours, he was told by them, what afterwards was confirmed to him by his own Observation; viz. that these exotic Birds had but within these few Years appeared in *Virginia*, and had never been observed there before.
>
> They arrive annually at the time that Wheat (the Fields of which they most Frequent) is at a certain Degree of Maturity; and have constantly every Year from their first Appearance arrived about the same time in numerous Flights. They have attain'd the name of Wheat-Birds.[41]

The Wheat-birds, better known as Horned Larks (*Otocoris alpestris alpestris* [Linnaeus]) are pinkish-brown in color, with whitish underparts. They sport black crescents under the eyes and on the breast. They nest in the area of Newfoundland and to the north but their range is tremendous. They have been reported in all parts of North America.[42]

Another bird had attracted Mitchell's notice, "the sharp-tailed grouse," (*Pediaecetes pasianellus campestris*, or the Prairie sharp-tailed grouse). He told Thomas Pennant that it had been reported in "the unfrequented parts of Virginia."[43] As it is today an inhabitant of southern

duce of North America Adapted to the Climates and Soils of Great-Britain, Ireland, and Most Parts of Europe, &c (London, 1767), p. 5.

41. *Philosophical Transactions* 64 (March, April, May 1747):443–44.

42. F. Gilbert Pearson, ed., *Birds of America* (Garden City, 1917), 2:212–14.

43. *Arctic Zoology*, 2 vols. (London, 1784), 2:306. Mitchell was evidently consulted

Canada and the northern United States, this seems unlikely but, of course, might have been possible at that time.[44] Pennant said that those which had been brought to England had all come from Hudson's Bay.

It was probably at Catesby's home that Mitchell met the Scot, Dr. Isaac Lawson. Fossils were one of his particular interests and his collection was one of the finest. He cultivated a large correspondence, particularly in Germany, and traveled widely. He was responsible for much of the writing in Cramer's *Ars Docimastica* (the art of assaying ores).[45] He had taken his medical degree at the University of Leyden at the time Linnaeus was in Holland. He and Dr. Gronovius had become enthusiastic supporters of the young Swedish doctor. In his diary, Linnaeus wrote of Lawson as his particular friend who "had many times asked him if he stood in need of money, and, on Linnaeus's answering in the negative, had given him sixty, eighty, or an hundred guelders; remarking that he had still enough for himself. He loved both Linnaeus and Gronovius very much, and was a man of great judgment."[46]

It was Lawson and Gronovius who had financed Linnaeus's *Systema Naturae* and sent a copy to Sir Hans Sloane. They were also responsible for similar help in the publication of more of his books during the period in which he was in Holland. Lawson took part in the small coterie of friends, including Linnaeus and Gronovius which met each Saturday night in winter for discussion of scientific matters. It was during these meetings that the practicality of Linnaeus's methods of classification were often tested on minerals, fish, insects, and plants. The last were often those which Clayton had sent to Gronovius via Catesby. Lawson made many trips home and acted as liaison between Continental scientists and the English ones. He brought news of the accomplishments of both, of the latest books, and delivered parcels.[47]

---

by numbers of people about American flora and fauna. George Edwards, writing about the "monax, or marmotte, of America," noted that "Dr. Mitchel, a physician of Virginia, now in London, has informed me this animal has much the actions of a squirrel; and, when wild, has a more bushy tail than this figure presents" (*Natural History of Birds*, 2 vols. [London, 1747], 2:104).

44. Pearson, *Birds of America*, 2:27–29.

45. Da Costa, "Notices," *Gentleman's Magazine* 82, pt. 1 (1812):206. At Lawson's death, da Costa bought some of his collection.

46. Dawson Turner, ed., *Extracts from the Literary and Scientific Correspondence of Richard Richardson* (Yarmouth, 1835), p. 345n.

47. Berkeley and Berkeley, *Clayton*, pp. 60–63, 102–3, 111.

When Mitchell met Lawson he was physician general of the British army in Flanders, a position which still allowed him to return home occasionally. It was interesting for Mitchell to talk with someone who had known well the illustrious Linnaeus in Holland. Mitchell told Lawson that he was trying to assess public interest in a natural history of Virginia.[48] Lawson must have encouraged Mitchell to write to Gronovius. The Leyden doctor wrote to Linnaeus in May that he had received a letter from him, in which he said that he had decided to undertake such a project.[49] Lawson and Mitchell did not meet again as the former died of a malignant fever, epidemic with his troops, in late May.

Having dedicated a paper to Sloane and being a staunch admirer of his, Mitchell must certainly have paid his respects to him soon after his arrival. Sloane was in his late eighties, very frail and quite deaf. Having a growth on his tongue, it was laborious for him to talk and difficult for his listeners to understand.[50] In spite of such handicaps to relaxed conversation, Sloane's friends always enjoyed their visits with the old gentleman and browsing among his superlative collections and library.

Sir Hans's home was two miles from London and known as the manor of Chelsea. The village itself was composed of "beautiful streets, well-built and handsome houses all of brick, three or four stories high." Lying close to the Thames and surrounded by market-gardens, it was restful after the city. Located on the manor's land was the garden of the Apothecaries' Society where Sloane had studied as a young man. It had been established well outside the city, since many plants were unable to flourish in London's coal-smoke.[51] In 1722, Sloane had turned over the land to the Society for a rent of five pounds per annum and the understanding that it would yearly send to the Royal Society fifty new plant specimens, properly mounted for a herbarium.

Philip Miller was gardener at Chelsea when Mitchell arrived in England. It was his experimentation with the cross-fertilization of cabbages which Mitchell had used to buttress his hypothesis in his essay on plant classification. He was delighted to make Miller's acquaintance and the two men became friends. Miller's *Gardener's Dictionary* was already a standard reference work and his reputation as a skilled horti-

48. J. F. Gronovius to Linnaeus, 24 March 1746/47, LCLS.
49. 12 May 1747, ibid.
50. *Kalm's Account*, p. 97.
51. Ibid., pp. 96–98. 106.

culturist well-established. His training in the field was impeccable. His father, a nurseryman, determined that his son should be scientifically educated in addition to the practical training which he was able to impart. As a result, Miller was proficient not only in botany but other sciences and several languages. He diligently cultivated other nurserymen in order to exchange information. He traveled widely in England and on the Continent to add to his knowledge but he always remained open to experiment. Through several trials, he finally designed new heating methods for his greenhouses.[52] Extremely successful in the practical aspects of horticulture, he did not limit his gardening to these alone but conducted experiments in cross-fertilization.

The Apothecaries' Garden was laid out along the river, from which a small canal entered. There grew a variety of water plants. The garden was filled with a myriad of medicinal plants and survives today as a very active horticultural establishment, where three century old brick walls and a tree given by Catesby may be seen. In the eighteenth century there were several Orangeries, only one of which remains now. They were heated by an ingenious system of bent pipes designed by Miller. In a room above an Orangery, there was a collection of great interest to Mitchell. It was that of the great John Ray, upon whose reference works Mitchell had depended when he first returned to Virginia from Edinburgh. It was a distressing sight to him and was described thus by a contemporary: "The plants in *Mr. Ray's Herbarium* were sewn with cotton onto the paper in large paper books. The whole collection consisted of about eight or twelve such paper books in folio. In some places the plants had been cut out, for *Dr. Sherard* had borrowed this collection from Mr. Dale, and when he had found any plant, which was either rare, or he thought much of, it was said that he had either clipped or cut it out, so that the books had been sufficiently mutilated."[53]

Although Mitchell did not specifically mention meeting Dillenius, it seems highly likely that he visited him at Oxford. He would have been eager to talk to the German doctor for whom he had such great admiration and for whom he had collected so many plants and seeds. He would have been interested to see how many of the latter had survived in the physic garden. In any event, there was little time for the

52. Ibid., pp. 92–93.
53. Ibid., p. 108.

friendship to develop as the sixty-three-year-old Dillenius died of apoplexy on 2 April, less than a year after Mitchell reached England.

When a letter from Linnaeus to Dillenius arrived, Collinson requested Mitchell to answer it. He was delighted at the opportunity to begin a correspondence with Linnaeus. He informed him that before his letter arrived, Dillenius had suffered a stroke, "the inevitable consequence of intense application, which ought to serve as a warning to others." Although Dillenius had applied himself so mercilessly to completing the *Pinax*, he had not achieved his objective. Mitchell wrote that "His loss to science is unspeakable, and perhaps, at this time irreparable . . ." unless Linnaeus could be persuaded to complete his work.[54]

Dillenius had been one of the few men who had not hesitated to challenge Linnaeus's statements. Ten years earlier, he had written him: "I have more reason to apprehend your anger, for not approving entirely of every thing you have done, and for speaking my mind so plainly. I cannot but observe that you are not very patient under the attacks of adversaries. For my part, I am not more pleased with my own opinion, than with that of other people. I am ready to listen to anybody's remarks, for the sake of discovering truth. . . ."[55] He continued this policy with Linnaeus through the years. He berated him for his attitude towards Catesby, "an honest, ingenuous man, who ought not to be suspected of error or fraud, as you seem inclined to do."[56] Unquestionably, Dillenius's honesty and frankness had been of incalcuable value to Linnaeus, whose distinguished reputation discouraged most men from questioning his pronouncements. While hardly of the same botanic caliber as Dillenius, Mitchell, too, met Linnaeus on an equal footing in having no hesitation in expressing his own opinion even if it were diametrically opposed to that of the Swedish doctor. This he demonstrated in his first letter. He cautiously advised Linnaeus to reexamine his description of *Stewartia*. In answer to his question regarding genera related to *Chionanthus*, he readily replied *Olea*.

In regard to current English news, Mitchell reported on Martyn's abridgment of the *Philosophical Transactions*, Catesby's completion of his *Appendix*, John Hill's proposed history of fossils. He admitted that

54. Mitchell to Linnaeus, 16 April 1747, CLO 2:442–44.
55. 28 November 1737, CLO 2:103-4.
56. 18 August 1737, ibid., p. 102.

he was "inclined to give the publick something on the natural and medical history of North America, if not a history itself, at which I have long laboured. I wish I could profit by your assistance." He was still of the same mind in May, when he wrote to Gronovius, sending his regards to Linnaeus.[57]

Although Mitchell apparently never completed this project, six months later Collinson could announce to Linnaeus that his botanic essays would be published under the direction of Dr. Trew. Unfortunately, Mitchell's addenda and corrections arrived too late to be included.[58] When Mitchell wrote to Linnaeus in September of the following year, 1748, he referred to the publication of his papers in the last volume of the Nuremberg *Transactions*: "They consist of a dissertation on a new botanical principle, derived from the sexual theory, which I think accords with your ideas, and, if I mistake not, our systems support each other; also characters of several new genera of plants sent, seven years ago, from Virginia. I long to know your opinion upon them, which I hold in high estimation. Some of these genera have, I believe, appeared in your last publications and those of Gronovius." Although Linnaeus commented on Mitchell's new genera in a letter to Haller, he never committed himself with an opinion of the proposed method of classification.[59]

During the winter of 1746/47, Peter Collinson was engaged in the publication of another friend's work. Cadwallader Colden's *History of the Five Indian Nations* had been published in New York in 1727. It was received so favorably that Collinson had persuaded Colden to write a sequel and with it to republish the first part. He promised to find a publisher for him. Since Colden had neglected to supply a title, Collinson asked Mitchell to draw up a title page.[60] Mitchell spent many hours devising one which he hoped would appeal to the prospective bookseller and yet not offend the author. Various friends who had written books had told him that the printers were highly disdainful of their efforts in this direction. They invariably discarded the author's

57. Gronovius to Linnaeus, 12 May 1747, LCLS.

58. Mitchell's addenda, corrections, and etymology were added to the original descriptions of the genera in the manuscript of this biography as an appendix, but had to be omitted. A copy of the manuscript will be offered to the Virginia Historical Society.

59. 20 September 1748, CLO 2:448; Linnaeus to Haller, 13 September 1748, ibid., p. 429.

60. Collinson to Colden, 27 March 1746/47, LPCC 3:369.

efforts and drew up their own, often so extravagant that they embarrassed the writers considerably.[61] Mitchell finally contrived a title page so attractive that in March Collinson was able to write to the New Yorker that the bookseller, Osborne, would print the two volumes at his own expense.[62]

Mitchell was hopeful that Colden would be as pleased as Osborne with the result of his efforts. Correspondence had been badly interrupted by the war, and it was not until two years later that he had a letter from Colden. To his dismay, his friend was highly indignant. In the first place, Colden had dedicated his original book to William Burnet, governor of New York at that time. The dedication of the English edition was to General James Edward Oglethorpe (1696–1785), one of the trustees of the colony of Georgia, with whom Colden had "no kind of Acquaintance." Moreover, as Colden did not write to "serve the same purposes for which the Booksellers print I never could have consented to such kind of Title page. . . ."[63] He did not object, however, when Collinson presented both Gronovius and Mitchell with a copy of his book a year later.[64]

Soon after Mitchell settled in England he involved himself in a chemical research project, an attempt to learn the best method for the production of potash. Precisely why he did so at this time is debatable. He eventually gave a long and detailed report of his research before the Royal Society, and it may be that he undertook it with this in mind.[65] On the other hand, there were great practical implications of the study for both England and the colonies, and Mitchell said that this was his motivation. In any event, he was characteristically thorough in his approach to the problem. He read everything available on potash production since ancient times. He wrote to people abroad for information on current practices, and he made laboratory experiments of his own.

Potash was at that time essential for the production of such basic materials as soap and glass, and was required in dyeing and bleaching, but "Altho Pot-ash is a thing daily used, and well known even to the Vulgar; yet, as the making it is a mechanic Art, practised only by the

61. Mitchell to Colden, 25 March 1749, Hornberger, "A Letter from John Mitchell," *Huntington Library Quarterly* 10 (1946–47):411.
62. Collinson to Colden, 27 March 1746/47, LPCC 3:369.
63. Colden to Mitchell, 6 July 1749, LPCC 9:19–20.
64. Collinson to Colden, 20 June 1748, LPCC 4:67.
65. Published in the *Philosophical Transactions* 48 (1749):541–63.

Vulgar, and neglected and overlooked by the Learned, so we have had no satisfactory Account of it; and they, who understand it, generally keep it a Secret, lest others should learn so beneficial an Art," as Mitchell put it.[66]

In Mitchell's first letter to Linnaeus he questioned him concerning the preparation of "Russian Ashes," and Linnaeus sent him a paper on the subject. Meanwhile, he read accounts by Boerhaave, Geoffrey, Houston, Kunkelius, Lemery, Merrett, Neri, Redi, and others. Methods of preparation varied considerably in different countries, and several methods used in England all produced an inferior product for which those requiring it paid an exorbitant price. So essential was that of better quality normally imported that a special order of King and Council authorized its importation from Spain even during war. At the time of Mitchell's studies England was importing potash from Germany, Poland (Dantzick), Russia, and Sweden, as well as Spain, although there seemed no fundamental reason why she should not produce her own either in England or the colonies.

Mitchell's studies revealed that quite a range of plant materials were in use for potash production. These included lees left over from winemaking in France, seaweeds in northern England, and tobacco stalks in America, as well as a variety of woods in different countries. Mitchell thought that most North American trees would be suitable, except those with resins and gums such as Pine, Fir, Sassafras, and Sweet Gum. He particularly recommended Hickory as being ideal and abundant. The best quality potash being produced in Europe at that time came from Spain, and was called "Barrilha," from an herb of the same name. Mitchell cited several authors' contentions concerning the identification of the plant, but favored that of de Jussieu, *Kali Hispanicum* or Alicant Glasswort. He believed, however, that much of the potash reaching England from Spain was adulterated, in spite of the high prices paid for it, and that England would never have an adequate supply of the real article unless she raised the plants herself. He thought this more likely to be successful in the colonies than in England, as he was informed that it grew well in Spanish American colonies.

Methods of extracting potash were as varied as the plant materials used, and Mitchell described them in some detail. Linnaeus had sent him a dissertation by a man named Lundmarck at the University of

66. Ibid., pp. 541-42.

Åbö, from which he quoted at length. He described the processes used in England and other countries, and discussed the relative merit and weakness of the product. Hoping to gain some personal insight which might suggest ways of improving the methods used, he made his own chemical analysis of the best Russian potash available and studied its properties. He described its physical appearance, hardness, odor and taste, solubility, tendency to deliquesce, sediments formed, ability to tarnish silver, etc. He found that pieces of the potash in boiling water "make a constant explosion, like gunpowder." This he thought was not caused by the release of "included Air" but by the expansion of its sulphurous parts. He boiled, filtered, evaporated, and crystallized samples with such chemicals as "Oil of Vitriol" (sulfuric acid) and noted the appearance and odor of the fumes produced.

Having gained a better understanding of the chemical nature of potash, Mitchell considered and discussed its use for various purposes, including medicinal ones. The Russian potash was specified by the College of Physicians for the making of soap to be used as a laxative and purgative in difficult cases for which it would be effective, even if "more offensive to the Stomach; which is much complained of by some People, who take large Quantities of the sharper kinds of Soap." Although medicinal use of potash was important and interesting, its chief use was as a commodity in trade and manufacturing, and for these purposes the English had to put up with a miserable quality. Seeking practical information Mitchell went to talk with workmen concerned in making white glass. They told him that the quality of available potash was so poor that they were forced to substitute saltpeter which was not only more expensive but inferior to good potash. He had no opportunity to consult men concerned with dyeing, but quoted others to the effect that French potash was best for it, as was Spanish for bleaching and soapmaking.

Mitchell's paper was too long for a single session of the Royal Society, so was given at two successive meetings, 17 and 24 November 1748.[67] It was apparently well received, if one can judge from contemporary comment of several members of the Society who were present and remarked upon it in their own writings. Stukeley, for example, referred to it in his diary as "an excellent account," and summarized it

67. Royal Society Journal Book XIX, pp. 579 and 581.

at some length.[68] Dr. Stephen Hales later wrote to John Ellis: "I believe the method of making potash is sufficiently explained by Dr. Mitchell."[69] Perhaps the compliment most welcome to Mitchell was when Franklin reprinted his article in *The Pennsylvania Gazette* on 18 December 1750. There, he knew his ideas and suggestions might possibly bear some practical fruit. The editor's introduction was short: "The following piece, wrote by a Gentleman not long since an Inhabitant of one of the Colonies, and who has their Welfare much at Heart, will, we doubt not, be acceptable to many of our Readers, and possibly be of publick Use."

68. Stukeley Correspondence, pp. 102–10, MSS Eng. Misc. c. 113, Bodleian Library OU.

69. 22 October 1755, CLO 2:36.

VIII ఞ Some English Gardens and Gardeners

"It is dangerous Conversing with these Strangers who keep Journals."

Franklin to Colden, 1773[1]

It was at this time that Mitchell made the acquaintance of a man who was to have a significant influence on the remainder of his life, John Stuart, third Earl of Bute. Either Catesby or Lawson may have introduced the two men as they were great admirers of his. It was they who had suggested that Linnaeus name the plant which Clayton had sent, the *Stewartia*, in his honor. It is possible that Collinson, who was also a friend of Bute, performed the introduction, or it may have been that Mitchell had met him through one of his kinfolk during his school days. Whatever brought the two men together, they immediately discovered a wealth of common interests in spite of their different background.

Bute was two years younger than Mitchell. His mother was Lady Jane Campbell, sister of his father's most intimate friends: John, Duke of Argyll and Archibald, Earl of Islay. Both brothers were extremely influential Scots. Bute had been sent to Eton at the tender age of seven. Since his father died very young, he spent many holidays with the Duke. The Campbells were a strange family and often his two uncles were not on speaking terms. At such times, arrangements for their nephew were made in writing. At twenty-three, Bute married Mary, daughter of Lady Mary Wortley-Montagu, who had been responsible for the introduction of smallpox inoculation into England.[2]

Beset by financial problems the first nine years of their married life, the young couple lived on the Isle of Bute, a rather austere place. Except for some fine trees around the house, there were no gardens. This

1. 5 March, LPCC 7:185.
2. J. A. Lovat-Fraser, *John Stuart, Earl of Bute* (Cambridge, 1912), pp. 2-4.

lack was compensated by the marvelous views across the water to the mainland and neighboring islands. Some financial misfortune in 1746 forced the Butes to leave Scotland. They rented a house for forty-five pounds a year at Twickenham, a fashionable village near London.[3] Bute's uncle, the former Lord Islay who had succeeded his brother as duke in 1743, had a country home there. There were many even more impressive establishments in the general neighborhood: Marble-Hill, home of the Countess of Suffolk; Mrs. Pritchard's Ragman's Castle, where cleverly situated mirrors duplicated the charming vistas of the gardens throughout the house; Horace Walpole's Strawberry Hill at Teddington; the Earl of Radnor's Cross-Deep and the former home of Sir Godfrey Kneller, who had died in 1723.[4]

In this same spring of 1747, the Butes' apothecary invited him to ride to the Egham races in his carriage. Frederick, Prince of Wales, was also there and when a sudden storm drove him to take shelter in a tent, it was found that one more was needed for a game of whist. Bute was invited to play, being the only man of sufficiently gentle birth present. When the game finally broke up, he found that the apothecary had departed, so the Prince took him back with him to spend the night. The Prince discovered that Bute shared his enthusiasm for theatricals and it was not long before the Earl was recognized as one of his favorites.[5] Recorded opinions vary greatly concerning Bute's personality. Many of them were definitely colored by his later political career or by jealousy.[6]

The many years of genteel poverty had provided Bute with the leisure to develop his interests in mechanics, botany, and mathematics. While he enjoyed all of these sciences, the second was to become his favorite and he achieved great skill in its practice and theory. He corresponded with many European botanists including Gronovius and was held in great esteem by them. His botanic library was so complete

3. Ibid., p. 5.

4. Henrietta Pye, *A Short Account of the Principal Seats and Gardens in and about Kew* (Brentford, n.d. but c. 1760), pp. 5–11. There was another printing in London in 1760 but no author was given and "Kew" was replaced by "Twickenham" in the title. Still another similar publication appeared in London in 1775, entitled *A Peep into the Principal Seats and Gardens in and about Twickenham by a Lady of Distinction in the Republic of Letters.*

5. Lovat-Fraser, *Bute*, pp. 5–6.

6. Dutens, *Memoirs of a Traveller Now in Retirement*, 5 vols. (London, 1806), 4:183 and 178.

that four years later he wrote to Gronovius that it only wanted three or four books, one of them Jacob Theodore's *Taberni Montani Icones*, published in 1590.[7]

The Virginia doctor, with his firsthand knowledge of North American plants, was cordially received by Bute, who was then living in a townhouse on Grosvernor Street. Now that royal favor was possibly his and his wife had received a handsome inheritance, Bute was considering repairing an old country house that his father had owned jointly with his brother-in-law, the Duke of Argyll. Known as Caenwood (now Kenwood), it was located five miles from London, between the villages of Hampstead and Highgate. It is a handsome situation, with a very fine view of London. The first house had been built around 1616 but the two-storied brick residence in Bute's day only dated to the turn of the century. Since 1690, the property had changed hands ten times and suffered consequent neglect. Bute had bought out the duke's interest in 1746 and was now starting to develop a garden.[8]

With eight acres devoted to this project, he began to collect every exotic which he thought might survive the English climate. In the spring of 1747, he discussed his ideas with Mitchell, saying that he would like seeds of various North American varieties, but particularly flowering shrubs and trees. He was especially interested in those of the new *Magnolia* and the White Cedar. Mitchell assured Bute that his friend, John Bartram, could readily supply them. In the course of conversation, Bute told Mitchell that he was certain that his uncle, the duke, would also like to put in an order but that he would only be interested in the new and rarer varieties. When Mitchell viewed Argyll's garden at Whitton, he readily understood what Bute meant.[9]

Archibald Campbell (1682–1761), was almost thirty years older than Mitchell. Educated at Eton and the University of Glasgow, he had studied law at Utrecht. A contemporary account of him said that he could write a letter in eight languages, and that he "understood Botany, Chemistry and the practise of Physic . . . all Branches of the Mathe-

7. 2 February 1750/51, Collections of the Marquess of Bute at Mount Stuart, Isle of Bute. We are very much indebted to the Earl's archivist, Miss Catherine Armet, who sent us copies of this letter and one of Mitchell's to Bute.

8. Sir John Summerson, *The Iveagh Bequest, Kenwood: A Short Account of Its History and Architecture* (London, n.d.), pp. 5–6.

9. Mitchell to Bartram, 2 June 1747, Darlington, *Memorials*, pp. 364–66, and Bartram Papers, 4:85, HSP.

matics, of Natural and Moral Philosophy,"[10] rather a large order. He owned one of the finest private libraries in Great Britain. After a short period in the army under Marlborough, he acted as one of the commissioners to arrange the English-Scottish parliamentary union and was created Earl of Islay. Sir Robert Walpole, in appreciation of Islay's and his brother's part in the suppression of the 1725 riots, permitted the two men free rein in managing Scottish affairs.[11] Islay had little compunction in using his brother and soon controlled the government to such an extent that he was known as the "King of Scotland." No one denies that his paternalistic attitude did much for his country, particularly in education and economic fields. When Mitchell met Archibald Campbell, he had already been Duke of Argyll for four years. "His vast domains, his extensive feudal rights, his almost boundless patriarchal authority, his great following of men bearing the same name as himself and looking to him as the head of their clan, gave unusual value to his support and weight to his influence."[12] A member of the Privy Council and keeper of the Great Seal, his power was unquestioned. In spite of these honors and responsibilities, Mitchell found Argyll a simple and friendly man, extremely informal in his demeanor and habits, considering his rank and the times.[13]

Although Argyll's public and private affairs were vast and complex, the greatest interest of his life seems to have been in plants. He owned great properties in Scotland, at Inveraray and elsewhere, and a house in London, but in 1723 he purchased a tract of land on Hounslow Heath, near London, where he began to develop the place he called Whitton. Since the Crown had permitted him to enclose some of the heath, he was later accused of "land-grabbing." The soil was poor and required many years of enriching.[14] Where plants were concerned, he was a patient man. He maintained a nursery on Hounslow Road where he raised trees from seed. It was far easier to obtain seeds than plants since he imported them from all over the world. He did purchase seed-

---

10. Andrew Henderson, *Considerations on the Question, Relating to the Scots Militia . . . Among Which, A faithful Character of Archibald Late Duke of Argyle* (n.p., n.d., 1761?), p. 43.

11. Sir James Balfour Paul, *The Scots Peerage* (Edinburgh, 1904), pp. 378–88.

12. J. A. Lovat-Fraser, *David Balfour's Duke of Argyll* (Inverness, 1928), pp. 6 and 15.

13. Alexander Carlyle, *Autobiography of the Rev. Alexander Carlyle* (Edinburgh, 1860), p. 352.

14. G. E. Bate, *And So Make a City Here* (Hounslow, 1948), pp. 209–10.

lings, however, for planting on his Scottish estates, in quantities which often exceeded 100,000. He was, in fact, one of the very early practitioners of forestation. His passionate arboriculture earned him the sobriquet of "tree-monger."[15]

To Mitchell, Argyll's garden was fascinating. Though he came to know it intimately in the next fifteen years, it continued to exert its charm for him. A great many of the plants were new to him, for they were international in origin. Argyll had ordered many of them, but no diplomat or traveler escaped his stern directives to collect for him wherever he went. Now that the garden was almost a quarter century old, it was truly impressive. It covered almost thirty acres, not including a nine acre tract for nursery and kitchen garden and sixteen acres of pasture. There was almost a mile of carefully tended gravel and grass walks.[16] Lofty trees shaded the paths. Argyll's famed Cedars of Lebanon, raised from seed, were now thirty-two feet tall, some of which survive today. These were dwarfed by a Spruce-fir fifty-five feet tall, while a New England Pine was thirty-five feet. Rarities such as Coffee and Banana Trees brushed against Chinese Peppers, a Palm, and even a Pistachio Tree in the greenhouse. There was a great display of all varieties of North American evergreens and Argyll questioned Mitchell concerning them. Virginia shrubs and trees of all sorts abounded but strangely enough no *Stewartia* nor *Magnolia*.

The garden was typically eighteenth century with fish-ponds, a canal, an aviary, and a sundial. There was the usual statuary glimpsed among the evergreens. One of these was Gabriel Cibber's statue of a Highland piper and his dog.[17] A Gothic tower, containing two rooms, crowned a man-made hill. From the brick battlements, there was a lovely view. It was furnished with chairs of the Duke's own design and a mammoth Chinese gong, a real curiosity at the time.

The contrived and artificial effect thus achieved was remarked upon by a contemporary clergyman:

15. Gordon Stanley Maxwell, *Highwayman's Heath* (London, 1935), p. 254.

16. In 1765, a catalogue was drawn up in preparation for the sale of the property: *A Particular of the Noble Large House, Gardens, the Tower, Temples . . . of the Late Duke of Argyle, Situate at Whitton . . .* (London, 1765). It describes the estate in great detail, including a list of the trees and shrubs, drawn up by Daniel Croft, the Duke's gardener.

17. Maxwell, *Highwayman's Heath*, p. 255.

Old Islay, to show his fine delicate taste
In improving his garden, purloin'd from the waste.
Bade his gard'ner one day to open his views
By cutting a couple of grand avenues;
No particular prospect his lordship intended,
But left it to chance how his walks should be ended.
With transport and joy he beheld his first view end
In a favourite prospect—a church, that was ruin'd;
But alas, what a sight did the next cut exhibit,
At the end of a walk, hung a rogue on a gibbet.
He beheld it and wept for it caused him to muse on
Full many a Campbell who died with his shoes on.
All amazed and aghast at this ominous scene,
He ordered it quick to be closed up again,
With a clump of Scotch firs that would serve as a screen.[18]

The greenhouse, like the gardens, was on the grand scale, being ninety-six feet long with two "genteel bedrooms with wainscot floors, marble chimneys," and two closets. Mitchell was intrigued by Argyll's ingenious water system. It consisted of a twenty-foot square brick building, fifteen feet tall, topped by a windmill. The eight sails were seven and a half feet by three feet broad and were capable of raising the water twenty feet. In a light wind, this was a slow process, but in a brisk one some of the doors had to be closed.[19] At the back of the house was a long wall, glassed on one side and at the top where orange trees were grown. A bowling green and a Chinese summer house added to the amenities.

Bute told Mitchell that the Duke wanted a great quantity of seeds but he was afraid that it would be too late in the season for much collecting by the time Bartram received the order. For that reason, he would limit his order to as much as could be sent for five pounds. Argyll was especially anxious to have seeds of the Pawpaw, the new *Magnolia*, the White Cedar, the orange *Apocynum*, the Scarlet *Spirea*, the "*Euonymus scandens*," the large "*Ketmia*" whose blossoms resembled cotton and the new pines which Bartram had mentioned. When Mitch-

18. Ibid., pp. 254–55, quoting the Rev. James Bramston. Both Argyll's grandfather and great-grandfather were beheaded.

19. "Duke of Argyll's Windmill," *Gentleman's Magazine* 19 (June 1749):249–50.

ell sent a letter to Bartram by Captain Teffin on 2 June concerning the order, he sent an abstract by another carrier as well. He already suspected that his letter to Colden had been lost and possibly others. He wrote to Bartram to send Argyll's and Bute's orders in Collinson's care. Peter had told him that the duke already had seven boxes on order through him. In closing, Mitchell asked to be particularly remembered to Mrs. Bartram and Dr. Bond.[20] It was not until 30 January of the following year (1747/48) that Bartram reported to Collinson that he had put on board the *Beulah* three boxes of tree seeds, one of which was for the Duke.[21]

Some time before Mitchell wrote to Bartram, he had written to Benjamin Franklin.[22] While in Philadelphia, he had heard much talk of two springs in the general vicinity of the city. One was the Yellow Springs in Chester County, about thirty-two miles out of town. They were named for their property of depositing a yellow tinge on the stones, due to iron in the water. It had become a fashionable watering spot not long after the medicinal properties of the springs became known in 1722.[23] The other was the mineral spring at Schooley's Mountain in New Jersey. First discovered by the Indians, it soon became popular with the whites. Now Mitchell wanted Franklin to procure some of the blue stones from the Yellow Springs, for what reason he did not say. He was more specific regarding the New Jersey spring, from which he wanted water samples. He had told his friends about the remarkable property of this water which was said to turn iron to copper. Understandably, they were skeptical, so he was anxious to make a chemical analysis.[24] He later wrote Bartram his reasons: "When I think of the many other Productions in the spring I cannot but think it as a sort of reflection on us among other things, that we should let it lye in obscurity, & not so much as acquaint those with it who would thank us so heartily for our pains but might like to give us some better

20. Mitchell to Bartram, 2 June 1747, Darlington, *Memorials*, pp. 364–66, and Bartram Papers, 4:85 and 86, HSP.

21. Darlington, *Memorials*, p. 180.

22. This letter has been lost, but Mitchell referred to it in his letters of 2 June to Bartram.

23. Harry B. Weiss and Howard R. Kemble, *They Took to the Waters: The Forgotten Mineral Spring Resorts of New Jersey and Nearby Pennsylvania* (Trenton, 1962), pp. 187 and 197.

24. Ibid., p. 27.

information of its nature & uses, if they were appraised of this thing. for this reason I have desired some of the water & of every production about it which I shall put to the most exact tryalls that I or any acquaintance are able to make."[25]

Mitchell's letter to Franklin was apparently lost and with it any further plans for examining the waters. Philadelphians continued to be an incurious lot. It was not until 1808 that the botanist, Dr. Benjamin Smith Barton, reported a chemical analysis of Yellow Springs. This indicated that it was a "simple carbonated chalybeate," containing a small quantity of iron. Two years later, the spring at Schooley's Mountain was examined by Professor Samuel Latham Mitchill, a chemist. While iron was present in the water, there was no indication of any copper, nor in any other such springs.[26]

On the whole, the Mitchells appear to have led a quiet life during 1747. The doctor was still collecting material for a natural history and doing research for his potash article. There is no documented evidence that he was also writing, as Carrier has suggested, "An account of the English discoveries and settlements in America." This appeared anonymously in Volume II of the revised edition of *Harris' Collection of Voyages and Travels*, published in 1748. It is true that the portions dealing with natural history are of higher caliber than those in *A New and Complete History of the British Empire in North America* (1756), which Carrier also attributes to Mitchell. Nevertheless, they both would appear to fall far below Mitchell's scientific standards. In the latter book the author even included both frogs and snakes under the heading of "stinging insects."[27]

Poor health again tormented Mitchell. With the coming of winter, he suffered a series of illnesses. To add to his anxieties, his wife became seriously ill. Just before they had sailed in 1746, she had been unable to leave her bed to sign the sales contract for their house. Now, the doctors despaired of her recovery. When Collinson wrote to Franklin in mid-April, 1748, he said that Mitchell "had near Lost her."[28] In view of the fact that this was the last mention of Helen Mitchell which has been found, it seems likely that she did die shortly after Collinson's let-

25. Undated letter (1749?), Bartram Papers, 4:86, HSP.

26. Weiss and Kemble, *They Took to the Waters*, pp. 191 and 27.

27. Lyman Carrier, "Dr. John Mitchell, Naturalist, Cartographer, and Historian," *Annual Report of the American Historical Association* 1 (1918):205, 209–10.

28. 12 April 1747/48, *Papers of Franklin*, 3:284.

ter was written. She remains a shadowy figure in Mitchell's life. No evidence appears as to her maiden name or where she came from or what she was like. Mitchell himself never mentioned her or any children in his letters, but this is not surprising. Few eighteenth-century gentlemen referred to anything as personal as their immediate family in their correspondence. Apparently, Mrs. Mitchell left no will. This, too, was not unusual, as few ladies had property of their own to leave. Another indication of her death in the spring of 1748, is that Mitchell's life thereafter certainly seems to have been that of a bachelor.

On 17 February 1747/48, a young professor of Oeconomy at the University of Åbö (Turku) in Swedish Finland, landed in London on his way to North America. He had been sent by the Swedish Royal Academy of Sciences to describe its "natural productions" and to determine which of them might thrive in Sweden and be of economic value. He was Peter Kalm (1716–79), son of a Swedish minister and protegé of Baron Bjelke. He had traveled in Russia and the Ukraine, and had written on the flora which he found there in articles for the *Flora Suecica*. He entered the University of Upsala in 1741, where he studied under Linnaeus. His first book was published the following year and he was elected to the Swedish Royal Academy of Sciences before he graduated. Accompanying Kalm to America was a young gardener and artist, Lars Jungstrom.[29]

Richard Warner, a wealthy gentleman whose hobby was gardening, took Kalm under his wing. He showed him the sights of London: Westminster Abbey, the Houses of Parliament, and St. Paul's. Kalm was charmed with the view of London from the church's tower, but disappointed that it was so limited "by the thick coal smoke." He visited Warner's home at Woodford where he met his four famous seagulls, two of which had come from Newfoundland. With one wing clipped, they patrolled his garden for caterpillars, frogs, snails, and other pests, following the gardeners about as they dug. They were so tame that they came to the call of "Gull, Gull." Kalm went with Warner to view the Apothecaries' Garden and Sloane's collections. Gradually his acquaintance widened among those with scientific interests in London. Peter Collinson invited him to attend a meeting of the Royal Society, which then met each Thursday afternoon at five. On 21 April, Kalm went with Collinson and heard papers concerning variations in the

29. *Kalm's Account*, pp. vii–xiii

magnetic needle, the *Coccinella*, and a comet seen by Richard Bradley. He was, of course, introduced to many people, including Dr. Cromwell Mortimer and Mark Catesby.[30]

It was inevitable that Kalm should meet John Mitchell. Just when they met does not seem to be a matter of record, but Collinson was doubtless responsible. Kalm did record that on May fourth he spent the morning with the Duke of Argyll, probably taken there by Mitchell, and the remainder of the day at Mitchell's house, and they spent much time together thereafter.[31] It was a welcome meeting for both men. Mitchell was delighted to discuss botanical matters with a friend and student of Linnaeus, as well as with one who had traveled and collected in Russia. Kalm was eager for first-hand accounts of the country to which he was going. Few, if any, in London were so well qualified to advise him on many aspects of its natural productions. Their discussion covered a wide range of topics, many of which Kalm later recorded in his diaries. Kalm inquired about candlemaking in America, and was advised that they were very readily made from a species of *Myrica*, or Bayberry, which grew in abundance in the swamps there. The berries of this plant are covered with a wax excellent for the purpose, and Mitchell described the process used to extract it:

They take the berries and cast them into a pot of boiling water, when the wax melts off the berries by itself and floats as a grease on the top of the water. When the water is cold, the wax hardens, and can then be taken off and kept till it is wanted. The candle is made from it in the same way as tallow or ordinary wax. They mostly mix this wax with the tallow they are going to make dip candles of, as it makes the tallow candle harder and firmer; for if the summers in Virginia are very warm then the tallow candles becomes so soft and weak from the great heat that it cannot stand straight but bends down; but if some of this wax is melted together with the tallow they never bend with the summer heat. Some of the poor people in that country are said to make their candles entirely from this wax.

Kalm expressed such interest that Mitchell told him that he could see *Myrica* plants in Argyll's gardens. It had flourished so well that the Duke had been able to have candles made from their berries by the Virginia method.[32]

30. Ibid., pp. 17–19, 26, 163, and 100.
31. Ibid., pp. 31–32.
32. Ibid., pp. 112–13.

Conversation was not limited to plants. Kalm was excited by Mitchell's account of the buffalo:

When the traveller in Virginia has gone some miles from the sea shore up country, or up towards the hills, he often gets to see a multitude of the wild Oxen which are found there. When they become aware of the presence of man, they run away, directly without doing any harm; but if any one shoots at them and they are only wounded by the bullet and not nearly killed, they come rushing at the one who has fired, and are dangerous enough unless one can find a means either to shoot them down directly and kill them, or to slip away. Their principal food is the great Reed (*Arundo*) which grows everywhere in the morasses. The Indians or the wild folk there, shoot them, sometimes eat up the flesh, or throw it away and use the skin, or sell it to the Europeans, who make the same use of it as of any other ox-leather.

Mitchell told Kalm that one of his friends tried unsuccessfully to tame some buffalo calves. No fence was capable of turning them and when let loose they returned to the wild. Other Virginians had been more successful, but eventually were forced to shoot their tame buffaloes which had eaten and trampled their crops.[33]

During the remainder of May, Kalm and Mitchell saw much of each other. They spent many hours strolling the streets of London when they were not visiting gardens. One sight never failed to intrigue them. This was a very ragged snake charmer, who was invariably surrounded by a fascinated crowd as he handled his fearsome pets. He kept them in a bag and, when offered a ha'penny, he would bring them forth and handle them. Sometimes he would horrify his rapt audience by stuffing the head of one of his vipers into his mouth.

Kalm and Mitchell asked him whether he had ever been bitten. Yes, he replied, but he knew of a safe antidote for the poison. They observed, however, that the snakes did not appear very vicious. In fact, so lethargic were they, that a stick poked at them hardly prompted a response. Some of the more daring of the crowd held the snakes themselves with no ill effect. The ever curious Mitchell, who was seldom satisfied with less than the truth, returned on 17 May and bribed the man to disclose his secret. He admitted that he had removed the poison fangs. Sometimes in doing so he had been bitten but suffered no ill

33. Ibid., pp. 113–14.

effects thanks to the "Snake-Oil," made from snake fat, which he carried in a glass bottle at all times.[34]

Mitchell explained the reason for the excellence of North American pork to Kalm. He said that swine there were fed principally on maize, which grew easily and abundantly. In the fall, the pigs were driven into the oak woods where they fed upon the acorns. Kalm made careful notations of all the information which he received from Mitchell and later in North America found it to be highly accurate.[35]

One day Mitchell went with Kalm, Herr Magister Burmester, an Oeconomy professor from Lund, and some other gentleman, to Hampstead, a small town a few miles north of London. It was a favorite drive or walk for Londoners, with "long-sloping hills," now covered with grass. The Swedish men were much impressed at its luxuriance so early in the year. It was comparable in growth to that of Swedish grass a full month later. Turning to Mitchell, Kalm asked, "What sort of grass is silk-grass, which is mentioned in the description of Virginia, and is said to serve the same purpose as hemp?"

"It is called by Morison in his *Historia* Yucca foliis filamentosis, and grows in Virginia on the sea-shore. It was formerly used like flax and hemp to make clothes of, but since they have been in the habit of getting clothes and other similar things from Europe, the method of preparing this has been so far forgotten that they no longer know in what way it was formerly prepared," Mitchell replied. He added, "I sowed it in my garden in Virginia, where it throve well. I attempted to treat it in the same way as hemp, when I obtained from the fibers in the leaves a sort of fibre not unlike hemp. Only a few of the wild plants grow in Virginia, but its home is farther south." Both professors were naturally interested in the commercial potential of this Yucca, but Mitchell said he was certain that it was "scarcely found" as far north as Pennsylvania as it was too cold for it even there. Kalm noted, "I have since found this was true, and that linen is prepared from its leaves."[36]

The afternoon following their expedition to Hampstead, 23 May, Mitchell and Kalm called upon Mark Catesby. Here was another man

---

34. Ibid., pp. 38–40.
35. Ibid., p. 114.
36. Ibid., pp. 47–50, 116–17. Bartram had transplanted one from the James River to his Pennsylvania garden but it had never bloomed; Darlington, *Memorials*, p. 311.

who knew North America well. Kalm pertinaciously questioned his host, literally bombarding him with his queries. Finally he turned to both men and very gravely asked them:

"Do you think that *Punch* is a useful or a baneful Drink?"

They replied that much depended upon the manner in which it was prepared. Catesby, evidently, could no longer restrain his latent sense of humor and seriously answered Kalm's query.

"My experience in Virginia and Carolina was as follows. The people there drank at one time Punch which was made of strong Brandywine or rum and water with much sugar in it, but only a little lemon-juice was added. The effect, which they gradually found, of this was, that after some time they got a kind of Paralysis, which was such that they could not hold anything with the fingers; for they had almost no strength in them, but were obliged to place everything they wished to take hold of between the two hands. For example, they could not hold the glass which they wished to raise to the mouth with the fingers, which they could not press together, but between the wrists."

Gazing at Kalm with his rather shortsighted eyes, Catesby continued: "Afterwards they began to diminish the quantity of Brandywine and sugar but to put more lemon-juice in it, after which they did not get such troublesome paralysis, although commonly the sad future consequence was that he who drank Punch generally became very palsied, in his old age."[37]

Ignoring tact, Catesby remarked to Kalm: "About twenty years ago we hardly knew here in England what a 'Wall-louse' was; but since that time they have travelled over here in ships from foreign countries that there are now few houses in London in which these least welcome guests have not quartered themselves."[38]

On a more helpful bent, Catesby recounted his method of preserving birds and fish when traveling for he was certain that the young professor would find it useful. After cleaning a bird, he stuffed it with snuff and placed it in a fairly warm oven, being careful that it was not so hot that the bird fat melted. He removed it after a short time. When it was cool, he again returned it to the oven until it was completely dry. The secret was to dry them very gradually. To pack them for traveling,

37. *Kalm's Account*, pp. 119–20.
38. Ibid., p. 51.

he placed them in a cask, packed in snuff which protected them from insects. His fish he preserved in wine.[39]

England's May continued to live up to her reputation for beautiful days that year and on the twenty-fifth, Mitchell, William Watson, Richard Graham, and several other Fellows of the Royal Society took Kalm out to Dulwich, in Surrey, to search out rare plants. Kalm was enchanted with the countryside and recorded:

The whole of this tract of country was most delightful. It went up and down in long sloping hills with valleys between. We had a continuous series of well-built villages, gentlemen's houses, ploughed fields, meadows, orchards and gardens, kitchen-gardens, &c. The country was everywhere divided into small inclosures, with hawthorn and other hedges round them, so that one could only suppose that he was travelling all the way through a garden. Here and there appeared small woods of all sorts of leaf-trees. When a view of the country was obtained from some of the highest hills, it looked pretty enough; but the great number of hedges caused it to look, a little farther off, as though it were entirely overgrown with woods, through which some brick house peeped here and there; for as the *inclosures* were for the most part small here, the hedges prevented the ploughed fields and meadows which lay between them from being seen.[40]

As they strolled along under the balmy May sun, talk again turned to grasses. Kalm was interested to see rye for the first time in England. He noted that it grew well and was curious that more was not planted although he realized that wheat was preferred. Mitchell commented that perennial grasses were rare in the New World, adding: "The grasses that are found there are generally *gramina annua*, which sow themselves every year. For this reason I think that I shall have a large number of seeds of *gramina perennia* collected here, and sent over to *Virginia* to be planted there. The grass in *Virginia* has not the beautiful vivid and green colour that it has here in Europe, but the colour of the grass there is brownish, and not so grateful to the eye."[41] This statement may come as something of a surprise to present-day Virginians. Mitchell was, of course, unfamiliar with the limestone areas of the Valley of Virginia where grasses are at their best. We have no record of

39. Ibid., pp. 51–52.
40. Ibid., pp. 53–54.
41. Ibid., pp. 55 and 120.

Mitchell sending seed, but many present-day grasses were introduced from Europe both intentionally and unintentionally.

The English in the group all agreed that the 1748 spring was the latest any of them had ever known—at least three weeks later than usual. Kalm had to confess that it was still three weeks earlier than in Stockholm. As they approached a hill, small cabins were to be seen near a series of pit-wells. They were very informal, constructed of walls of sod, floors of dirt, and roofs of furze. In these stayed the summer visitors who came to drink from the wells. Kalm thought that the water tasted like any from an "ordinary" clay-pit and that any benefit existed "only in folks' imagination." There was a supposedly genuine mineral spring in Dulwich, "walled round deep down into the earth." The hot and thirsty travelers drank long and lustily from it despite its reputation for purging.[42]

Argyll had insisted that Kalm must see his house at Whitton. Sunday, 29 May, was selected by the Duke as the day for the visit. There were several other guests, including Dr. Mitchell and William Watson, who had brought good news with them. The nine-year War of Jenkins' Ear had finally been concluded and Spain was willing to begin peace preliminaries.[43] In spite of all that he had heard, Kalm was amazed at what Argyll had accomplished, working with such a barren soil as the heath presented. It was the type of project in which Scandinavians, with their own meager, poor soil, were particularly interested. He later noted: "There was here a very large number of *Cedars of Lebanon*, which appeared to have the best opinion of a dry and meagre earth, and it seems that it might be suitable for planting on our great heaths and sandy tracts, in Sweden and Finland." The healthy plantations of North American pines, firs, cypresses, and other trees impressed him equally.[44]

Kalm's host took him on a tour of the house. It was surrounded by gardens and ponds and faced the canal at whose end could be seen the Gothic tower. A contemporary has left a lively account of the house:

. . . a regular handsome Building: There is on the Ground Floor one fine well proportioned Room, where stands a Chinese Pagoda of Mother of Pearl, of exquisite Workmanship; at the upper End of it is a Collection of China,

42. Ibid., p. 56.
43. Entry dated 29 May 1748, in Andrew Fletcher's Common Place Book, Acc. 4423, Box 413 (1755), National Library, Edinburgh, subsequently referred to as NL.
44. *Kalm's Account*, p. 58.

consisting of the greatest curiosities in Porcelaine: In the Next Room is a beautiful Collection of Butterflies and other Insects, and also Drawings of Birds, Fishes, and Fruits colour'd and highly finish'd. The upper Floor is in the Chinese Taste; a with-drawing Room hung with fine India Paper, the Curtains and Chairs of painted Taffeta; next to that is a Bed Chamber in the same Manner, with a most elegant painted Taffeta Bed, and a Palampour [bed-cover] of the same: On each side of the great Room below Stairs, is a long Gallery, in one of which are all the Instruments which the Duke used in his Mechanical and Chymical Experiments; and along the opposite Side, are a Set of Admirable Drawings; the other is fill'd with Books and Drawings also.[45]

Interesting and attractive as it was, Kalm could not repress his feeling that it was a most unpretentious house for a man of Argyll's rank and wealth. The Duke was accustomed to this reaction:

Your wonder . . . probably is why I have not a larger and grander house here than this; but I have first decided to prepare this meagre soil, and make it available to plant all kinds of trees in, and after setting the trees in the order, and in the positions they ought to occupy so that they may grow, then, as I have the money, I can always build the most handsome Castle in one year, and even a shorter time, when I choose to do so, which it would take a poorer man 10 years to build, but to effect so much as that a single tree shall take root and grow as much in one year as it would otherwise grow in ten, that can I never effect with money, but Nature must have its time; therefore he who intends to build a house, and lay out a garden round it, ought to make a beginning with planting trees to gain time.[46]

With the coming of night, the joys of the day had not ended, for Mitchell, Watson, Kalm, and several of Argyll's other guests went all the way to London by water, under a radiant moon.[47]

Kalm did not record further meetings with Mitchell although they certainly did meet again. He delivered to Mitchell some dissertations and a letter from Linnaeus sent in his care.[48] Before he sailed on 5 August, Mitchell gave him an enthusiastic letter of introduction to Benjamin Franklin which Kalm delivered the day he arrived in Philadelphia, along with one from Collinson. In spite of Franklin's urgent invitation to stay with him and an offer of any service, Kalm would not accept.

45. Pye, *A Short Account of the Principal Seats*, pp. 14–15.
46. *Kalm's Account*, p. 59.
47. 29 May 1748, Fletcher's Common Place Book, Acc. 4423, Box 413 (1755), NL.
48. Mitchell to Linnaeus, 10 August 1748, CLO 2:444.

It was not until 30 October that he finally dined with Franklin. He had spent the interim mainly in the country and was reluctant to come to the city until winter.[49]

Kalm spent almost three years in North America, traveling over Pennsylvania, New York, New Jersey, and southern Canada. On a trip to Niagara Falls, he was accompanied by John Bartram. He managed to collect a large variety of seeds to be forwarded to Sweden, a great deal of information and notes on the country and a wife.[50] On his return home, he spent a month in England. Kalm saw Mitchell only briefly as the doctor was in the country at the time[51] but he did see quite a bit of Collinson.[52] Kalm began to publish his *Travels* two years later. They were almost immediately translated into German but did not appear in English until 1770–71 so Mitchell never had the pleasure of reading his friend's account. However, Franklin did and wrote a rather scathing denunciation of it in a letter to David Colden on 5 March 1773: "Kalm's Account of what he learned in America is full of idle Stories, which he pick'd up among ignorant People, and either forgetting of whom he had them, or willing to give them some Authenticity, he has ascrib'd them to Persons of Reputation who never heard of them till they were found in his Book. And where he really had Accounts from such Persons, he had varied the Circumstances unaccountably, so that I have been asham'd to meet with some mention'd as from me. It is dangerous Conversing with these Strangers that keep Journals."[53]

In spite of Franklin's thoughts on the subject, Kalm's account of his North American years today is considered a most interesting and valuable contribution to eighteenth-century history. Undoubtedly, Mitchell was very helpful in preparing Kalm for his visit to the New World. Matti Kerkkonen has written: "An important acquaintance with a view to Kalm's American journey was J. Mitchell, who had been born and

49. Franklin to Logan, 30 October 1748, *Papers of Franklin*, 3:323–24.

50. *Kalm's Travels in North America*, 1:ix–x. Kalm married the widow of Johan Sandin, a Swedish clergyman who had come to New Jersey the previous year. Sandin forwarded seeds to Linnaeus for Clayton but it is doubtful that the two ever met (Berkeley & Berkeley, *Clayton*, pp. 105–7).

51. Mitchell's report to the Board of Trade, 14 April 1752, C.O.5/1327, PRO. A transcript of this is in the Library of Congress.

52. Collinson to Bartram, 24 April 1751, Darlington, *Memorials*, p. 184.

53. LPCC 7:185.

had lived a large part of his life in Virginia. . . . Sometimes Kalm met him every day for they lived close to another. 'He is an incomparably good man,' Kalm wrote to Linnaeus."[54]

Ten days before their visit to Whitton, Kalm had attended a meeting of the Royal Society as the guest of Dr. Watson. Mitchell was also present with Richard Graham.[55] This was not the first time that he had attended a meeting by any means. His first appearance there in December, 1746, was with Henry Baker, well-known in scientific circles for his work with the deaf mutes and an essay on the microscope. Mitchell's name was already familiar to members of the Royal Society from his papers read by Peter Collinson while he was still at Urbanna. The two doctors, Mortimer and Parsons, who were members of the informal philosophical discussion group to which Mitchell belonged, often took him to the meetings as their guest, as did several others: Dr. Alexander Russell, James Theobald, a Lambeth businessman, and a Mr. Sherwood.[56]

On the ninth of June, 1748, Mitchell was proposed as a candidate for a Fellow. The proposal read: "John Mitchell of *Catherine Street* London Doctor of Physick. A Gentleman of great merit and Learning, who Some time since communicated to the Royal Society a very curious dissertation concerning the Colour of the skin in Negroes, and who from his long residence in *Virginia*, & from his great application to the Study of Natural History, especially Botany, is very well acquainted with the Vegetable Production of North America, being desirous of being admitted a fellow of the Royal Society, is recommended by us from our personal knowledge of him as highly deserving the Honour he desires, as we believe he will be (if chosen) a usefull and valuable member of our Body." The certificate was signed by an impressive group of men. Not surprisingly, Mark Catesby and Richard Graham were among them. Another friend and a very active member, William Watson, also signed. He too was a physician and naturalist and one of the few Fellows interested in the new study of electricity. He was one of those who had been present at Whitton on 29 May, and he and Mitchell found many areas in which they were most congenial. Two

---

54. *Peter Kalm's North American Journey, Its Ideological Background and Results* (Helsinki, 1959), pp. 81–82.
55. Royal Society Journal Book XIX, p. 523.
56. Ibid., pp. 166, 176, 187, 212, and 344.

of the signers were Secretaries of the Society: the current one, Dr. Cromwell Mortimer, who wrote an Index to Willughby's *Plates of Fishes*, and the man who succeeded him, Thomas Birch.[57]

Even the president of the Royal Society signed Mitchell's certificate. Martin Folkes (1690–1754), had been vice-president under Sloane and was a controversial figure. In any event, a contemporary description of him is memorable. It came from the jaundiced pen of Dr. William Stukeley:

> Martin Folkes has an estate of near £3000 got by his fa[the]r in the Law. he is a man of no oeconomy, before at age, he marryed Mrs. bracegirdle off the Stage. his mo[the]r grieved at it so much that she threw herself out of a window & broke her arm. his only son broke his neck off horseback at Paris. his Eldest da[ughte]r ran away with a bookkeeper, & who used her very ill. quarreling with Sir Hans Sloan about the presidentship of the Royal Society & being baffled, he went to Rome with his wife & da[ughte]rs, dog, cat, parrot & monkey. there his wife grew religiously mad. he went to Venice & got a dangerous hurt upon his leg. returning he was successor to Sr. Hans, presidt. of R. S. losing his teeth he speaks so as not to be understood. he constantly refuses all papers that treat of longitude. he chuses the Councel & officers out of his junto of sycophants that meet him every night at Rawthmills coffee house, or that dine with him on thursdays at the Miler, fleet street. he has a great deal of learning, philosophy, astronomy; but knows nothing of natural history. in matters of religion an errant infidel & loud scoffer. professes him self a god f[athe]r to all monkeys believes nothing of a future state: of the scriptures of revelation.[58]

On 17 November, Mitchell was present at a meeting of the Royal Society as a guest of William Watson. He gave part of his paper on potash, the remainder of which was read on 24 November. He was again present on 8 December, as a guest of Martin Folkes. The following week he was elected a Fellow and signed the obligation three days before Christmas at which time he was admitted a Fellow. The colorful John Hill became a Fellow at the same meeting. Having no financial problems, Hill paid twenty guineas, thus being relieved of further contributions.[59] Evidently Mitchell was less affluent.

57. Raymond Phineas Stearns, "Colonial Fellows of the Royal Society of London, 1661–1788," *William and Mary Quarterly*, 3d ser. 3 (April 1946):239–40; Nichols, *Literary Anecdotes*, 5:423–24.

58. Stukeley Notebook, fol. 24, MSS Eng. Misc. e. 260, Bodleian Library, OU.

59. Royal Society Journal Book XIX, pp. 579 and 581; Journal Book XX, pp. 14 and 17.

IX ❦ Mitchell and His Fellow Botanist, the Duke of Argyll

"If you can send any of these to the Duke of Argyll they will be acceptable."

Mitchell to Colden, 25 March 1749[1]

The heat of a London July sent many to seek relief in the country. Mitchell spent some of the summer days of 1748 at Whitton. He may have been there on the nineteenth when both the Duke of Richmond and Philip Miller dined there, for Andrew Fletcher referred to the event as "a vast Colledge on Botany."[2] Fletcher, oldest son of Lord Milton, was M.P. for East Lothian. Parliamentary affairs required so little of his time that he was able to serve as Argyll's private secretary as well. He and Mitchell found many mutual interests, especially a love of gardening and botany in general. Together they visited the nursery garden of James Gordon at Mile End, three days after the dinner.[3]

Singularly gifted in his field, Gordon had been trained under Lord Petre and Dr. Sherard. He was one of the very few who were successful in raising plants from the "finest Dusty seeds," such as those of the Mountain Laurel, Azaleas, and Rhododendrons. He was equally gifted in rooting cuttings. Collinson never ceased to marvel at his skill and it was to Gordon that he brought his most precious seeds for germination.[4] He often shared his North American seeds with him, particularly those from Bartram.

Both Mitchell and Fletcher were fascinated by Gordon's display of so

---

1. Hornberger, "A Letter from John Mitchell," *Huntington Library Quarterly* 10 (1946–47):416.

2. Entry in Fletcher's Common Place Book, Acc. 4423, Box 413 (1755), NL.

3. Ibid. Fletcher's father, the influential Lord Milton, was a nephew of the famous Andrew Fletcher of Saltoun (Carlyle, *Autobiography*, pp. 260–61).

4. Collinson's notes in his Common Place Book, 2 September 1763, p. 4, Linnean Society of London, subsequently referred to as LS.

125

very "many Curious plants" which had come from all over the world: three sorts of Cytisus from Siberia; an "Azed Tree from Persia"; a white flowered Clematis from Persia "that blows twice in the season"; "Aconitum from Virginia"; "Bartram's Sweet Dittany"; "Apocynum called in Virginia Wild Hemp"; a "new sort of Magnolia"; a "cal-thoides commonly called the Sea Marigold"; "Cassida from Persia"; a "purple Hypericum—a rare plant"; a "Double Batchelors button"; "Barbae Jovis Africana pinnatis foliis"; "Delphinium orientale, a very beautiful flower"; "Linum perenne from Siberia"; "Poligala Africana buxi foliis"; "Perennial Convovulus from Virginia"; "Rosa Sylvestris Virginiana (Delights in moist soil)"; "Leonurus Canadensis in great abundance"; "Peristrea or Barbadoes Gooseberry." All of these and many others were duly recorded in one of Fletcher's many notebooks. A few days later he also recorded "Mr. Gordon's short list of Curious Plants," containing still others not included above: "An African Milk-wort Tree"; "Two sorts of Virginia Fox Glove"; an "Evergreen Afri-can Hyacinth"; a "Perrenial Pea with a Red flower from Virginia," etc. etc.[5]

Charles Lennox, second Duke of Richmond and a grandson of Charles II (1701–50), invited Mitchell to spend some time at his coun-try estate, Goodwood, in August. Richmond was an old friend of Col-linson. Through him the duke had acquired many of the fascinating plants that graced his impressive gardens. Collinson placed large orders with Bartram for him.[6] He procured some of Argyll's Swamp Pine for Goodwood.[7] He did not hesitate to act as mentor on occasion. In December of 1742, he wrote to Richmond: "I was greatly delighted to find in the Close of your Letter that when all pleasures abroad fail'd, that you found those that was Real & more Certain at Home."[8]

To a genuine love of gardening, a common interest in medicine was added to insure congeniality between Richmond and Mitchell. The Duke had been "created a doctor of medicine" at Cambridge in 1728 and was elected a Fellow of the College of Physicians the same year. It

5. This notebook is now in the manuscript collections of the Alderman Library, Uni-versity of Virginia (Ac. #9897).

6. Aylmer Bourke Lambert, "Notes Relating to Botany, Collected from the Manu-scripts of the Late Peter Collinson," *Transactions of the Linnean Society* 10 (1811):273.

7. Duke of Richmond to Collinson, 5 December 1742, B.M. Add. MSS 28,726.

8. Same to same, 17 December 1742, ibid. Collinson has added this note on the bot-tom of the Duke's letter.

was said of him that "his doors were always open to men of learning, science and ingenuity."[9] On 24 August, he wrote to Collinson: "Can't you come about the latter end of next week, & then I will bring you down, for I shall go up in three or four days to town myself; & by that time your Law affairs may I hope be settled, if not your [st]ay here may be the shorter, but pray come [when] you can for I would fain have you here with Dr. Mitchell."[10]

Kalm's visit had inspired Mitchell to get up a packet for Linnaeus in June, to go in the care of Magister Burmester, previously mentioned. When Argyll heard about it, he decided to send some plants to the Swedish scientists. He selected a group of North American ones, mainly trees: Larch, Fir, Birch, *Rhus*, *Myrica* and others. He asked Mitchell to inform Linnaeus that he would send him "a kind of Bear called the Racoon" as soon as he had the opportunity.[11]

Kalm had delivered a letter from Linnaeus to Mitchell in July but it was several weeks before he had a chance to answer it, as he was out of town so much. He was delighted with the essays that Linnaeus had sent, particularly with one on the manufacture of potash which he needed to complete his own dissertation. Recollecting his discussions of tar-water with Colden, he asked Linnaeus if he had any papers on Scandinavian methods of making pitch. He had just received a shipment of seeds which he had requested from American friends to replace those which he had lost on his ill-fated voyage to England. He made up a parcel of some of these and some *Polygala* root, which he had freshly gathered, to accompany his letter. Two of John Tennent's latest publications on the subject of the root were included. Mitchell informed Linnaeus that his earlier ones, distinctly inferior, were no longer in print.[12] He did not mention that the Virginia doctor had been bailed out of prison by Sir Hans Sloane and had gone to Jamaica.[13]

It was not until two months later that Collinson, to whom Mitchell had entrusted his package for Linnaeus, found a safe passage for it and the final volumes of Catesby's work. Both boxes, in the care of Mr.

9. Nichols, *Literary Anecdotes*, 5:319.

10. Duke of Richmond to Collinson, 24 August 1748, B.M. Add. MSS 28,727.

11. Mitchell to Linnaeus, 10 August, CLO 2:444–45.

12. Ibid., pp. 444–46. Later, he again queried Colden about the New England Pitch Pine as he was anxious to determine the most suitable North American pine for tar and pitch manufacture.

13. Stearns, *Science in the British Colonies*, p. 290

Biork, were placed on board Captain Tornland's ship, the *Assurance*, consigned to a Stockholm merchant.[14] When Catesby learned that Mitchell was writing to Linnaeus, he asked Mitchell to inquire of Linnaeus if the plants that he had sent three years earlier were flourishing.[15] They had been the gift of Dr. Isaac Lawson, who had asked Catesby's advice in selecting them. Catesby had strongly recommended those which were hardy in the English climate so that hopefully they might survive a Swedish winter. Among them were the Tulip Poplar, the Dogwood, the *Robinia*, and the *Catalpa*. Lawson's gift had also gone on the *Assurance*, but in 1745 with a Captain Fisher in command.[16]

Over a year had passed before Linnaeus had replied to Mitchell's first letter so he was astonished when a letter arrived from Sweden in the middle of September. It had been written two days after his own. In his reply, he told Linnaeus that he was pleased that they were in agreement about the genus *Napaea*, or Glade-mallow, and the *Althaea*, though in what connection he did not mention. He hastened to correct Linnaeus concerning news in Sweden of Philip Miller's death. Mitchell was certain that this rumor was due to a mixup between Philip Miller and Joseph Miller, who had died at the beginning of the summer. In fact, Philip Miller had just told him that he was ready to publish "some Figures of Plants." Mitchell was embarrassed not to know the *Linaria Scoparia* (*Chenopodium Scoparia* L. or Belvedere) which Linnaeus wished the English botanists to examine microscopically.[17] Linnaeus had had a plant of it to flower the previous year but it had been killed by frost. He had already sought Haller's assistance in discovering the stamens.[18] Mitchell concluded his letter with the wish that Kalm's travels would be highly successful and assured Linnaeus that he had done everything in his power to be of service to him during his stay in England.

Mitchell reveled in Linnaeus's letters, with their wide range of curious subjects, but found them tantalizingly brief. He had given such a short description of his "Botanical Clock" that it only titillated his friends' curiosity. When Collinson read of it, he wrote to Linnaeus, "But pray consider what will become of the clockmakers, if you can find out

14. Collinson to Linnaeus, 3 October 1748, CLO 1:21.
15. Mitchell to Linnaeus, 20 September 1748, CLO 2:448.
16. Catesby to Linnaeus, 26 March 1745, ibid., pp. 440–41.
17. Mitchell to Linnaeus, 20 September 1748, ibid., pp. 447–48
18. Linnaeus to Haller, 23 October 1747, ibid., p. 418.

vegetable dials?"[19] Likewise, Mitchell was anxious to hear more of Linnaeus's experiments on the plant food of domestic animals. Linnaeus's bare reference to Steller's reaching Canada by way of his Russian journeyings was especially maddening. Mitchell immediately wanted to know by what route, in what part of Canada did he land, and on what authority was Linnaeus quoting. If Linnaeus had also included the fact that he had just discovered how to grow pearls that same summer, Mitchell's curiosity would probably have exploded. Collinson's comment, when he learned, was typical: "Next, I am afraid you will be spoiled for a gardener, you will grow so rich with the breeding of oriental pearls."[20] Linnaeus had inquired in his previous letter about Mitchell's botanical essays, to which the Virginian could give no definite answer. Now, he was able to tell him that Dr. Trew had written Collinson that they had appeared in the current Nuremberg *Transactions*. Letters to Mitchell in which Linnaeus might have commented on them have been lost, but he did write to Albrecht Haller on 13 September, remarking on Mitchell's *Nova Genera*, but he did not mention the proposed method of classification.[21]

In the early fall, letters from Virginia brought Dr. Mitchell word of the death of his father on 8 August. He had served as Burgess until a year before his death and had been active in other ways.[22] His inventory was presented in the Lancaster County Court on 13 October and was substantial. His estate included forty Negroes, seventy-one cattle, one hundred and twenty-one pigs, forty-six sheep, and seven horses, in addition to a house and store. The store was well supplied with a large and varied merchandise. Eighty-one thousand pounds of tobacco and one hundred and seven pounds of currency were due to the estate. Over one hundred pounds in cash were found in the house and in England

19. Collinson to Linnaeus, 3 October 1748, CLO 1:21–22. This had been published in the *Pan. Suecus Amoen. Acad.* 2:225.

20. Collinson to Linnaeus, 3 October 1748, CLO 1:21–22; Linnaeus to Haller, 13 September 1748, CLO 2:428–29.

21. Ibid., p. 429.

22. Between 1737 and 1741, he acquired ninety acres from William Miller (Lancaster County Deed Book 13, p. 67). He added fifty acres adjoining his own land in 1739. These were bought from William and Elizabeth Kelley for £2700 (ibid., p. 36). One hundred and fifty acres were purchased from John and Jane Rogers in 1740 (ibid., p. 168). Isaac White sold him seven acres in 1747 (Lancaster County Deeds & Wills, Book 14, p. 133—all records at VSL).

there was a credit of three hundred and seventy-five pounds as well as the current shipment of tobacco not yet paid for.[23]

Nothing was left to his son, Dr. Mitchell, but in the event of his half brothers' deaths without heirs, he would become the residuary legatee.[24] He was, however, with Robert, Jr., and Richard, an executor of his father's will. Robert, Jr., inherited the plantation in Richmond County where he and Hannah were living. His father had bought it the previous year from the widow of Thomas Wright Belfield and her son, John. It consisted of six hundred and ninety-five acres.[25] He also left him twelve slaves. To Richard, his father left the plantation on which he was living and two others, lying in Farnham Parish: "Upper & Lower Quarter," as well as all land adjoining in Richmond and Northumberland Counties. This included the mill. If Robert, Jr., left no heir, his inheritance first went to Dr. Mitchell, second to Richard, then to the daughters. This applied also if Richard left no heirs.[26]

Since his father did not leave Mitchell anything in his will, one assumes that either he had already settled a sum on his oldest son or that he considered him well-provided for through inheritance from his mother. This was probably turned over to him when he purchased the property at Urbanna. There seems little doubt that he possessed investments of some sort as he could not have survived financially in England, unable to practice his profession. It is possible that when Dr. Reade purchased the Mitchell home in Urbanna, he turned over his interest in some of the property which he owned in England. When Reade died he still possessed several houses in the city of Bedford there. Mitchell's account with Coutts's bank, which still survives, shows deposits from time to time: John Spotswood's bill on Thomas Knox for £325; John Knight's note for £21; Nicholas Lilley & Co., bill on John Tozier & Co., for £27.3.9; Archibald Arbuthnot's bill on George

23. Ibid., pp. 227–30.
24. Ibid., pp. 212–14.
25. Richmond County Deed Book #10, pp. 425–27, VSL. The land adjoined that of a Mrs. Hopkins and Sir Marmaduke Beckwith. Some of the land remained in the family's hands until this century and several were buried there. See will of Adelina S. Mitchell (Richmond County Wills #30, 18 February 1908, p. 238, VSL). At that time, Mrs. Mitchell had three surviving children: a son, R. S. Mitchell, and two daughters, Mrs. Willie J. Harrison and Mrs. Bessie L. Motley. There were also several grandchildren.
26. Mr. Mitchell directed that his unmarried daughters, Frances and Judith, should receive their patrimony upon their marriages or when they reached the age of twenty-one.

Ouchterbery for £9.6.3; Robert Baldwin's note for £25, and James Richardson's for £16.[27] It is apparent that the income that he deposited was scarcely adequate for his living expenses but he may have deposited only what he did not need. He was able to supplement his income by other means. One of these was staying for long periods with the Duke of Argyll. It is not possible to judge whether this was in the capacity of a paid employee or merely as a guest who was entertaining. No regular payments to Mitchell by Argyll have been found and yet there is definite indication that Mitchell and a Dr. Stuart may have acted in the capacity of private physicians to the duke and his household. In any event, Mitchell's relationship to Argyll over a long period was quite close and involved many favors on both sides of the friendship.

When Mitchell described Franklin's ingenious new stove, the duke immediately requested him to order one, which he did, paying the printer, William Strahan, three guineas as Franklin had designated. He also acquired one of the pamphlets describing the stove for Argyll.[28] Mitchell recommended to Argyll that Richard Corbin of Virginia be appointed one of the council there.[29] Argyll was in a position of influence as an important member of George II's household. He was on the Privy Council and Keeper of the Great Seal as well as lord justice general. It is impossible to know how much influence Mitchell's recommendation had but the fact remains that Corbin was appointed to the council by the king on 19 January 1749/50.[30]

Mitchell's North American botanical knowledge was very welcome to the duke and the garden at Whitton Place sheer heaven for the doctor. In 1748, Mitchell drew up a catalogue of the "Curious Collection from all parts of the World," which was intended to be published.[31]

---

27. Spotswood's bill, 18 August 1756; Knight's note, 25 August 1756; Lilley & Co., 24 March 1757; Arbuthnot's note, 28 March 1757; Baldwin's note, 20 December 1760; Richardson's note, 3 January 1761. Miss M. Veronica Stokes, Archivist and Curator of Coutts & Company, was exceedingly generous with her help and time in making the records of Mitchell's account available to the authors.

28. Franklin to William Strahan, 23 November 1748, *Papers of Franklin*, 3:327. The catalogue of Argyll's library shows an "Account of Pensylvania [sic] fireplaces, Philadelphia" (p. 211).

29. "Excerpts from the Cattle Book," p. 4, Box 414 (1756), Saltoun MSS, NL.

30. C.O. 5/1327, p. 159, P.R.O. Argyll, as Keeper of the Great Seal, received £3000 per annum and, as lord justice general, £2000.

31. Mitchell to Colden, 25 March 1749, Hornberger, "A Letter from John Mitchell," *Huntington Library Quarterly* 10 (1946–47):415–16.

Evidently this was never done, for it was not listed in the brochure of Argyll's library in 1758. It may have been in manuscript form but would not have survived as the duke's library was later lost in a fire. A portion of it may be extant in the Whitton Place sales catalogue printed in 1765.[32] In it, Daniel Crofts, the duke's gardener, listed 368 trees and shrubs on 17 July of that year. Sixty-six of these are definitely attributed to Virginia and included such diverse plants as *Acacia*, *Azalea*, Ash, Benjamin-tree (Spice Bush), Chinquapin, Dogwood, Hemlock-spruce, Haw, Hawthorne, Hornbeam, *Itea*, Laurel, Maples, Oaks, Pines, Paw-paw, Service tree, Tulip-tree and Walnuts. Many others flourished in Virginia but were not designated as such. Unfortunately, Crofts did not include the Latin name, which Mitchell would have done in his cata-logue. Although the majority of the plants were natives of North America, there were trees and shrubs from most of the areas of the world known at the time: Siberia, Turkey, Portugal, Lebanon, Malta, Russia, Spain, China, and Switzerland.

Argyll had no hesitation in impressing his friends to collect for him and there are many notations in Andrew Fletcher's notebooks of the receipt of such gifts: Pine seeds from General St. Clair in Geneva; Afri-can Bay seeds from the Duke of Bedford; Evergreen-willow cuttings from the banks of the Po River from General Sinclair; Juniper seeds from Hungary from Lord Hyndford; a Red Bay, a Water Tupelo, and a Sumach from General Oglethorpe in Georgia; Carolina Yellow Hawthorne and "Candel Berry" from Sir James Carnegie; a parcel of seeds from Robert Dinwiddie, Governor of Virginia; plants from Mr. Crokatt, a South Carolina merchant; a list sent to the British Consul in Spain of seeds available there; a list of seeds of Newfoundland Pines, Firs, and Monarch Oaks sent to a Lieutenant Fletcher; German seeds from Collinson; St. Peter's Wort seed from Majorca; Chilean Straw-berries; seeds from Aleppo and China. The duke was as generous with his own plants and seeds as he expected his friends to be and long lists of them are noted to be sent to various people. Fletcher listed thirty-eight different types of seeds which were collected at Whitton in 1749, many of which were given to friends.[33]

32. See chap. 8, note 16.

33. Green leather notebook in Box 436, pp. 14, 53, 57, 67, 11, 62, 99, 40, 97; "Din-woodie" seeds, 28 January (a catalogue was enclosed but is now missing), Box 415 (1756); old green notebook marked "1749–1757," in Box 35, pp. 17, 4, 15, 100. All of these are among the Saltoun MSS, NL.

Mitchell was able to relieve Fletcher of some of his seed-collecting duties, particularly those from the New World. For the Virginian, the dream of every gardener came true: access to a rather plentiful money supply for acquiring plants in quantity including some rare and unusual ones, even though it was done for someone else. The order to Bartram, which he had placed in June 1748, arrived on 21 January, and included a wide variety: Sassafras, Red Cedar, Candle Berry, Small *Magnolia*, great-leaved and small-leaved Willow Oaks, Chestnut and Black Oaks, Red Oak mixed with Willow, Swamp Spanish Oak and Red, Poison Ash, Arbor Judae, Scarlet Sumach, Tupelo, Cluster Cherry, White Cedar, Sweet-leaved, fine-twigged Hickory, coarse-leaved rough Hickory, White and Black Walnuts, Great Champlain Oak, Benjamin, Red Spirea, and Mountain White Oak.[34]

In late January, Mitchell gave Fletcher some Virginia seeds to be delivered to Mr. Crofts. Unfortunately, Fletcher did not record from whom Mitchell had obtained them. They included a *Convolvulus*, an evergreen *Euonymus*, and a *Laburnum*. Later, he added a gift of *Lilium Canadense*.[35] On 4 February, he was able to hand over a parcel of seeds received from Barbadoes: Arigalo Pear seed; the Hog or Gully Plum, *Acacia*, Soap Berry, Okra, *Lignum vitae*, Cassada Tea, French Physic Nut, Seaside Hops, Sand Box Tree, Hura and Evergreen *Euonymus*, Maahite, "small 6 weeks beans," Bully Berry, Cotton seed, and Chick stone.[36]

Ten days later, Mitchell visited Oxford, where Dr. Humphrey Sibthorpe (1713?–1797) had been appointed Dillenius's successor. The professor welcomed him and proceeded to make up a packet of seeds for the duke. It included *Mesembryanthemum Geniculi florem*, Neapolitan and Egyptian *Teiorda*, Neapolitan *flore Candido*, and Balm of Gilead Firr which was "supposed to be different from that at Whitton," *Paliurus* and *Arbutus*. Sibthorpe promised to send later seed of the *Caraganae*, a genus of Asiatic trees or shrubs of leguminous character.[37]

When Mitchell presented Argyll with a new type of Indian corn in March, he also gave him a description of the method of planting, cultivating, and harvesting it in Virginia, which Fletcher carefully recorded:

34. Green leather notebook, p. 45, Box 436, Saltoun MSS, NL.

35. Old green notebook, 1749–57, p. 24, Box 35; green leather notebook, p. 37, Box 436, Saltoun MSS, NL.

36. Old green notebook, 1749–57, pp. 4–5, Box 35, Saltoun MSS, NL.

37. Ibid., p. 17.

Method of planting Mays or Indian Corn fr. Dr. Mitchel 1749

The Ground should be first Tilled for this as for other grains Altho the frequent Stirring of the ground in weeding the Corn makes it unnecessary to Plow it so much before; After the ground is thus slightly broke up Run Single Furrows across it at the Distance of About five foot each. Cross these furrows again with others at the Same distance till the whole field is finished in this manner.

At the place where these furrows cut one another plant the corn by droping four or five grains in each hole made by the furrows Crossing one another.

To Save time in the Spring of the year as well as their Horses which are then weak it may be Sufficient to cross plow the ground in Single furrows in this manner before it is all plowed over or at the most to run three furrows in a place close together and Cross them with a Single one about five foot distance plowing up the ground between these Ridges at any time of leisure after the Corn is planted.

When the Corn is about a foot or two high it must be wed Either with a Hough or a Plough, For this purpose a Breast Plough Seems to be the most Convenient of any used in Britain.

The most Convenient way to weed it with a Hough is to draw the weeds from about the Corn on Each Side into the middle between the Rows. This makes a Ridge between Each row of Corn which you again lay up to the Roots of the Corn at the Second weeding.

After the Corn is wed go over it and pull up the Suckers that come up from the Root and leave no more than two Stalks Standing in a Hill.

As Soon as the weeds begin to grow again it must be wed a Second time in doing which the Earth Should be laid up in a Hill about the Roots of the Corn which makes this work most Conveniently done with a Hough Either at first or after plowing This Second weeding Should always be done before the Corn begins to blossom or tassel at top. Nothing hurts a Crop of Corn more than to Suffer it to be overrun with Weeds.

As Soon as the Lower blades of the Corn begin to Change Colour and turn dry Especially nigh the Stalk they may be pulled off as far as the Ear and made in Bundles of the Size of an armfull which are tyed up with two or three of the Blades and hung upon the Stalks to dry for Fodder. After that the tops of the Stalks are cut off with a knife Immediately above the Ear and laid on the ground to dry in like manner for Fodder. This is Commonly done in the month of September and the Corn is Usually Ripe after the first frost in October or November which is known by the grain turning hard. Then it is pulled off the Stalks and the Husk upon it is taken off which with the blades and tops Serve as Hay and makes Very good Fodder for Cattle.[38]

Andrew Fletcher's notebook also gives "The Method of raising & Curing Tobacco in Virginia." Although he does not specifically attribute it to Dr. Mitchell, there seems little doubt that he was the author:

They dig up a Bed for the seed, then cover it with wood as thick as a Babbin & set it on fire; the ashes after the fire is out is raked and mixed well with the Earth.

The seed is sowed within 12 days of Xmas: When the leaves of the plants are as broad as a Crown piece, they are planted out upon hillocks scraped up with a Hoe, about a foot high, and 2 ft Diameter in the bottom, 4 ft distance from each other; when the plants are about 18 inches high or 2 ft the tops are to be broke off and all the leaves from the Root upwards except 8, some leave 12, but 8 is best. The Succors are to be taken away as fast as they come out, and the Tobacco Worms taken off and destroyed; When the leaves are Crisp enough to snap, when when [sic] bent double between the Finger and thumb, they are ripe and fit to gather: The Plant is to be Cut off above the root early in the morning and set with the head downwards till noon in order to wilt, it may then be laid flat on the Ground, till night; and then carried into the House, and hung upon sticks, as red Herrings, in the Herring houses, for about a month: During this time the leaves will become very brittle; for which reason it is not taken down till the next rain, they will then give, and become very tough; it must then be laid in a great heap upon boards (or any thing that will keep it from the Earth) to sweat for above fourteen days, it is then stript from the Stalks, and tyed in bundles or hands, about twelve leaves in each hand, and must be then put into Hogsheads, and pressed hard down in them.[39]

That same month (March), Mitchell again wrote to Colden. He suspected that his previous letters had been lost.[40] He enclosed some seeds and said that he would welcome any of the common wild seeds that Colden might send to him, especially those of trees and shrubs.

38. Ibid., p. 40; the method of planting corn is in one of Andrew Fletcher's notebooks, pp. 59–63, Acc. 4423 (Seven Commonplace books of members of the Fletcher family of Saltoun, 1748–1826), Saltoun MSS, NL. A hough was the Scottish term for "hock," a strong handled hook.

39. Ibid., pp. 54–55.

40. 25 March 1749, Hornberger, "A Letter from John Mitchell," *Huntington Library Quarterly* 10 (1946–47):411–17

He added, "If you can send any of these to the Duke of Argyll they will be acceptable, & I shall present them in your name. You will hardly find any more ready or able to return the favour. What he wants most are a good quantity of Red & White Cedars, Pitch & all other Pines, Chesnut oak of the red, white & swamp sorts, small shrubby oaks frequent in the Woods, with a Specimen with them to see if they are different from what he has, which are very many." To this, Mitchell added: "His Grace wants likewise a Bull & cow of your American Buffaloes, which I thought you could procure him from the Indians of N. York, if it is not too much trouble. He will pay any expence that may be necessary to procure them, if it is not too much trouble to you." Undoubtedly, he had been regaling Argyll with the tales which he had told Kalm of the buffaloes.

Mitchell also sent another order to Bartram for Argyll. The shipment arrived in December. Unfortunately, the first part of Mitchell's letter is missing, which must have contained both the date and directions as to the order's content.[41] It was far more varied than that received in January:

List of Seeds from John Bartram, Pennsylvania
Dec. 1749

Sugar Maple	Golden Rod
Ash	Apios, which Indians
Cherries	Eat
White Cedar	Narrow leavd Clinopodeñ
Evergreen Euonymus	Little small leav'd
Red oak	Onobrachrys
Scarlet Sumach	Great Convolvus climbing
Beach leav'd sumach	wt a Red Eye
N. England Pine	Golden Rod from the
Shrubby White oak	Desart
Hemlock spruce	Fine Aster from Do.
White Walnuts	Virginia Ditany
Pignuts	Ketmia from a sea marsh
Acorns No. 4 & 5th	Sennae Major Minorae
Sassafras	foliis
Euonymus Scandens	3 sorts seeds unknown

41. Undated, Bartram Papers, 4:86, HSP.

Acorns different sorts	Oswego Tea
Chamaerhododendron	Virginia Foxglove
Crane berries	Shrubby Hypericum
Wild oats	Fine pea—Jersey
flower from the	
Desart[42]	

It was only a few weeks after the Pennsylvania seeds arrived, that some came for Mitchell from Jamaica. Unfortunately, there is no indication of this order:

Ketmia Egyptica . . . musk
Ketmia Brasiliensis . . . Brazil okra.
Parkinsonia Aculeata, foliis minitis . . .
Palma Humilis Dactylifera Palmetta.
Anona foliis Laurinis, Sapodilla Caenito
Acajou, or Cashew Tree. A note added that it should never be
    removed from the place in which it was originally planted.
Ketmia Indica, or Indian red Sorrel.
Ketmia Sinensis . . . Martinico Rose
Ketmia Indica . . . Long okra.
Anonymous . . . flourishing shrub.
Orobus Americanus—wild Liquorice
Another anonymous plant
Sapindus foliis costa alata . . . Soapberry
Papaya fructu maximo . . . large pawpaw tree
Granadilla american . . . Passion Flower from Panama which
    "continues flowering and fruiting all the year."
Mahogany[43]

Mitchell served as adviser not only to Argyll but to others as well. When he was asked by Fletcher which botany books he would recommend, he gave him a list of seventeen, and included the prices of most of them:

Tournefort's Institutions   1.10   1719
Boerhaves Index alter 9to

42. Green covered notebook, p. 101, Box 435, Saltoun MSS, NL.
43. Ibid., p. 102.

Hortus Cliffortianus
Linnaei Fundamenta Botanica
      Systema Naturae Edit. 6th
      Flora Lapponica

Royen's flora Leydensis	.6 sh.
Flora Virginica	3
Morison's Historia Plantarum	2.
Lobel Icones Plantarum 4to	5 sh.
Herman Paradisus Psalavias	5 sh.
Raii Synopsis Briton Edit. 3	4 sh.
Cornuti Historia Plantarum Canad.	3 sh.
Dale Pharmacologia 4to	8 sh.
Tournefort's Plantes des Paris	4
Chomel Histoire de Plantes	6
Gmelin Flora Siberica	10
Miller Botanicum officinale[44]	4

Lord Bute, likewise, received occasional assistance from Mitchell but once it was not too helpful. Knowing that Gronovius would be interested in some "bute-shells" from the Isle of Bute, he had asked Mitchell to oversee the packing of a box of them to send to Leyden. Somehow, in the process of making up the parcel, the doctor and the servants between them had managed to lose it.[45]

Much of Mitchell's time was spent in the country during the first six months of 1749. He arranged for his mail to be sent to James Buchanan, a London merchant.[46] When in town, he seldom missed the meetings of the Royal Society, often bringing a friend with him. In January, he was accompanied by the Reverend Clark, minister of the parish of Houghton-Conquest in Bedfordshire, who, in February, gave a paper on a stone removed from a boy. Once Dr. Pieter Camper (1722–89), of Leyden, was his guest. Camper became a Fellow in 1750.[47]

Interest in the snake-killing powers of the Virginia Dittany or Wild

44. Ibid., p. 13.
45. Earl of Bute to J. F Gronovius, 2 February 1750/51, in the Bute Archives, Isle of Bute.
46. Mitchell to Colden, 25 March 1749, Hornberger, "A Letter from John Mitchell," *Huntington Library Quarterly* 10 (1946–47):417.
47. Vol. XX of the Journal Books of the Royal Society, pp. 48, 72, 54.

Pennyroyal was again fascinating the Royal Society. Mitchell triggered some of the discussion by stating that he had seen "the sweet scented dittany" used in such an experiment to no effect. He wrote to Bartram that in checking later the description of Dittany supposedly used, as printed in the *Philosophical Transactions*, he discovered that it was a different plant, the *Trichostema* which appeared in the *Flora Virginica*. Mitchell described it as a small weed, rank in odor, and with a blue flower, rather like an *Hypericum*. Mitchell knew that "it will kill worms in the body & why not other reptiles?" He had seen it growing luxuriantly in Bartram's fields, so he wrote to his friend, asking him if he had time to test its snake-killing properties. The Royal Society would like to have the claims tested further. If Bartram would send him the results of his experiments, he would present them to the society and make certain that they appeared in the *Transactions*. If he had any success, he hoped that Bartram would send some of the dried plant "that I may convince our Philosophers of the truth of it, for they are otherwise great Infidels in what they do not see."[48] Bartram was otherwise occupied and did not follow Mitchell's suggestion.

Another joint venture did result in a paper for the society by Dr. Watson.[49] In mid-May, he and Mitchell visited John Tradescant's garden in South Lambeth. Tradescant was a widely traveled Dutchman who had visited Greece and Egypt as well as most of Europe. As a result, his collections of birds, fish, minerals, insects, and plants were justifiably famous. He began his garden, with his son's help, in the 1620s. Except for John Gerard's garden, it was probably the first botanic garden in England.[50] He was credited with many plant introductions that bear his name: Tradescant's Spiderwort, Tradescant's Aster, and Tradescant's Daffodil. At the death of his son, his friend Elias Ashmole (1617–92) acquired the museum that subsequently found its way to Oxford.[51]

Watson and Mitchell found the house in ruins and the garden neglected for years. It was depressing, but under the mass of weeds they

48. Mitchell to Bartram, undated (1749?), Bartram Papers, 4:86, HSP.
49. 25 March 1749, Royal Society Journal Book XX, pp. 128–29; Watson's account was published in *Philosophical Transactions* 46 (1749):668–69. He was known by contemporaries as "the living lexicon of botany."
50. Stearns, *Science in the British Colonies*, pp. 48–49.
51. 25 May 1749, Stukeley Corres., p. 56, MSS Eng. Misc. e. 128, Bodleian Library, OU.

found evidence of the former glory: *Borago latifolia sempervirens, Polygonatum vulgare latifolium, Aristolochia clematatis erecta,* and *Dracontium.* More remarkable were two huge *Arbutus* trees which somehow had survived the severe winters of 1729 and 1740, which had killed all the others of this species. As the doctors wandered back into Tradescant's orchard, they were delighted by a *Rhamnus cathartica,* twenty feet tall and almost a foot in diameter. Mention of a huge Cypress (*Taxodium distichum* [L.] Richard) also appeared in Watson's account. He said that Tradescant had first introduced this species to English gardens "which has since been so much esteemed, and is now one of the great ornaments of the Duke of Argyll's Garden at Whitton." Watson did not go into the more sordid details supplied by Philip Miller. Since the Cypress stood in a "common yard" the neighboring housewives had no compunction about making use of it. Its century old dignity might have been humiliated by the hooks and clothes lines, but not its "Health and Vigour."[52]

Mitchell and Watson may not have seen the entire garden. In 1773, a Dr. Ducarel published a letter to Watson in which he referred to Watson's account of their visit. He was of the opinion that they had only seen a small part of it. He wrote, "In it, Sir, you seem to confine the extent thereof to that now belonging to Mr. Small's house. I believe it was otherwise; and on the account of the great number of plants, trees, etc. am inclined to think that Tradescant's garden extended much farther. Bounded on the West by the road, on the East by a deep ditch (still extant) it certainly extended a good ways towards the North, and took in not only my orchard and garden, but also those of two or three of my next neighbours; and some ancient mulberry trees, planted in a line towards the North, seem to confirm this conjecture."[53]

Continued reports of the prevalence of yellow fever in New York revived Mitchell's interest in the disease. He had had to postpone completing his account of yellow fever because of involvment in other affairs and the fact that such a project required close concentration and undisturbed attention, both of which were impossible in his weakened

52. Watson, "Some Account of the Remains of John Tradescant's Garden at Lambeth," *Philosophical Transactions* 46 (1749):668–69.

53. *A Letter from Dr. Ducarel, FRS and FSA to William Watson, MD, FRS upon the Early Cultivation of Botany in England and Some Particulars about John Tradescant* (London, 1773), pp. 9–10. This copy of Ducarel is in the Gough Survey 30, Bodleian Library, OU.

health. Now, he was feeling stronger and there was more time for such studies, so he asked Colden for an account of the New York epidemics and also about the victims of the disease who had been on troop transports which he had seen at Hampton Roads.[54]

He had other questions for his friend as he was again collecting information for his "Natural & medical History of N. America." He was particularly concerned with the uses which could be made of various natural products, both medical and commercial, but found his research into such matters blocked by the lack of materials with which to conduct experiments. He had some Canadian Balsam, whose medicinal properties he found of value as a diuretic and detergent. A friend of his who was threatened with diabetes had found great relief by taking Balsam. Mitchell asked Colden if it was available in his neighborhood and whether it came from the Hemlock Spruce or the Balm of Gilead Fir.

Both Colden and Bartram received Mitchell's inquiries concerning red and black dyes used by the Indians. In Virginia, Mitchell knew that they used a small *Rubia* to be found in the swamps, for their red dye, but he had no idea from what they derived the black. Kalm was to learn from the New Jersey inhabitants that the common field Sorrel (*Rumex acetosella* [L.] Small) produced an acceptable black dye which fact may well have come from the Indians.[55] Mitchell was still anxious to improve his knowledge of the Oaks which had so impressed Catesby. He queried Colden as to whether the New England Monarch Oak was the same as the "White Swamp or water Chesnut Oak." He wanted to know what other varieties they had. He also desired information on other northern timber trees, saying that he had found the Locust, the Honey Locust, the Mulberry, the old Red Cedar, the Ring Oak, and the Tulip Tree the most durable. He considered, however, the Chestnut Oak and the small White Swamp Oak the best. Since he had come to the Mother Country, he had heard innumerable complaints concerning American timber which the English claimed not only shrank but rotted. For these reasons, they purchased wood for their beer vats and barrels from Germany. Mitchell discovered that this was Chestnut

54. Hornberger, "A Letter from John Mitchell," *Huntington Library Quarterly* 10 (1946–47):411–17.

55. *Kalm's Travels*, 1:185.

so he thought it advisable for the colonies to export that wood rather than Oak which they had been doing. In Virginia, it would be a welcome idea as they had found no real use for Chestnut.

Pines had again become the subject for Mitchell's inquiry. He had been studying Dudley's description of the New England evergreens and wondered if the Pitch Pine which he mentioned could possibly be the same as the southern. He was of the opinion that it was not. He was trying to determine the Pine which was best suited for the production of pitch and tar. He had been studying the manner of making these products by the Norwegians and others. In his research he had become convinced that the poor product coming from North America was due to the method of manufacture rather than the trees themselves.

Letters from home brought Mitchell interesting news. With the signing of the Treaty of Aix-la-Chapelle, the previous October, Virginians again were thinking of expanding westwards. Before he had left Urbanna, the migration to the west had been stimulated by the treaty with the Six Nations at Lancaster and King George's War. The former removed much of the danger and the latter had resolved the necessity for trying to avoid offending the French. Mitchell remembered the aspirations of the Greenbrier Company which had been granted 100,000 acres on the river of that name in April of 1745. He had known some of the men involved, including John Robinson, John Robinson, Jr., and William Beverley. So many others had applied for Trans-Allegheny grants at that time that the Council ordered that no further surveys would be considered for the time being.[56]

From Collinson, Fothergill, and other Quakers, he had heard much of the Ohio Company established in 1747 by the president of the Virginia Council, Thomas Lee, for the London representative was John Hanbury, a well-known Quaker merchant. Many of the twenty-five Virginians who had organized the company were from the Northern Neck and some were known to Mitchell, particularly those of the Carter family. They were applying for land in the area of the Forks of the Ohio River. Mitchell understood the government's reason for granting the company land the summer of 1749 without payment of quitrents for ten years and the insistence that a fort be built.[57] It was

56. Richard L. Morton, *Colonial Virginia*, 2 vols. (Chapel Hill, 1960), 1:570–71.
57. Ibid., pp. 573–74.

the strategy of barriers between English and French land interests. The English had learned something from their old adversary.

The French were far from unaware of the English activities and countered immediately. Mitchell was amused by and yet indignant about the new French surveys of their colonies which, he told Colden, brought them "as far as to your doors, if not beyond them." In fact, D'Anville, the King's Geographer, had been criticized for attributing ownership of the Appalachian Mountains to the English. Mitchell realized that the French were encouraging more settlements in Louisiana. He was fascinated by D'Anville's new maps and promised Colden a set if he did not already have them. He wondered how accurate they might be and questioned Colden as to the location of the New York mountains in relation to the sea. In Virginia, he knew the distance was two hundred miles and he had heard that it was three hundred in Carolina. He wanted to know what passes there were, and where they were located.

The old fascination which Mitchell had with exploration and surveys still intrigued him now that all London was becoming concerned with the subject. The actual mechanics of map making were beginning to interest him. There had never been a precise way in which to determine longitude. In 1715, Parliament had offered £2000 reward to the man who invented an accurate marine timekeeper. Those of metal proved sensitive to temperature and humidity. Rewards eventually went to John Harrison, a carpenter's son, who developed a workable wooden clock.[58]

58. For a full account of Harrison's work, see Lloyd A. Brown, *The Story of Maps* (New York, 1949), pp. 228–40.

X ⚜ A Journey to Scotland

> *"I have taken a long and laborious journey, with the Duke of Argyl, to the uttermost parts of Scotland, over the mountains and wilds of that country, as well as through various counties of England."*
>
> Mitchell to Linnaeus, 1 May 1750[1]

In his letters to both Bartram and Colden, Mitchell referred to his growing intimacy with men of influence. He had met many such men through his friendship with Collinson, Fothergill, and Catesby, and later Argyll and Bute, but it was his own attractive personality that made such introductions develop into friendship. To Bartram, he suggested that he look about for some modest office whose salary would enable him to spend more time on his plant collecting than he was able to do while supporting his family by farming. If he did learn of such a place, Mitchell would be delighted to use what influence he had to insure his appointment: "I am pretty well acquainted wt. several in power, & can easily propose such a thing to them & even urge it."[2]

To Colden, Mitchell wrote that he had presented a copy of the New Yorker's book to Argyll, who was much impressed with it. He added, "If you think my representation of any thing relating to your Interest or wellfare can be of any service, you may depend upon it, as I have the good fortune of frequent access & conferences with several in power, who are frequently asking me about what happens in our Colonies."[3]

It was quite true that Mitchell, through his association with Argyll and Bute, found himself meeting and dining and talking more and more with some of the most influential men in England. Much of that spring and summer of 1749 was spent at Whitton, where he met various important gentlemen at Argyll's table.[4] There were two frequent guests who were later members of George II's Household: Sir Harry

1. CLO 2:449.
2. Mitchell to Bartram, 1749? Bartram Papers, 4:86, HSP.
3. Mitchell to Colden, 25 March 1749, Hornberger, "A Letter from John Mitchell," *Huntington Library Quarterly* 10 (1946–47):412.
4. Dinner guests listed in Andrew Fletcher's "Catalogue," Saltoun MSS #435, NL.

Erskine, who became Keeper of the Private Roads and Sir Henry Bellenden, who was appointed Knight of the Black Rod. Erskine's son was often present as well. Lord Dupplin and Mr. Crockatt were guests, as were General and Mrs. St. Claire, back from Switzerland. Sir Hew Dalrymple (1690–1755) was another of Argyll's friends. He was a Scottish judge and was always a lively addition to any dinner table, for he "had as much conversation and wit as any man of his time, having been long an M.P."[5] John Murray was another Scot. He had married his cousin, Charlotte, daughter of the second Duke of Atholl, and would succeed to the title upon his uncle's death. Of all those whom Mitchell met at this time, the two who influenced his future the most were Lord Dupplin and James Oswald, both Commissioners of Trade and Plantations.

Fifteen to sixteen persons were usually present at Argyll's Sunday dinner and Mitchell found himself often among them. As today, meat was the main dish in eighteenth-century England and appeared either boiled or roasted. Kalm attributed the delicious flavor to the fat resulting from fine pastures, but added: "The Englishmen understand almost better than any other people the art of properly roasting a joint, which also is not to be wondered at; because the art of cooking as practised by most Englishmen does not extend much beyond roast beef and plum pudding. . . ." Potatoes, accompanied by a cup of melted butter, were served with roasts and whole carrots accompanied boiled meat. Green vegetables included Brussels sprouts, cabbage, spinach, peas, beans, cucumbers, and lettuce. For beverages there were wines, small beer, punch, and cider. Tarts and cheese concluded the meal.[6]

Argyll appears to have been a pleasant and popular host to his friends, in spite of some very adverse descriptions of his character by his enemies. Horace Walpole, who disliked him intensely, described him as "slovenly in person, mysterious, not to say with an air of guilt in his deportment, slow, steady, when suppleness did not better answer his purpose, revengeful, and if artful, at least not ingratiating." The second Earl of Stair was quite as acrimonious in his remarks and said that Argyll was "as little useful in his public character as amiable in his private one; one as mean in his conduct as in his aspect, and who acts

5. Carlyle, *Autobiography*, p. 278.
6. *Kalm's Account*, pp. 14–16, the quotation being on p. 15.

[no] more like a man of quality than he looks like one; a man of as little weight as principle, and no more fit to be trusted with any commission that requires ability and judgment than with one that requires honesty and fidelity."[7] To his friends, the duke was an entirely different person. Mitchell and others found that he "never harangued or was tedious" and that his informality made his guests relaxed and welcome. He did have some unusual customs as when, after dinner, he retired to an elbow chair beside the fireplace, pulled his black silk night cap down over his eyes, and proceeded to nap for an hour and a half. After tea, he enjoyed a game of sixpenny whist for several hours. Then everyone adjourned to a sideboard generously laden with a cold collation and wine, to which they helped themselves.[8]

Whitton was very lovely that spring. The gardens were mature and beautiful after twenty-five years. The trees and shrubs were becoming very handsome. Argyll's patience had been astonishingly successful in converting a barren piece of earth into a beautiful garden. On 5 March, the Mycabolan Plum bloomed, the Russian *Larix* was completely green and buds could be seen on the Prussian Balm of Gilead. In the nursery, there were fifty of these last, twenty New England Three-leaved Pines, and 1312 of the Five-leaved variety, sixty Frankincense Pines, twelve Virginia Cedars, and many others. In February and March, the gardeners were busy planting seeds of Portugal Oak, Black Haw, *Magnolia*, *Acacia*, Pitch Pines, Persimmon, and Pennsylvania *Sassafras*. By mid-March, the Virginia "red-flowering maple" was in bloom and in April the Horse-chestnut leaves were out and those of the Carolina Cherry. Just as the blue *Iris* began to blossom on 3 May, there was the usual gardener's gambling loss: two nights of hard frost. Nevertheless, the June garden bore little mark of the disaster for it was a mass of bloom: *Spirea*, Poppies, Mallows, Geraniums, and "Candy Tufts."[9]

Besides enjoying the pleasures of the gardens, Mitchell reveled in the apparatus which was in the duke's laboratory in the Gallery. There he could study many of the latest ideas and discuss experiments with his friend. Argyll was not only an expert in chemistry but was singularly

7. Both quotations from Lovatt-Fraser, *Argyll*, p. 7.

8. Carlyle, *Autobiography*, pp. 399, 328, 352.

9. Fletcher's green leather notebook, pp. 31, 33, 40, 41, 72, and 81, Box 436, Acc. 2933, Saltoun MSS, NL.

gifted in mechanics, such as the construction of watches and clocks.[10] It was he who could explain the principle of Harrison's new maritime clock to Mitchell. The application of this to the problem of longitude interested both men, with their mutual liking for mathematics. Hours in the library passed far too quickly, interrupted only by the occasional melodious note of the Chinese "Gom" in the Gothic Tower.

Each summer, the duke spent several months in Scotland, attending to various affairs of his estates there. To Mitchell's delight, this year he was invited to accompany him. He probably went as Argyll's physician, although there is no evidence of actual payment for any services rendered. The two men had often chatted about the flowers to be found in Scotland. Now, they planned a field trip to the Highlands and the northernmost areas of Scotland. They would also collect in the English counties as they proceeded north. Andrew Fletcher busied himself with preparations for the journey. On 6 July, he arranged for the Franklin stove to be sent to Scotland on the *Happy Samuel* in Captain John Dick's care.[11] "A young Buffaloe Bull & a young black New England bitch" had arrived in London from Cadwallader Colden. Fletcher entrusted them to James McKenzie, master of the *Peggy*.[12] Finally, all was ready and the duke and his entourage could depart.

After dinner on Thursday, July twentieth, the duke in his coach, accompanied by his attendants, departed from London. They did not go far the first day, spending the night at Waltham. There, they visited the Abbey and the ancient Tulip Tree, thought to be two hundred years old. Its age was surprising since it appeared to be "the tender sort." When Fletcher wrote to his father, Lord Milton, on Sunday, he reported that Argyll was well "as also Capt. Sir Duncan Campbell and Dr. Mitchell who are on duty in the coach." Eight days later, they were in Scotland, dining with Milton at Saltoun.[13]

From there they proceeded to one of the duke's estates, Whim, where there were huge plantations of trees. Mitchell was impressed with the magnificent results of time and money. Through the years,

---

10. Henderson, *Considerations*, p. 43. In the following year a bill to Argyll gives some idea of the wide range of his interests: one "portable measuring barometer" and box, 3 "Steel joints," mending telescope and 2 pairs of "Microscopic Spectacles" (Box 408, 1750, Saltoun MSS, NL).

11. Box 407 (1749), Saltoun MSS, NL.

12. Green leather notebook, p. 88, Box 436, Saltoun MSS, NL.

13. Ibid., p. 91.

consignments of fifty to one hundred twenty-five thousand tree seed-lings were sent to Whim. Seeds were also forwarded to William Brown, the gardener and included all varieties from Pines to Spruce Firs.[14] Ponds were stocked with carp, delivered by the "fish-carrier." In 1747, additional work had been done on the laboratory there for Argyll had no inclination to forgo his scientific interests even for the short period of a yearly visit.[15]

After a week's visit at Whim, they left on August tenth for Glasgow and Roseneath, which they reached on the twelfth.[16] Raining as it was the following day, they still went down to view the duke's new twenty-foot boat. He also owned the *Princess Augusta*, a 95-ton yacht which had been built by Lord Baltimore. She was quite a ship, with four anchors and eleven brass guns. Leaving Roseneath, Argyll's party made their way north and west to Inveraray, twenty-three miles from the county town of Argylshire. Everywhere they went, the duke was greeted by people, many of whom bore his name.[17]

From Fletcher and others, Mitchell had heard of the beauty of In-veraray and still he was quite unprepared for its majesty. The castle stood in a magnificent setting, a thirty-mile demesne of mountains and water. Through the grounds ran the Aray River with its charming cascades and falls, with the romantic Lock Dubh at the bottom of the glen. Majestic trees, on all sides, gave shape and color to even the misti-est of mornings.[18] As at Whim, Argyll had repeatedly sent shipments of seeds and plants for Inveraray and even, on occasion, oysters for the salt water pond there.[19] He was interested to read the list made 12 June of the seeds which had come up. One was a "Spindle Tree," planted four years previously.[20] He checked the progress of the year-old plants raised from the New England Pine seeds sent the last February.[21] He was especially partial to this species, finding that they produced seed in sixteen years after sowing. His method of cultivating this Pine was so

14. Box 411, Saltoun MSS, NL.
15. Box 408, Saltoun MSS, NL.
16. Green leather notebook, p. 91, Box 436, Saltoun MSS, NL.
17. Box 427, Saltoun MSS, NL.
18. William Rhind, ed., *The Scottish Tourist* (Edinburgh, 1845), pp. 157–59.
19. "Excerpts from the Cattle Book," Box 414, Saltoun MSS, NL. A note adds that they stopped importing the oysters as they became "mudded."
20. Old green notebook, p. 78, Box 35, Saltoun MSS, NL.
21. Box 406, Saltoun MSS, NL.

successful that he later gave the Royal Society of Arts a description of it.[22]

The old castle had been in the Campbell family for three hundred years but the duke had begun a new one in 1745. Robert Adam was responsible for the new design. When completed it was described as being "in the castellated style," with "bold and imposing appearance, with towers at the angles, surmounted by a square pavilion, which rises high above its circular towers. The blue granite with which the structure is built, gives a severity to its whole aspect that harmonises well with the surrounding objects."[23]

Twenty-four years later, Boswell said that Dr. Johnson "was much struck by the grandeur and elegance of this princely seat," but thought it should have had another story. He admired the fine old trees which were a contrast to "the nakedness" on the eastern coast.[24] He remarked on Argyll's typical Scottish sense of thrift. When Boswell protested that such a character did not build "so great a house," Johnson replied, "Sir . . . when a narrow man resolves to build a house, he builds it like another man. But Archibald, Duke of Argyle, was narrow in his ordinary expences, his quotidian expences."[25]

In 1749, however, building had barely been begun and it was difficult for Mitchell to imagine what it would be like. He would hear about it for many years to come, for it was always the duke's favorite project and never far from his thoughts. This was known by many. When his architect, Robert Adam, was interested in filling a vacancy on the Board of Works in 1758, he wrote to his brother James: "I have fast Hold of his G[race] at present as I have Brunius busy making out a large view of Inveraray in oil Colours which if it Succeeds Well, will surely lay him under obligations to me, on a favourite subject. I intend not to take anything for it."[26]

There was a steady procession of visitors all during their stay at Inveraray. Although Mitchell thought that he had been well aware of the duke's importance in London, he realized now the truly feudal character of his friend and patron, with his far-reaching domains, count-

22. Archives of the Royal Society of Arts, London, n.d., 2:3.

23. Rhind, *Scottish Tourist*, p. 158.

24. George Birbeck Hall, ed., *Boswell's Life of Johnson*, 6 vols. (Oxford, 1950), 5:355.

25. Jack Werner, ed., *James Boswell, The Journal of a Tour to the Hebrides with Samuel Johnson, LLD.* (London, 1956), p. 303.

26. 17 June, GD18/4848, Clerk of Penicuik MSS, Scottish Record Office.

less retainers, innumerable obligations, and responsibilities. The recital of his titles became more than a series of honorable appellations: "Duke of Argyle, Marquis of Kintyre and Lorn, Earl of Campbell and Cowall, Viscount Lochow and Glenila, Lord of Inveraray, Mull, Morven, and Tyrie, Admiral of the Western Isles, Heritable Master of King's Household in Scotland, Heritable Keeper of Dunstaffnage and Carrick, &c, one of the sixteen peers for Scotland, one of His Majesty's Privy Council, one of the trustees of . . . the annexed estates, Chancellor of the University of Aberdeen, and an honorary fellow of the royal college of physicians of Edinburgh."[27]

From conversation overheard, the duke's promotion of Scottish trade, his attention to the improvement of education, his interest in medical schools were all most apparent to Mitchell. From the great tree plantations, Argyll's continual concern with reforestation and agriculture impressed the Virginian. From the large number of callers, he could have well believed the statement made later that at least 54,000 people had the Duke to thank for their positions at one time or another. Mitchell was quite overcome by the extent of Argyll's power, at least in his native Scotland.[28]

The end of the summer found Mitchell and Argyll starting upon their botanical tour through the awe-inspiring western Highlands and across to the western islands. It was a wild country, sparsely inhabited and subject to strong winds and rains sweeping across the hills. The journey was anything but easy, even with the comforts and little luxuries which Argyll was able to command.

Argyll and Mitchell took with them Linnaeus's volume on the Lapland flora. To their disappointment, they discovered no new plants but this was not surprising. The Highlands, like the slopes of the Welsh mountains, exhibit few Alpines and hardly any of the more showy types. They did manage to collect some of the plants mentioned by Linnaeus, and they found their travel delightful in many ways. The great Scottish meadows were filled with *Anthericum*, or False-Asphodel, a member of the Lily Family. In addition, there was Ray's *Phalangium Scotium minimum*, which Mitchell considered a variety of the common species. He remembered that Simon Paulli had described a disease prevalent among cattle feeding in such meadows, a gradual dissolution

27. As listed in his obituary in *The Scots' Magazine* 23 (1761):222.
28. Henderson, *Considerations*, p. 43.

of the bones due to this plant. When he inquired locally, he found that their cattle succumbed to the same ailment. He determined to query Linnaeus in his next letter as to the prevalence of the disease in Sweden. He was interested to find that the islanders, like the Virginia Indians, distilled their red dye from the root of a *Rubia*. In this case it was the *R. minima* "of Lobel and Gerarde" which was used. It produced a beautiful coral color.[29]

The Scottish autumn was well under way, when the duke and his party began their long journey back to London on October tenth. They went by way of Edinburgh, which gave Mitchell an opportunity to renew old friendships and revisit favorite places. The trip had been an expensive one for Argyll. Even the short distance to Edinburgh cost him over twenty-seven pounds, including the rental of four saddle horses and a chaise horse. Corn and hay for one night came to six shillings four pence which was considerably under the night's white wine ration of four bottles at eight shillings! In every place a small tax was extracted for "the poor."[30] While no itemized accounts appear for the meals consumed on this trip, their dinners were probably similar to one of the duke's on another occasion: "Hotchpotch [a thick vegetable soup], Roast Beef & plum pudding, Kidney beans, apple pie, 2 Turkies, 2 ducks, artichokes & eggs, Cauliflower & sausages, shoulder of mutton & petetos, Bread, 1 doz. Ale," which came to two pounds, eight shillings, six pence. An additional five shillings was charged for a "China dish broke."[31] From Edinburgh, the Argyll entourage continued on to Glasgow which they left on the fourteenth. It was late October when they were at last back in London. Strenuous as the summer had been, Mitchell had enjoyed every moment and he felt much more fit than he had for many years.

To his delight, he found a letter from Franklin waiting for him. It had been written on 29 April and contained "Observations and Suppositions towards forming a new Hypothesis for explaining the several Phaenomena of Thunder Gusts."[32] In 1746, Collinson had sent Franklin "a glass tube" or Leyden jar with directions for its use. It proved to be the most fascinating toy that Franklin had ever possessed. He spent

29. Mitchell to Linnaeus, 1 May 1750, CLO 2:449–50.
30. Box 407, Saltoun MSS, NL.
31. 1752, Box 410, Saltoun MSS, NL.
32. *Papers of Franklin,* 3:365–76.

hours in experimentation, repeating the demonstrations which he had seen Dr. Spencer perform in Boston. Then he began to devise ones of his own. Having had a local glass blower construct additional tubes, he drafted his friends and neighbors to join him in the fun. One of these was a Mr. Kinnersley who, being unemployed, Franklin persuaded to demonstrate such electrical experiments for money. Using specially constructed apparatus, his lectures proved so popular that he had traveled not only the colonies but the West Indies.[33]

Franklin sent several accounts of his experiments to Collinson but this time he decided to share his thoughts with his friend, Dr. Mitchell. His essay consisted of fifty-six numbered points concerned more with the interrelations between electricity and heat than merely "Thunder Gusts." They contained much that is correct by present-day interpretation, even if very differently expressed. There were also many interpretations with which we would disagree. The fifty-six points cover a wide range of territory and deal with the distinction between gases, liquids, and solids; the cause of dew and rain; conductors and nonconductors of electricity, and many other items.

Knowing Watson's interest in and knowledge of the subject of electricity, Mitchell showed him Franklin's letter and it was decided that the former would read it to the Royal Society on 9 November. Because of its length, it was continued again the following week and Mitchell, himself, may have presented the remainder of the essay. The society's secretary seems to have been as confused by Franklin's theories as many of the Fellows for his brief notice of the paper in the journal is not very enlightening: "The Ingenious Author of this Essay endeavours to account for the several Phaenomena of Thunder and Lightning from Electricity: But as his paper contains a long chain of deductions it is impracticable to give any tolerable account of it without running out into too great a length, or doing injury to his argument. Thanks were ordered to Dr. Mitchell and to Mr. Franklin for this communication."[34]

Whether it was ill health, a lost letter, or reluctance on Mitchell's part to inform his friend of the Royal Society's less than enthusiastic reception of his paper, Franklin had still heard nothing from him by

33. *The Works of Benjamin Franklin*, ed. Jared Sparks, 10 vols. (Boston, 1856). 1: 208–9.

34. Royal Society Journal Book XX, pp. 165, 170–71.

the following June.[35] Mitchell finally wrote and there was an eventual vindication for Franklin's theories as he noted in his autobiography: "One paper, which I wrote for Mr. Kinnersley, on the sameness of lightning with electricity, I sent to Mr. Mitchell, an acquaintance of mine, and one of the members also of that Society; who wrote me word, that it had been read, but was laughed at by the connoiseurs. The papers, however, being shown to Dr. Fothergill, he thought them of too much value to be stifled, and advised the printing of them. Mr. Collinson gave them to Cave for publication in his *Gentleman's Magazine*; but he chose to print them separately in a pamphlet and Dr. Fothergill wrote the preface. Cave, it seems, judged rightly for his profession, for by the additions, that arrived afterwards, they swelled to a quarto volume; which has had five editions, and cost him nothing for copy-money." Besides Franklin's letter to Mitchell, several others to Collinson were included in the book which was published in 1751.[36]

In spite of Franklin's pleasure in the several editions, few in England paid them much attention. On the other hand, Buffon was impressed and immediately had it translated into French. Abbé Nollet, who felt that Franklin was invading his private territory, could not believe that an American could have been so successful in his field. After the book was translated into Latin, Italian, and German, the Royal Society had second thoughts and decided to reconsider the colonial's papers.[37]

Even more interesting to Mitchell than Franklin's letter on electricity was the map which he had sent him. This was a map of Pennsylvania made by Lewis Evans, the surveyor.[38] He was the man who had copied Mitchell's yellow fever essay for Colden, who later helped him with his map. Evans and Mitchell may have met in 1744 and their mutual friends were numerous. Evans was a friend of Bartram and had accompanied him and Conrad Weiser to Onondega in 1743. He was Welsh and had come to Pennsylvania sometime before 1736. There he had married Martha Hoskins. Their daughter was the godchild of Mrs. Franklin. Like his other friends, he knew Collinson and made Kalm's acquaintance in 1748.[39] Sharing an interest in natural history, Kalm and

35. Franklin to Colden, 28 June 1750, *Papers of Franklin*, 3:48.
36. *Works of Franklin*, 1:209.
37. Ibid., pp. 209–12.
38. There is a photostat of Franklin's gift to Mitchell in the Library of Congress. It was made from the original belonging to a Boston dealer, Dr. A. S. W. Rosenbach.
39. Lawrence Henry Gipson, *Lewis Evans* (Philadelphia, 1939), pp. 2–7.

Evans were most congenial and saw much of each other. However, Kalm may not have had the same respect for his friend's map-making abilities as others did. He wrote to Bartram from Quebec in 1749: "If you do see Mr. EVANS, pray remember my most humble duty to him, and tell him that I hope to satisfy his curiosity in true maps of Canada: but the map of Canada he was so kind and write for me, had once (it was not far from it) thrown me in the other world. The reason was, that he has not put down a great river between Fort Ann and Crown Point, that runs in Woodcreek. My guides did not very well know the way, and we did go down this river, where such Indians did live that do kill all the English they see; but to our happiness we did by good time find that we were wrong, and returned."[40]

Nevertheless, Evans was considered a good map maker, although the one that Franklin sent Mitchell was not as accurate as the one that he made in 1755. Mitchell was delighted to have it for he was becoming more and more involved in cartography. Having always liked the subject, he had found it necessary to make a study of it for the book he planned on the natural and medical history of North America. With the current interest in the French challenge to the English settlements, he was so often questioned as to boundaries, distances, physical features, and history of the various colonies that he developed a habit of collecting maps and information wherever he could. Already, he was roughing out sketches that clarified missing information. He talked to any geographers, travelers, and historians he met, read widely, and sought facts from his friends.[41] Many of the men whom he met at Argyll's home were deeply concerned in settling limits with the French, so he was exposed often to the challenge of discovering the proofs which they sought.

For this and other reasons, Colden's letter of 7 July was very welcome since it gave some enlightenment on the New York political scene. Colden had written Collinson at the same time, saying, "I have at last receiv'd a very obliging letter from Dr. Mitchel wherein he tells me that he wrote largely to me several times but as none of these letters have come to my hand, I believe they have been intercepted by

40. Darlington, *Memorials*, p. 369. The only impressive body of water between Fort Ann and Crown Point seems to be Lake George!

41. Mitchell to Colden, 25 March 1749, Hornberger, "A Letter from John Mitchell." *Huntington Library Quarterly* 10 (1946–47):413, 416–17.

some villainous people here who have done so with several other letters directed to me. . . . I have wrote largely to Dr. Mitchel by this conveyance & as few can be so well inform'd as to the public actions in this Province since the commencement of the War as I am & others indeavour what they can to misrepresent them I have given him a particular acct. of them."[42] Collinson promised to give Colden's "pacquet" to Mitchell the moment he returned from Scotland.[43]

Colden was very pleased that Mitchell had spoken of him to Argyll for his father had "great regard . . . for that noble family." Colden's father, who was then living in Ireland, had been of assistance to the duke's grandfather after his escape from the Castle of Edinburgh. He had helped him to go from Ireland to Holland. Argyll's father visited the Coldens whenever he was near their home and he could remember his visits. He would prepare a summary of Indian affairs for the duke.[44] Because of Mitchell's concern in Colden's personal affairs, the New York doctor was writing at length concerning events in the province.

Upon receipt of the letter, which Collinson had forwarded to Scotland, Mitchell discussed its contents with Argyll. When they returned to town, he immediately gave it to one of the Lords of Trade and Plantations, whom he knew rather well. He was pleased to have Colden's account as there were conflicting reports of the situation in New York, much of which had been misrepresented. Since discussion of the boundaries between British and French possessions was still the most important topic, Colden's letter was very timely. From his talks with historians and geographers, Mitchell agreed with Colden that both French settlements at Niagara and Crown Point had been illegally made on British territory. He felt that the New Yorkers had been delinquent in disputing this claim.

Mitchell suggested that the Lords of Trade and Plantations consult with Colden to get a record of New York Indian affairs, which had been done. Nevertheless, actual proof was needed when negotiating with the French and he hoped that Colden would supply it.

Mitchell wrote this request to Colden in the spring of 1751,[45] as his letter of the previous year, containing much of the same information,

42. LPCC 4:114.
43. Ibid., p. 131.
44. Colden to Mitchell, unsigned draft, 6 July 1749, LPCC 9:19–34.
45. Mitchell to Colden, 5 April 1751, ibid., 87–91.

had been lost. Now that the Board of Trade had about completed their discussion of Nova Scotia, Mitchell wrote Colden that New York's boundaries would be next. He had been told that Colden had given an account on this topic to Governor Shirley and, if he would send him a duplicate of it, he would present it to the Board of Trade. From them he had learned of the handling of the incipient revolt of the Five Nations by Clinton. He hoped that the proposed meeting with the Indians at Albany would likewise be successful. He still thought that New York should seize the land at Niagara since it was a focal point for the French to foment trouble among the Indians.

XI ⚜ *Distractions of a Botanist*

> *"I have been obliged to give over my botanical pursuits for some time. . . ."*
>
> Mitchell to Bartram, 1 August 1750[1]

Barely two months after Mitchell's return from Scotland, he received word that his good friend, Mark Catesby, had died on 23 December 1749. Catesby had not been well for many years and the swelling in his legs the previous summer had been so severe that his doctors doubted that he would survive many weeks.[2] In spite of this, he rallied and was again up and about by December. While walking with his son one day, he fell and never regained consciousness, dying a few days later.[3] Catesby's death was a great blow to all of the natural history circle. Mitchell felt it particularly. In addition to a warm affection for his friend, he no longer had one who had known and lived in Virginia, with whom to discuss his native land.

There were, of course, new friends, and his acquaintance among the influential continued to widen. Sometimes, he and Dr. Stuart were Argyll's only guests listed by Fletcher, but much more often there was a good sized group. Some were present fairly regularly: Sir Harry Bellenden, Lord Erskine, General and Colonel Campbell, Lord John Murray, Sir Hew Dalrymple, and the two architect brothers, Robert and James Adam.[4] Some guests appeared seldom or only once. Mitchell found that there were some faces new to him among his fellow guests. He had met several before under other circumstances, but it was far more interesting to meet them in the warm informality of Argyll's home.

There was D. Campbell (1671?–1753), a prosperous Glasgow merchant and member of Parliament, who had bought the island of Islay. Charles Cathcart (1721–76), 9th Baron, had been one of the two hos-

1. Darlington, *Memorials*, p. 366.
2. Thomas Knowlton to R. Richardson, 18 July 1749, Turner, *Richardson*, pp. 400–401.
3. Frick and Stearns, *Catesby*, pp. 48–49.
4. Andrew Fletcher's "Catalogue," of dinner guests for 1749–50, Box 435, Saltoun MSS, NL.

tages held by the French to guarantee the return of Cape Breton under the 1748 Treaty of Aix-la-Chapelle. He had served under the Earl of Stair and was now a colonel. Baron Maule was often present. There was a great-grandson of Robert Baillie, a Scottish judge by the name of Henry Home, Lord Kames (1696-1782). He was an indefatigable writer of whose literary efforts Dr. Johnson had a low opinion. In April, and often thereafter, John Carmichael, 3rd Earl of Hyndford (1701–67), was Argyll's guest. His arrival was preceded by the Hungarian Juniper which he had sent in March on his way back to England from Russia, and his luggage contained a choice variety of Russian seeds. This alone would have endeared him to the duke and Mitchell, but he was an interesting man in many ways. Born in Edinburgh, he had served in the footguards until he succeeded his father to the title in 1737. He had acted as a mediator between Frederick III and Maria Theresa. Carlyle, in his life of Frederick, described Carmichael thus: "We can discern a certain rough tenacity and horse-dealer finesse in the man; a broad-based, shrewdly practical Scotch gentleman, wide awake."[5] In 1744, he was sent on another mission to Russia and spent six years there. Now that he was back in England he was appointed not only a Privy Councellor but a Lord of the Bed-chamber.

As previously noted, it is difficult to determine Mitchell's exact position, if any, in Argyll's household. From his ubiquitous presence, it would certainly seem that he and Stuart were employed in some capacity, possibly as doctors to Argyll and his large household. Mitchell may very well not have practiced medicine at all but made himself useful in other ways. In his case, it seems unlikely that this was a firm commitment since he apparently came and went at will and he may not have stayed in the duke's home at all. Whether he received financial compensation is unknown. In Argyll's account with Coutts and Company, only four payments were made to Mitchell over a period of ten years, ranging from eleven to seventeen pounds. These were probably to reimburse him for such things as plants ordered from Bartram, the Franklin stove, or even the buffaloes.[6] Of course, there could well be a record of payments to Mitchell in some other bank accounts of the duke.

5. Information from the *Dictionary of National Biography*.
6. 9 May 1749, 27 February 1751, 1 February 1754, and 18 September 1759.

During the winter and spring of 1750, Mitchell found himself more and more involved in seeking information and writing reports for the Lords of Trade and Plantations. Such confining work, requiring great concentration and many hours at his desk, did not agree with him and his health suffered. He wrote to Bartram that such a life "gives me pain even to set down to take a pen in my hand & very often I am unable to do it, on account of a vertiginous disorder which it has occasioned & brings it on."[7] He had to give up all unnecessary writing and his correspondence suffered. His friend Franklin lamented " 'Tis a loss to us all."[8]

Mitchell did manage a short letter to Linnaeus the first of May, thanking him for his letter which he had received before he left for Scotland the previous year.[9] He reported on his travels and that Catesby's book had already fallen in price to seventeen and a half guineas. He made up a packet of American seeds for Linnaeus and sent two papers on pitch and tar water, one by Dr. Stephen Hales. Two years before he had questioned Linnaeus on the Swedish methods of preparing tar but had received no reply on the subject. Now, he again requested information:

The learned here differ about the manner of preparing tar, on which, it is to be hoped, you can give us information. The chief question is, whether it is obtained from old wood, or from the fresh sap, of the growing tree, and whether from the roots, or the whole trunk? Is the wood in the furnace allowed to burn with a gentle not violent flame, or is it only surrounded by fire? and, if the latter, how is it contrived? We learn, from the periodical publications, that a work has lately appeared in Sweden upon this very subject of making tar, which I beg of you to send me by the first opportunity, in whatever language it is written. Our people are daily swallowing this article, as a medicine, especially its acid spirit described in the publications I send you, and yet we are ignorant of its true preparation.

Linnaeus may have been reluctant to give away his country's trade secrets for this appears to be the conclusion of his correspondence with Mitchell. In a postscript, Mitchell indicated that he was no longer

7. 1 August 1750, Darlington, *Memorials*, p. 366.
8. Franklin to Colden, 11 October 1750, *Papers of Franklin*, 4:67.
9. CLO 2:449–51

having his mail sent to Mr. Buchanan but desired that Linnaeus address him "FRS at the apartments of the Royal Society."

One March day, Lord Bute and Mitchell dined with Argyll and gardening must certainly have been a principal topic of conversation. Since he had left Scotland, Bute had had no opportunity to indulge his great love of gardening. Unable to afford a country place near London, he had felt frustrated, although he had been assiduously collecting a botanical library. Now that he was Lord of the Bed-chamber and his future prospects appeared bright, he was preparing to renovate Cane Wood (now Kenwood), which he had acquired from Argyll.[10]

For a year, the Butes had been making their plans for renovation. Lady Mary Wortley Montagu was delighted and wrote to her daughter in 1749: "I very well remember Caenwood House, and cannot wish you a more agreeable place. It would be a great pleasure to me to see my grandchildren run about in the gardens. I do not question Lod Bute's good taste in the improvements round it, or yours in the choice of furniture."[11] The house was far from elaborate, being a two-storied brick, with kitchens and an orangery on the western side. At that time the Hampstead-Highgate Road passed close to the house which was given privacy by a high brick wall.[12] The grounds, while not developed, were well adapted for gardening. Dillenius had often collected at Cane Wood, where he found *Mnium Trichomanis* and Doody had earlier discovered *Lichenastrum Ambrosia* there.[13]

When Mitchell showed Bute a letter from Gronovius in February, 1751, Bute was embarrassed to realize that he had neglected his Dutch friend so long. He hastened to write him about the revival of his dormant love of botany and included a description of Cane Wood: "at a very great expense, I repaired, a great house my father had within five miles of London, in a scituation that yields to none; You may remember hearing of the Villages of Hampstead & Highgate, plac'd on two high hills; My house is betwixt them defended from the north by a great wood, tho in anothers possession, to the South an old wood of 30

10. Sir John Summerson, *The Iveagh Bequest, Kenwood* (Pamphlet published by the Greater London Council, n.d.), pp. 5–6.

11. Ibid., p. 6.

12. Ibid., pp. 14–16.

13. Abridgment of his *Historia Muscorum* with notes, #236 and #511, Sherard MSS 210, Bodleian Library, OU.

Acres belonging to me, over which the whole city, with 16 miles of the River appears from every window; a garden of 8 acres betwixt me and the wood, I am filling with Every exotick our Climate will protect. . . ."[14]

Bute was not only collecting rare plants for himself but also for Frederick Louis, as Thomas Knowlton wrote to Mr. Richardson: "The Prince of Wales is now about preparation for building a stove three hundred feet in length, for plants and not pines; and my Lord Bute has already seatled a correspondance in Asia, Africa, America, Europe, and every where he can: as, to be shure, my Lord is the most knowing of any in this kingdome by much of any in it; such is his great abilitys therein; and he is the person as has prompted the young prince; and from such, what may not be expected? And next spring it will rise and grow apase, as all glasse and frams will be ready."[15]

The Prince of Wales had been born and educated in Germany, remaining there when his grandfather, George I, succeeded to the English throne, although his parents, brothers, and sisters had all gone to England. He felt a complete stranger not only to his new country but to his family when he went to London upon his father's accession in 1728. For some reason George II disliked his son and failed to provide for the maintenance of a separate household for him although Parliament had provided ample funds. When Frederick and Princess Augusta were finally ejected from the palace, they rented Kew House, a few miles from London. It belonged to the astronomer, Samuel Molyneux, and the prince was fascinated by his observatory and planetarium.[16]

The grounds of Kew House had once been very handsome, for the previous owner, Sir Henry Capell, a well-known horticulturist, had laid out the gardens. He had filled them with rare plants and trees from France and constructed two greenhouses. His friend, John Evelyn, said that "his garden has the choicest fruit of any plantation in England." In 1688, he described the tall reed palisades which Capell had constructed to protect his oranges in the summer. Among the more unusual plants were Mastic Trees, White-striped Hollies, and Silver Firs.

14. 2 February 1750/51, Bute Archives, Mount Stuart, Rothesay, Isle of Bute.
15. Knowlton to R. Richardson, 13 November 1750, Turner, *Richardson*, pp. 406–7.
16. Averyl Edwards, *Frederick Louis Prince of Wales 1707–1751* (London, 1947), pp. 11–17, 57

Two parallel walls protected the gardens. When they bought Kew House in 1730, Frederick and Augusta directed William Kent, the landscape gardener, to restore what had been neglected for years.[17]

Kew House provided a happy country life for the prince and his family for they enjoyed tennis, cricket, walking, and other outdoor activities. The prince wrote poetry and both he and his wife were very fond of the theater. Even the children presented plays for their parents. Frederick and Augusta gathered round them a small court of congenial people, many of whom were also opera buffs.[18] George Bubb Doddington (1691–1762), later Lord Melcombe, was one of these and he recorded a whole week of plays at Kew House in April, 1750. He had been Lord of the Treasury under George I but lost favor with his son and gradually attached himself to the Prince of Wales. Doddington was known for his wit and Horace Walpole later described him on one occasion: "In the stage box was Lady Bute, Lord Halifax and Lord Melcomb—I must say the two last entertained the house as much as the play—your King was prompter, and called out to the actors every minute to speak louder—the other went backwards and forwards behind the scenes, fetched the actors into the box, and was busier than Harlequin."[19] Doddington had his serious side as well and was interested in many topics of national concern, as he noted in his diary.[20]

This was the group with which the Butes associated. As a matter of fact, it could be said to be a family tradition in the case of Lady Bute for her mother was supposedly the only Englishwoman whom George I could abide.[21] At Argyll's dinner that March day mentioned above, Bute probably recounted his recent activities at Kew. He, Doddington, and several others had been invited to dinner with their Royal Highnesses on 26 February. The next day everyone, "men, women and chil-

17. W. T. Thistleton-Dyer, "Historical Account of Kew to 1841, Royal Gardens, Kew," *Bulletin of Miscellaneous Information* #16 (December 1891):287–89.

18. Edwards, *Frederick Louis*, pp. 114–15.

19. Walpole to Montagu, 27 July 1761, W. S. Lewis and Ralph S. Brown, Jr., eds., *Horace Walpole's Correspondence with George Montagu*, 2 vols. (New Haven, 1941), 1:382.

20. 3 December 1749, Henry Penruddocke Wyndham, ed., *The Diary of the Late George Bubb Doddington, Baron of Melcombe Regis, From March of 1749 to February 6, 1761* (London, 1809), p. 25. In December, 1749, he recorded a visit from Dr. Sharpe, with a map and an account of the importance of Nova Scotia. It is likely that he was the same Sharpe who was Mitchell's fellow guest for dinner at Argyll's in May (Fletcher's "Catalogue," Box 435, Saltoun MSS, NL).

21. Edwards, *Frederick Louis*, p. 12.

dren," worked on the new walk at Kew. They were likewise occupied the following day, with only a cold dinner for their pains.[22]

Bartram, in far-off North America, benefited from Bute's intimacy with the Prince of Wales. In the summer of 1750, Bute asked Mitchell to order a box of seeds worth five guineas for Prince Frederick from Pennsylvania. Since Mitchell had last written, several letters had come from Bartram, but he had had no time to answer them. Now he reported the receipt of the plants and seeds which Bartram had sent to Argyll and said that he had paid Collinson for them "long ago." Collinson had also given Mitchell two or three seeds of the "new Magnolia" for Argyll but unfortunately none of them germinated. The duke did not want any more seeds unless it was something new, as he now collected seed of his own. However, Mitchell had found two other commissions in addition to that of the prince. Although he had warned the two gentlemen that it was late in the year to be ordering seed on 1 August, it did not seem to worry them and they each wanted five guineas' worth, too. One of the men was the Earl of Galloway. The other was William Wentworth, Lord Strafford (1722–91), who had married Lady Anne Campbell.[23] Strafford's father had a country place at Twickenham, near that of Argyll, and Mitchell had dined with him at the duke's home in April. Mitchell also told Bartram that he had mentioned him to several "great men" but with no particular success. They had all been interested in Bartram's "Industry & laudable endeavours, but are backward in rewarding them, at least with any thing that is real & substantial."

Mitchell was horrified to learn early in the next year that not only did Bartram not receive his letter with the orders but had not even gotten any payment for the plants and seeds sent to Argyll. He immediately wrote to his friend:

Mr. Collinson indeed made some mistake about the payment of the seeds sent the year before this last for the Duke of Argyll, and demanded payment for them again, after I had his Receipt for it, by which I suppose he might forget to write you about the Receipt of that Money, which he stands indebted to you for by his own Receipt to me, to wit £5..14.. charges included. I have likewise paid him lately twenty guineas for two Boxes received this

22. Wyndham, *Doddington*, p. 58.
23. Mitchell to Bartram, 1 August 1750, Bartram Papers, HSP. A shortened version of this letter is printed in Darlington, *Memorials*, p. 366.

year by the Duke of Argyll, & the Prince of Wales, and wanted another that I wrote for but could not get it.

This is to advise you of another Box of Seeds that is wanted by the Earl of Hyndford, for which he desired me to give you particular Instructions that they might be sent to him by the first opportunity & of the best of your for-rest Trees. He wants a box of Ten Guineas price, like the one you sent this year.[24]

There seems to have been misunderstanding on all sides, for Collinson wrote to Bartram the next month that he had never informed him of the value of the boxes which he was sending in his care for Governor Shirley, Mr. Pownall, Mr. Williamson, and Dr. Mitchell. As a consequence, he could only take whatever they chose to pay him.[25] With such informality in accounts, mistakes were bound to occur.

Upon Argyll's return from his annual visit to Scotland, Mitchell dined with him several times in the next four months. Lord Hyndford and Mr. Lind were usually the only other guests present aside from the two doctors.[26] Mitchell continued far from well for most of the winter and spring of 1751.[27] Franklin sent him his regards through Collinson and promised to write to him and to Dr. Fothergill by the next ship.[28]

In March, Collinson turned over to Mitchell a paper on a "Cure for Cancers," which Colden had sent to him, but he was uncertain as to when the doctor would feel well enough to consider it.[29] By April, Mitchell was sufficiently recovered to look over Colden's manuscript. From Connecticut, Colden had heard of the efficacy of the Juice of *Phytolacca*, or Pokeweed, in the treatment of cancer.[30] Colden described the plant in detail but could ascribe no specific reason for its apparent curative qualities. Interestingly, he theorized: "there seems some kind of analogy between cancers and the tumours made by some insects, laying their eggs in leaves, or the bark or fruit of vegetables, and in the flesh of animals. The whole texture and composition of the plant, so

24. Mitchell to Bartram, 30 March 1751, Bartram Papers, HSP. This particular passage does not appear in the printed version in Darlington, *Memorials*, p. 367.

25. 24 April 1741, Bartram Papers, 2:86, HSP.

26. Fletcher's "Catalogue," Box 435, Saltoun MSS, NL.

27. Collinson to Colden, 11 March 1751, LPCC 9:85.

28. 4 February 1751, *Papers of Franklin*, 4:113.

29. Collinson to Colden, 11 March 1751, LPCC 9:85.

30. "Cure of Cancers," From an eminent physician in New York, *Gentleman's Magazine* 20 (1751):306–8.

far as the influence of the little embryo extends, is altered, and the nature of the juice likewise. . . ." This analogy has been the subject of recent research.[31]

When Mitchell wrote to Colden in April, he did not express his opinion of the "Cure of Cancers." He did promise to make an abstract of it for the Royal Society, but there is no record that it was ever read there.[32] The article did appear in print later in the year, for Collinson gave it to the editor of the *Gentleman's Magazine*. He also wrote to Dr. Trew that the *Phytolacca* had been found to be of use in the treatment of cancer.[33] Mitchell did another favor for Colden in doing what he could for his friend, Mr. Jones, who was visiting England. When Jones left for Paris, Mitchell supplied him with several letters of recommendation, being impressed with his character.[34] Mitchell was obliged to cut short his letter to Colden as it was to be delivered by their mutual friend, Dr. Alexander Colquhun, who was leaving that day for America. He had been at Edinburgh at the same period that Mitchell had. In fact, he had lived at Dr. McFarline's home the year following the one Mitchell had spent there.

Only one reference has been found to Mitchell as a physician in all of his London years. This appears in Dr. (later Sir) John Pringle's book, *Observations on the Diseases of the Army*. This was so popular that its sixth edition came out in 1768. Pringle (1707–82) was one of the most distinguished medical men of his times, later becoming physician to George II and president of the Royal Society. In discussing the use of *simaruba* in the treatment of dysentery, he wrote: "Dr. MITCHELL, who formerly practiced in Virginia, where the dysentery is frequent, also informed me that he had likewise used this vegetable; but not with success, except when the patient voided an immoderate quantity of blood during the height of the disorder, or had a *diarrhoea* after the inflamnatory state was passed. He added, that he had usually made a stronger decoction than that which DEGNER prescribed; who probably was led to give the *simaruba* with more caution, as the bowels were so much inflamed when he began it."[35]

31. See research reports of the late I. F. Lewis and Lucille Walton on the Witch Hazel gall.
32. 5 April 1751, LPCC 9:91.
33. Collinson to Trew, 1 July 1752, UE.
34. Mitchell to Colden, 5 April 1751, LPCC 9:91. For Colquhun, see chap. 1, note 31.
35. Sixth edition, p. 282. The Simarubaceae, the *Ailanthus* family, are West Indian

There were two great losses to English botany that spring, as Mitchell wrote to Bartram: the death of both the Duke of Richmond and the Prince of Wales.[36] In both cases there was the suspicion that their enthusiastic love of gardening played some part in their fatal illnesses, as they had each been supervising work in their gardens just prior to their deaths. In the case of the prince, Mitchell knew there was little doubt of it as he had stood in the wet watching trees being planted "thro' a sort of obstinacy agst. any precautions of that kind, which it seems the whole family are blamed for. . . ."[37]

Meetings of the Royal Society were suspended for a month in respect to the prince and Collinson's eulogy in a letter to Bartram clearly expressed the feelings of the botanic world on this occasion:

> The death of our late excellent Prince of Wales has cast a great damp over all the nation. Gardening and planting have lost their best friend and encourager; for the prince had delighted in that rational amusement, a long while: but lately, he had a laudable and princely ambition to excel all others. But the good thing will not die with him: for there is such a spirit and love of it, amongst the nobility and gentry, and the pleasure and profit that attends it, will render it a lasting delight.[38]

Peter Kalm returned to England with his wife and other North American collections in late April, 1751. Mitchell eagerly inquired about his travels and questioned him closely on the colonial scene.[39] Collinson, too, spent much time with the visitors. He wasted no time in reproaching the patient Bartram, saying that Kalm "commends Thee in most things, but much Blames thee for not Enriching thy Journal with many Curious Articles which He had colected from thy Mouth."[40]

By June, Mitchell was once again a regular guest of Argyll. Others present that month were a most impressive group. Among them were the earls of Litchfield, Hyndford, and Northumberland on the second; John Murray and his wife, Lady Charlotte, her parents, the Duke and

---

and South American trees and shrubs. Today *Quassia* is employed as a bitter tonic and in the treatment of thread worms in children.

36. 30 March 1751, Darlington, *Memorials*, p. 367.

37. Doddington gave a lurid account of the last days of the Prince's life (Wyndham, *Doddington*, pp. 85–87).

38. 24 April 1751, Darlington, *Memorials*, p. 184.

39. See p. 186.

40. Collinson to Bartram, 24 April 1751, Darlington, *Memorials*, p. 184.

Duchess of Atholl, Lord Somerville, General Mackay and Mr. Oswald on the ninth; lords Edgecomb, Willoughby, and Panine, Sir D. Campbell and Mitchell's old friend, William Watson, on the fifteenth.[41]

As his acquaintance with those in power widened, Mitchell was encouraged to think of applying for a post for himself. The post that interested him was that of deputy postmaster general of the North American colonies. Although his health was still precarious at times, he felt that it would be no worse in his native land. He would not necessarily be required to live in Virginia, but could seek a more favorable climate. Moreover, his duties should be far less strenuous and confining than those of a physician. Colonel Alexander Spotswood, former Virginia governor, who had held this position from 1732 until his death in 1740, had been the first man to successfully establish a continental postal system which included the south.[42] He had lived not too far from Mitchell in Virginia. The accounts of Spotswood's Philadelphia agent, being inefficiently kept, he had appointed Franklin in his place. Franklin was delighted in spite of the small salary, for it meant that better postal service resulted in better newsgathering and an increase in both circulation and advertising for his newspaper. He was so meticulous in his accounts that he was shortly put in charge of several offices as comptroller.[43]

The deputy postmaster general's office had not been filled for a number of years. It had never been run to the satisfaction of the postmaster general, for it had never yielded a cent of revenue to the English government. It was hoped that a new man might be able to reorganize the operation so that it could be put on a paying basis. Several others besides Mitchell had applied for the position, but it was generally agreed that he was the most likely candidate. Not only were his friends the most influential but he was working on a post-office map, which should be of great assistance in working out postal routes, since it was in such detail that it included roads.[44]

Much to Mitchell's embarrassment and dismay, he received a letter from Colden, written in July, requesting Mitchell to ask Argyll to sup-

41. Fletcher's "Catalogue," Box 435, Saltoun MSS, NL.
42. Morton, *Colonial Virginia*, 2:530–31.
43. Franklin, *Autobiography*, p. 126.
44. John Rutherford to Colden, 16 August 1751, LPCC 4:287, and Colden to Franklin, 3 June 1752, *Papers of Franklin*, 4:318–19.

port his application for the same office.[45] At the same time, Colden had written to Collinson of his intentions. Collinson told Colden's friend, John Rutherford, about his application. When the latter wrote to Colden in August, he told him, "We were sorry you had been too late, Dr. Mitchel 'tis thought will be appointed, I sent him your letter by my Servant, but have not seen him."[46]

Colden's letter to Mitchell gave his reasons for wanting the position: "It is now time to beg your excuse for giving you so much trouble. I have been above 35 years out of Gr. Brittain & all my personal acquaintances in London are Dead   I have no correspondent besides your self & Mr. Collinson   In a former this summer I presumed so far on your friendship as to pray your assistance in obtaining the Contract for the office of D Post Master Genl of America   By what I have heard of the persons who enjoy'd this office last I cannot think that it requires any great interest to obtain the same contract they had."[47]

Colden had not forgotten Mitchell's questions on the New York situation. He had hoped to make inquiries when he was in Albany with the governor but there was no time. However, he felt that he could add little to the report which he had sent to Governor Shirley.[48] With his letter, Colden included a copy of his treatise on the "Principles of Action in Matter and the Motion of the Planets." Although it had been translated into both German and French, few read it. Hindle summarizes Colden's work in this field thus: "His approach to this basic problem in theoretical physics was rational, non-experimental, and uninformed."[49]

Colden's remarks on the Indians were of great interest both to Mitchell and the Board of Trade. They were written in mid-August and sent to his friend, James Alexander (1691–1756) for forwarding. Alexander was another Scot who achieved prominence in the New World, being a member of both the New York and the New Jersey Councils. Alexander wrote to Colden on the twenty-ninth that he had sent some remarks on the Canadian governor's letter to Clinton as well as some extracts taken from the Indian register. Copies of both of these docu-

45. Colden to Mitchell, 18 July 1751, LPCC 9:101–2.
46. 16 August 1751, LPCC 4:287.
47. Colden to Mitchell, 18 July 1751, LPCC 9:101–2.
48. Ibid., pp. 98–99, 102.
49. Hindle, *Pursuit of Science*, p. 44.

ments he was sending to Mitchell along with Colden's letter.[50] He informed New Jersey Chief Justice Robert Morris, who was on the point of departure for England, about these papers sent to Mitchell. He also wrote to Collinson suggesting that he introduce Morris to Mitchell.[51] This Collinson did and Morris later went to join Mitchell for a five-day visit at Whitton on December twenty-ninth. Mitchell had spent Christmas with Argyll.[52]

It must have been a great relief to Mitchell when he received a letter from Colden written in November. From Collinson, he knew that Rutherford had informed Colden that Mitchell had also applied for the postmastership. He naturally worried that his friend might be upset. He was reassured when Colden wrote him that "no other of your friends wishes you more heartily joy than I do."[53] Colden's disappointment in his personal ambition was much nullified by the thought that he would assuredly see his friend before too long. He had heard that postal accounts in his area had never been settled since Spotswood's death. This deplorable state would certainly require Mitchell's presence in the north and the two friends could actually meet face to face at last. Always a realist, Colden added that he had three sons, any one of whom would be quite competent to fill the position of Comptroller! He closed his letter by urging Mitchell to inform him in advance when he could be expected in New York city that he might meet him as Coldengham was sixty miles from there.

As far as meeting his friend in New York within the near future was concerned, Colden was an optimist. Even the following July Mitchell was still uncertain when he would take passage for home. The affairs of the colonial post office were in a sorry state. It had never yielded any income to England and the government was now determined that it should more than pay its way. This would require many improvements in the present establishment, the cost of which was unpredictable. From the time that he first applied for the position in 1751, Mitchell was involved in discussion and negotiations with the post office for the next two years. They could reach no satisfactory agreement, for the govern-

50. Alexander to Colden, 29 August 1751, LPCC 4:295.
51. Same to same, 17 September 1751, ibid., p. 296.
52. Fletcher's "Catalogue," Box 435, Saltoun MSS, NL.
53. Colden to Mitchell, November 1751? unsigned, unaddressed, and n.d., LPCC 9:108-9.

ment insisted that he should guarantee them a certain income when he was unable to estimate what income, if any, there might be. Finally, in August, 1753, he withdrew his application.[54] Collinson wrote to Franklin in January that "it is really very hard for poor Doctor Mitchell who was really Bambozelled per the Office. It is too Long a Story to Tell."[55]

Whether Collinson thought his friend Franklin had likewise been bamboozled he did not say. Franklin and William Hunter, publisher of the *Virginia Gazette*, had been appointed joint deputy postmasters, probably just after Mitchell had given up all pretensions to the office the previous year. From their experience in the next four years, Mitchell had been wise to forgo his interest, for they lost nine hundred pounds. Their contract called for six hundred pounds per annum to be divided between the two men, provided they could make that much profit. This would have been an impossible hardship for Mitchell, whereas Franklin and Hunter, as publishers, enjoyed fringe benefits which did much to equalize any monetary loss. With various improvements, after 1757 they were able not only to reimburse themselves but to pay to the Crown a profit three times that of the Irish post office.[56]

While waiting for a decision on the postal position, Mitchell turned to another moneymaking idea. His friend, Emanuel Mendez da Costa, was writing a history of fossils, but was also an ardent mineralogist. He had long wanted a translation of Joachim Friederich Henckel's *Pyritologia*. It apparently occurred to Mitchell that this might be a lucrative project. In November, 1751, he sent da Costa a copy of a proposal to republish the *Pyritologia*, informing him that "the Author" of the proposal had written a few copies to show his friends. When he was unable to interest any bookseller in underwriting the translation, he considered financing it himself, if there was sufficient interest.[57] Apparently he received sufficient encouragement in the form of subscriptions, for the English translation was printed by Andrew Millar in 1757. Henckel's book was concerned with many aspects of mining but since, as the advertisement said, he was "a rather indifferent writer," the translator had "abridged, cleared up & unfolded." The translator was not identified except as "a gentleman of uncommon eminence in this sort of

54. Collinson to Colden, 1 September 1753, LPCC 4:405.
55. 26 January 1754, *Papers of Franklin*, 5:192.
56. Franklin, *Autobiography*, p. 160.
57. Mitchell to da Costa, 15 November 1751, B.M. Add. MSS 28,540.

knowledge who was pleased to take upon him the revisal of the sheets."[58]

Argyll continued to invite Mitchell to dinner throughout 1752, although he was only present once again in January after his long Christmas-New Year visit and once in February, both times being the only guest except for Dr. Stuart. He dined there only once in March but Lord Home, Messrs. Doddington and Warburton, and Sir Harry Belleden were also there. For the next three months he was present much more often, along with other guests: Chief Justice Morris, Lord Bute, Sir John and Lady Gordon, Lord and Lady Stamford, Lord Henry Bell, Mrs. Water, Mr. Rhenolds, Lord Egmont, and Sir John Wistar.[59]

In spite of his many interests and projects, Mitchell probably did not forgo the pleasure of attending meetings of the Royal Society. It is impossible to determine how regular he was in his attendance, as members were only noted as being present when they brought guests or were elected to an office. Thus, in 1751, his name appeared but once in the journal on 7 March.[60] His guest that time was Erskine Baker (1730-67), son of Henry Baker. Erskine's mother was Daniel Defoe's youngest daughter and he was considered something of a child prodigy. He had been sent to the Tower of London to be trained as an engineer in the drawing room there. At the age of twelve, he had translated two dozen books of *Telemachus* from the French. At sixteen, he had written a treatise comparing Newton's *Metaphysics* with that of Dr. Leibnitz from the French of Voltaire. As sometimes happens with such young geniuses, when he finally married he declared his independence of intellectual pursuits by becoming a strolling player!

During 1752, Mitchell twice signed certificates of recommendation for prospective Fellows. One was for the portrait painter, Arthur Pond, of Great Queen Street. Cosigners included Henry Baker, Thomas Birch, Collinson, and da Costa.[61] The other certificate was for Dr.

58. *Pyritologia: or, a History of the Pyrites, the Principal Body in the Mineral Kingdom* . . . translated from the German of J. F. Henckel, Late Chief Director of the Mines at Friberg in Saxony (London, 1757), printed for A. Millar, in the Strand; and A. Linde, in Catherine Street, in the Strand.

59. Fletcher's "Catalogue," Box 435, Saltoun MSS, NL.

60. Journal Book XX, p. 463.

61. Journal Book XXXI, p. 51. Pond (1705?-58) was also well-known for the great number of etchings which he produced of Rembrandt, Raphael, and other Old Masters. In collaboration with George Knapton, he worked on "Heads of Illustrious Persons," between 1743 and 1752.

William Brackenridge, rector of St. Michael Bassishaw, a member of the Society of Antiquarians and Librarian of Sion College.[62] This last was an organization of the incumbents of the parishes within the City and the Liberties of London. On 23 November, Mitchell was accompanied by two guests: the Baron de Thienin and Mr. C'Angeul.[63]

It was during this same year, too, that Mitchell entertained briefly the idea that he might find time to again pursue his botanical interests. On 1 July, Collinson wrote to Trew: "Docr. Mitchell gives you his Humble Service & begs the favour of you to send Him a Coppy of his Vires *plantarum* Virginiana that I formerly sent you   He kept no Coppy Himself, so is in great Want of It. I hope you will be so good not to fail to do It, for I am much blamed for sending it so farr off—"[64]

To say that Collinson's request astounded Dr. Trew would express it far too mildly. Indignantly, he wrote to him on 30 September:

But it is more disturbing, my friend, what you have written to me concerning the sending of the other part of Dr. Mitchell's most distinguished work. That which was sent to me on March 20 in the year 1745/46 is the first part of this work which contained descriptions of some new genera of Virginia plants, to which you had added, on the 18th day of February 1746/47, by sending the dissertation on the principles of botany and zoology. This first part was printed in the year 1748 in the appendix of the Actae Academiae Curiosae Naturae, Vol. VIII. However, in order that I might be able to help you, oh clever man, and the esteemed O.[ptimus] D.[ominus] Mitchell beyond this, I ordered 50 copies begun, in which are preserved the dedications both to you and the well-known Sloane, which I reported to Dominus Ehret on August 30, 1748. Indeed, at the same time, I warned that these copies were not yet entirely finished, perfect and complete, since the other part concerning the medicinal plants I was expecting from your promise in March would follow. In letters to D. Ehret on 11 November of that same year, I repeated my request about the other part most recently communicated, inasmuch without that the copies, illustrated with small figures, which I had finished would, by no means, be allowed since there would be a mention of this in citing the dedications.

Trew added that, although he and Mitchell had exchanged several letters, the third part was never forwarded to him.[65]

62. Journal Book XXI, p. 94.
63. Ibid., p. 182.
64. ENU.
65. Ibid.

When Collinson received Trew's letter, he was understandably embarrassed. Apologetically, he wrote:

It really gives Mee concerne that I could forget the Title of the papers I sent you, for I really thought it was the Vires plantarum I sent & carried your letter to Docr. Mitchell,—& requested Him to lett Mee have the *Vires plantarum* to compleat your 50 copies. His answer was that he intended to make great additions to that Work; *his first leisure*, I know he is full of Employe.—and I have little or no hopes of his compleating It, so I pressed Him then the more, to lett Mee have It, as it was. He then putt Mee off untill next Spring,—my

Dear Friend I am sorry it happened, unfortunately—(att Present,) it is not in my power to help It,—but this I will assure you,—I will not forget to re-remind Docr. Mitchell, when your next Box goes, in the New Year, to trye if I can prevail with Him to send the Vires plantarum In It—[66]

Although Collinson continued to try to obtain Mitchell's manuscript for Trew, he had no success. On 28 April 1753, he wrote to the Nuremberg physician, "I hope to prevail on Docr. Mitchell to send you the Vires plantarum."[67] Two years later, he again wrote to Trew, "Do all I can I cannot prevail on Docr. Mitchell to send you His *Vires plantarum*."[68]

Final reference was made to the Vires plantarum when Trew wrote to Collinson on the twenty-seventh of June 1757.[69] Their correspondence had become somewhat erratic due to the loss of several of Collinson's letters and the lack of time for letters on Trew's part. The latter wrote, "I desire to mention again that I might share in those certain manuscripts of Dr. Mitchell even now." Trew said that when Mitchell had promised not to add to the Vires plantarum, he had sent him a number of printed copies of the first part, thus hoping to stimulate his forwarding the remaining manuscript. His devious ploy was no more successful than his outright requests had been and Mitchell retained his manuscript.

It is unfortunate that Mitchell was reluctant to part with the Vires plantarum for it might have been preserved. However, it is understandable. Mitchell had many literary ambitions. He had never aban-

66. Ibid., 15 November 1752.
67. Ibid.
68. 5 August 1755, ibid.
69. Ibid.

doned his idea of writing a complete medical and natural history of North America. One of the features of such a book would be a section on newly discovered plants, some of which might prove important additions to the known pharmacopoeia. There was always, too, the hope that publication of such a book might add materially to Mitchell's financial security.

The incomplete copies were bound into books in 1769, the year after Trew's death, by parties unknown, thus providing the mystery of the dedicatory letter to Sloane as he had feared. Apparently its reference to the medicinal plants of Virginia has been ignored for many years.

XII ❧ Mitchell, the Map Maker

"Dr. Mitchell has left Botany for some time and has wholly employed himself in making a map or chart, of all North America. . . ."
Collinson to Linnaeus, 10 April 1755[1]

In December, 1752, the Royal Society received a gift of a copy of "A Map of the Discoveries toward the Northern parts of the South Sea, with an explanation of it, by Mons. de Lisle of the Royal Academy of Sciences." Rather naturally, this was referred to Dr. Mitchell for an evaluation as he was known to have been working with maps for several years.[2] Two years previously, in 1750, Mitchell had completed a map of North America.[3] Few Englishmen had attempted such an ambitious project, covering almost the entire continent. In fact, the only previous large-scale map of this area had been made by Henry Popple in 1733. From this, some realization of the French encroachments were apparent but it "did not clarify the picture much. His facts were faulty and the sources of his information contributed to a badly distorted map. . . ."[4] Mitchell had collected facts wherever he could: from maps made on the Continent, from travelers, from historians, and from geographers. Of the last two, he told Colden "there are none I believe but what I have consulted. . . ."[5] He garnered knowledge of certain areas unknown sixteen years previously but, like Popple, his foremost interest was to point up the growing threat to British ambitions of French expansion. As a Virginian, he had long been aware of this. As many other colonials, he was fascinated by the possibilities of the vast, unexplored land to the west. Tales of its fertility and mineral treasures continually filtered back from scouts, Indians, and traders. He was unwilling that lands of such promise should go to the French by default. From letters of friends and relations, he learned that the current situation was becoming more critical daily. He determined to bring it to the atten-

---

1. CLO 1:34.
2. Collinson to Franklin, 27 January 1753, *Papers of Franklin*, 4:414, and Journal Book XXI, 14 December, p. 203.
3. According to Mitchell's statement on his map.
4. Lloyd Arnold Brown, *Early Maps of the Ohio Valley* (Pittsburgh), 1959, pp. 85–86.
5. Mitchell to Colden, 5 April 1751, LPCC 9:88–89.

tion of those in power, now that he had met many of them through Argyll. He concluded that there was no better way to achieve this than by a map. No matter how many words were written, only a map could clearly and forcefully delineate British and French claims and the incomparable challenge of the western lands. Crude as his 1750 map was, and Mitchell was only too conscious of this, it was of immense value in that it underlined the great lack of knowledge of boundaries, roads, and exact locations.

When the Lords Commissioners of Trade and Plantations heard of Mitchell's map and finally saw it, they were impressed by his meticulous dedication in completing the work. They were even more impressed by the realization that there were so many gaps in geographical knowledge. They had been immersed already in a search for such facts, since they were negotiating with France over boundaries at the very moment. The map probably came to the commissioners' notice through Lord Dupplin, a member of that body, with whom Mitchell had dined at Argyll's home in 1749. Another member was the second Earl of Halifax (1716-71). Born George Montagu, he had taken the name Dunk when he married Anne Richards in 1753, for her fortune had been inherited from an uncle, Sir Thomas Dunk. Halifax had been "Master of Buckhounds" in the Prince of Wales's household and, in 1748, was appointed president of the Board of Trade. He was a fortunate selection. He was not only intensely interested in the subject, particularly North American trade, but highly efficient. It was he who had helped to found the capital of Nova Scotia, which was given his name. Because of his accomplishments in promoting American commerce, he had been called the "Father of the Colonies."[6] It was Halifax who apparently was most impressed by the map for he and Mitchell were soon on intimate terms and remained so for many years.[7]

From 1750 on, Mitchell was retained in some capacity by the commissioners.[8] He was to redraw and improve his map and apparently to study and evaluate some of the reports coming in from the colonies. There is at least one of his evaluations in the board's collections in the

6. *Encyclopedia Britannica*, 12th ed., and *Dictionary of National Biography*.
7. Collinson to Colden, 10 June 1753, LPCC 4:393.
8. According to John Pownall, Secretary to the Board of Trade and Plantations (see Mitchell's map).

Public Record Office in London today.[9] It seems probable that he received no monetary remuneration for his services, since he was given the rights to publication of the finished map. This was a generous grant. Maps enjoyed great popularity in the mid-eighteenth century. Their sales were large and consequently afforded handsome profits. Mitchell now had access to the great storehouse of maps contained in the board's archives, which can still be tentatively identified from existing records.[10] Many were old and outdated, but many were of great interest to him.

Over the years, the commissioners had received reports in answer to their inquiries to the governors of the various provinces. These dealt with the number of inhabitants, products, and boundaries. For example, Lieutenant Governor Gooch, in 1743, replied that the ridge of mountains seemed to be a natural boundary which would limit settlements for many years to come. If mines were discovered, this might not be the case. Beyond the mountains, he said, lay another barrier, namely Lakes Erie and Huron. When English expansion reached to them, there might be "Contests with the French about the Boundaries."[11] The Lords Commissioners were now studying and reviewing papers describing French hostilities and encroachments in North America in violation of the Treaty of Aix-la-Chapelle, marking the end of King George's War.

At the meeting on 18 July 1750, five gentlemen were present: Halifax, Pitt, Grenville, Dupplin, and Townshend. They gave orders that would greatly facilitate Mitchell's task. Each of the North American governors was directed to supply a map or chart of his own province, which would give the exact boundaries and any incursions by the French.[12] Accordingly, on 25 July, a letter went out to the governor and company of Hudson's Bay, which began: "My Lords Commission-

9. "Some Additions to the Account sent from Virginia concerning the Extent and limits of that Colony, and the Encroachments that have been made upon it," C.O. 5/1327, ff. 429–40, Public Record Office, London, subsequently referred to as PRO.

10. It is possible to tentatively identify the maps available to Mitchell from a manuscript list in the Map Division of the British Museum, "List of Maps, Plans, etc. Belonging to the Right Honble the Lords Commissioners for Trade and Plantations under the Care of Francis Aegidus Assiotti, Draughtsman, 1780," Index 8315, PRO.

11. 22 August 1743, C.O. 5/1326, ff. 18–40, PRO.

12. Journal of the Commissioners for Trade and Plantations, vol. 58, f. 89, PRO.

ers for Trade and Plantations judging it necessary for His Majesty's Service and for the Benefit of the Plantations, that the Limits or Boundaries of the British Colonies on the Continent of America should be distinctly known, more particularly so far as they border on the Settlements made by the French or any Foreign Nation in America, have directed me to desire you will send their Lordships, with all possible Dispatch, as exact an Account as you can of the Limits and Boundaries of the Territory granted to the Hudson's Bay Company, together with a Chart or Map thereof, and all the best Accounts and Vouchers you can obtain. . . ."[13] Similar letters went to the other governors.

Not content with just the maps supplied by the colonials, others made on the Continent were purchased. Between Lady Day, 1750, and 5 January 1755, the large sum of one hundred and four pounds was spent on maps and charts.[14] It took time for the provincial maps to be made, but by 1752 they were at last beginning to arrive in England. Mitchell had to share his excitement with Peter Collinson. The latter wrote to Franklin in June: "Docr. Mitchell showed Mee a New Mapp of Pensilvania sent over by your Governor. The Doctor is Makeing a New Mapp of all our Colonies for the Board of Trade, Haveing the Assistance of all these Manuscript Mapps and which are Abundance in particular a Mapp sent by an Officer of the York forces, which much fuller Discribes the Country and Settlements on Mohawk, Oswego and the fork of Susquehanna than your Governours Mapp. Docr. Mitchell gives his Service but his prodegious Engagements as Above, prevents his Writeing by these Ships so hopes to be Excused."[15]

The Pennsylvania map which Mitchell showed to Collinson had taken almost two years to complete from the time of the commissioners' request. Lieutenant Governor Hamilton had written them in February, 1750/51, that he would have answered sooner had he been able to procure a map sufficiently accurate for their purpose. Since the only map maker whom he considered precise enough was away, it would be some time before the map could be completed. In the meantime, he sent a written description of the boundaries. He did not limit his comments to Pennsylvania. Much of the land belonging to Virginia along

13. From the Library of Congress transcript of C.O. 324/15, f. 1, PRO; Crown-copyright is acknowledged.

14. Board of Trade, C.O. 388/83, PRO.

15. 3 June 1752, *Papers of Franklin*, 4:318–19.

the Mississippi from the mouth of the Ohio to the head, including all the waters running into it, had been claimed by the French, who were worried by the activities of the Ohio Company. Hamilton said that the French had even gone so far as to place "Leaden Plates in the Earth with pompous Inscriptions." He enclosed a copy of one sent him by the governor of New York. Hamilton asked an Indian's opinion as to the accuracy of the map which he sent and he said that he considered that the western part was correct as to the placement of the mountains and Indian towns. The southern and eastern area Hamilton could guarantee as it was based on actual surveys. He urged the board not to limit the boundaries to the mountains as there was rich land beyond them.[16]

In October, 1750, Hamilton had written to Thomas Penn, the proprietor who lived in London. He reported what Conrad Weiser had told him of French machinations observed on his way to Onondago. He had given Hamilton a copy of his journal which the latter had directed Richard Peters, secretary of the province, to forward to Penn.[17] For some reason, Penn did not receive it until November, 1753. When he had finished reading it, he turned it over to Halifax, as he had done with other documents from Pennsylvania.[18] That same summer, he had had a long conversation with Halifax and Sir Danvers Osborn, on the subject of improving relations with the Indians.[19] Penn was extremely helpful to Mitchell, sharing with him his dispatches from Pennsylvania and his wide knowledge of that region, where he had spent many years.[20] It is probable that Collinson introduced Penn and Mitchell. He had sent the proprietor many parcels of seeds when he was living in Philadelphia and had introduced Bartram to Penn by correspondence.[21] Penn was greatly impressed by the meticulous care with which Mitchell worked and did all that he could to assist him.

The reports interested Mitchell almost as much as the maps. In the spring of 1751, one arrived from Lieutenant Governor Spencer Phips of Massachusetts, which gave the history of the English and French

16. 8 February 1750/51, C.O. 5/1233, pt. 3, PRO. Another was found in 1845 and is now in the museum of the Virginia Historical Society.

17. 13 October 1750/51, ibid.

18. Penn to Governor Hamilton, 1 November, Penn Letter Books, 3:266, HSP.

19. Penn to his nephew, John Penn, 14 August 1753, ibid., p. 243.

20. Penn to Peters, 21 February 1755, ibid., 4:39.

21. Collinson to Bartram, 8 September 1737, n.d., 26 January 1738/39, 24 February 1738/39, and 25 July 1762 (Darlington, *Memorials*, pp. 100, 114, 123, 127, 239).

settlements in Arcadia. Phips wrote that he would forward a map as soon as the artist completed it. Later, a report of Governor Shirley's speech to the council was received. In it, he rather bitterly remarked that the English had been unsuccessfully requesting the Indians' permission to settle lands already within the province and paying them an annual tribute as protection money. Meanwhile, he said, the French took by force the most distant areas without any justification at all. In fact, they went even further, forbidding the Indians to grant land to the English and enforcing their orders by building a chain of forts.[22]

Mitchell was not surprised to read reports that the Six Indian Nations were worried when they realized the English were starting to settle the lands, rather than building trading posts as the French did. They regretted the Treaty of Lancaster and, when the Virginians met with them in efforts to renew it in order to protect their settlers, they were far from enthusiastic. The French continued to stir them up. A report forwarded to the commissioners by Lieutenant Governor Hamilton gives an interesting glimpse of the state of affairs. The account of various disasters came from the Virginian, Captain William Trent, who later built Fort du Quesne.[23]

Naturally, reports from Virginia were of particular interest to Mitchell. In May, 1750, one arrived from Lieutenant Governor Sir William Gooch, answering the commissioners' queries of the previous year. Regarding the western boundaries of the province, he stated that they extended to the South Seas and included the island of California.[24] It was apparent that there was still great ignorance concerning the western areas of the North American continent. Gooch had resigned that same month because of ill health. The province then saw a succession of chief executives. On 4 September, the fifty-nine-year-old Thomas Lee, as senior member of the council, became acting governor. He and William Beverley had been the two Virginians who had met with the Indians at Lancaster in 1744. He lost no time in traveling over his domain so that he could better answer the board's questions which he did

22. The governor's speech to the Council and the Massachusetts Bay House of Representatives was delivered 28 March 1754 (C.O. 5/14, f. 177, PRO). Such French conduct was completely unjustifiable as the 15th Article of the Treaty of Utrecht declared the Indians of the Six Nations subject to Great Britain (C.O. 5/1344, f. 101, PRO).

23. C.O. 5/1065, PRO.

24. C.O. 5/1327, f. 167, PRO.

on 29 September.[25] Lee, whom Mitchell may have known, died in November. A week later, Lewis Burwell took office as his successor. He wrote the commissioners in January that he had employed skilled people to draw up an account and draft a map of Virginia. These he would forward with the appropriate vouchers as soon as they were finished. He had chosen Joshua Fry, a former professor of mathematics at The College of William and Mary, to make the historical and geographical report.[26] Fry also drew the requested map with the assistance of Peter Jefferson, Isham Randolph's son-in-law and father of Thomas. The two men were accustomed to working as a team, having served together surveying the Virginia-North Carolina line and the boundaries of the Fairfax grant. They had unsuccessfully tried to persuade the assembly to order a map of Virginia, on which they had already started.[27] Burwell was exceedingly well pleased with the map when completed and remarked that since "we are yet a country of woods, it is surprising how he could draw so beautiful a map of it." Burwell forwarded the documents to London in August where Fry's report was published the following year.[28] He, like his predecessor, died in November and was succeeded by the Scot, Robert Dinwiddie. Former surveyor general of customs for the southern district, he was no stranger to Virginia. He had returned to England in 1749 and gone into trade. His experience in business and politics was to serve Virginia well.

When Burwell's reports arrived on 9 December, Mitchell pored over them. He found Fry's letter to the acting governor, dated 8 May, most interesting. The professor had painstakingly documented Virginia's claims to her far-flung boundaries, using Stith's recently published history. To supplement it, he had enclosed Salley's journal and one of Dr. Thomas Walker. Walker was only four years younger than Mitchell and it is extremely likely that the two men had known each other, as Walker had lived in Williamsburg many years. There, he had trained as a physician under Dr. George Gilmer, a University of Edinburgh graduate, and later practiced in Fredericksburg. Walker

25. Ibid., f. 171.
26. 17 January 1750/51, ibid., ff. 221–22.
27. Coolie Verner, "The Fry and Jefferson Map," *Imago Mundi* 21 (1967):70–94.
28. 21 August 1751, C.O. 5/1327, ff. 263–64, PRO; Crown-copyright is acknowledged. Included in the packet was Stith's history.

was an incurable explorer, spending long periods hunting and traveling the little known western parts of Virginia. In 1749, he went with a surveying party as far as what is now Tennessee. During the years, he took out huge grants of this western land. In 1750, Walker and five other men found their way through the Cumberland Gap into present-day Kentucky.[29] That spring they built a cabin there, which Mitchell carefully recorded on his map: "Walker's—the extent of the English settlements 1750."

Fry's account was read at the meeting of the commissioners in March, 1752. A month later, on 15 April, "Some Additions to the Accounts sent from Virginia, concerning the Extent & limits of that Colony, and the Encroachments that have been made upon it" were given.[30] This report had been meticulously compiled by Dr. Mitchell and is a most interesting and carefully researched article, which required months of hard work. It is not surprising that his friends saw little of him at this time. His background made him a fine choice to supplement the Virginia report. Not only was he a native of that colony but, with the idea of a future book, he had spent many years collecting information on its history. Moreover, in drawing up his first map he had been concerned with the boundaries of the various colonies.

It is apparent throughout his paper that Mitchell was determined to give the Mother Country the benefit of every doubtful point when it came to delineating English boundaries in relation to those of the French. Nonetheless, he supported claims with documentation, frequently citing French sources. Virginia's first grant was that of Queen Elizabeth I to Sir Walter Raleigh in 1584, and it included all the land between Latitude 26° and 46°. This meant that part of Nova Scotia was considered Virginia. As early as 1613, Virginia orders drove the French from there. Mitchell gave Hakluyt's Voyages, Vol. 3, p. 243, as his source. With Raleigh's execution, the land reverted to the Crown. Mitchell wrote that when the Virginia Company was formed, two grants were made in 1606 and 1609, as the memorial from there had stated. These boundaries were far smaller than those of Raleigh's grant, being but 200 miles to the north of Point Comfort and the same distance to the south, which included part of present day North Carolina. At the dissolution of the company, the land again reverted to the

29. Morton, *Colonial Virginia*, 2:575–76.
30. C.O. 5/1327, ff. 429–40, PRO.

Crown in 1624, Virginia becoming a Royal Colony. Then the southern limits along North Carolina only went to 36° 30′ and on the Maryland boundary to the Potomac River. Along the Pennsylvania line, it was approximately 5° west of the Delaware River, but still unsettled. Beyond that, to the north, Virginia and New York claims came together and were still undetermined. Mitchell suggested that Lake Erie might be a satisfactory limit to Virginia. In any event, he thought it important that the boundaries of the various colonies be determined as soon as possible. Otherwise, with no one taking any responsibility for them, they could easily fall into French hands.

To the west, Virginia now extended to the Mississippi. Howard's and Salley's accounts made this distance to be 1,600 miles but Mitchell thought it far less. He considered extant maps grossly in error on this point. He had come to this conclusion from studying the most recent French maps which seemed to indicate a distance of 700 miles. By the same Maps, the French made it clear that they considered all the land from the headwaters of rivers running into the Mississippi to that river, theirs, and the land on the watershed to the Atlantic, English. Thus, Mitchell pointed out, they limited the English to a strip barely 200 miles wide along the coast, while they claimed a 500 mile corridor north and south, a ratio of two and a half to one.

Mitchell noted that the French claim to this territory was "only by virtue of a few Settlements they have made on the Mississippi. This they Claim by Right of the *first Discovery*, the *first Possession*, and *Grant* from their sovereign." He disposed of the French claim to these areas as follows, citing Coxe's *Carolina*: 1. The English discovery of the Mississippi in 1678 had inspired La Salle's later exploration; 2. The territory where the river was later discovered had been included in the grants to the Virginia Company in 1609 and to Sir Robert Heath in 1630, as well as to the Carolina proprietors. La Salle had not taken possession in the king's name until 1683 and the French king's grant to Crozat was not until 1712; 3. When the French went to the Mississippi in 1698, they found English settled there already and named it the English Reach, as Charlevoix stated. Salley, too, had been told the same story.

As an even stronger bulwark to his argument, Mitchell referred to the actual purchase of these lands from the Six Nations eight years previously at the Treaty of Lancaster. He gave French references confirming this ownership: Charlevoix and F. Gabriel's *Lettres Edifiantes & Curieuses*, p. 12. He said that the only French encroachment noted in the memorial was the French Fort of Crevecœur on the Illinois River in 1680. The fort no longer existed, but two French settlements along the river still survived. Further down on the Mereneg River were several more, near the mines claimed by the Mississippi Company in 1719. All were mere Indian trading posts with small garrisons except for Kaskasquies. Salley had mentioned these places where salt and lead were mined. Another product there was the manufacture of a cloth finer than English wool, from buffalo hair. All of these settlements were within Virginia's limits. Mitchell referred his readers to his map.

There was only one post in the 500 miles between Kaskasquies and the mouth of the Mississippi, where the French were well and strongly settled. This information Mitchell had acquired from a reliable source, a man who had lived with the Cherokees for fifteen years. He had found additional confirmation from Conrad Weiser's journal of his 1749 trip to the Ohio. There, the Indians had told Weiser the same thing. The French books concurred in this opinion although their maps noted two forts, as did Polle's. One was "Old Fort," where the Ohio flows into the Mississippi and Fort Prudhomme in the land of the Chickasaws. Actually, they had been two of La Salle's camps and were no longer in existence.

From his years spent studying this western area in the preparation of his map, Mitchell had come to the conclusion that the most important point was the Forks of the Mississippi where the Ohio, the Cherokee (Tennessee) and the Wabache flowed together (today's Cairo, Illinois). A fort there would command an area 500 miles square. The French recognized its value but had been discouraged from building a fort because of the incursions of the Cherokees. Mitchell would like to see the English construct one but the location was so distant from present English settlements that it was impracticable. Yet, with future expansion, a French fort could be a very real menace.

Mitchell traced English settlements from 1730, when they first ventured beyond the Blue Ridge Mountains as soon as the Six Nations had defeated the warlike Indians there. Not long after, settlers went beyond the Alleghanies where they found a branch of the Ohio, Wood River. Now, they had penetrated still further to the west, five hundred miles from the coast. There, a beautiful level country opened up to them along the Cumberland River.

In such expansive settlement, Virginia was well ahead of her sister colonies, who had stopped at the mountains. Unfortunately, this meant that Virginia settlers were in a very exposed position. While the Ohio Indians were friendly, there were some of the Six Nations who were not. On the west were the French at the forks of the Mississippi.

The major portion of these settlers were foreigners, mainly Germans, according to Mitchell. They came from New York and Pennsylvania, being unable to find land there. They settled in the middle and southern parts, although the Ohio Company had a handsome grant to the north. He felt that this last area was extremely important and went into great detail as to his reasons. The Ohio River leads directly from Lake Erie through Pennsylvania towards the mountains in Virginia where two rivers flow into it. There it proceeds northwest towards Lake Erie again and eventually to the Mississippi and the Bay of Mexico. Thus, the Ohio affords a magnificent water carriage for all Virginia's back settlements. At the forks of the Ohio previously mentioned, there were many Indians. Mitchell had seen lists of them given to the public interpreter by the Ohio Indians and the Six Nations. The latter counted no less than fifteen different tribes, all of which were allied to the French.

A letter from the Canadian governor to the chief executive of New York persuaded Mitchell of the urgency of the situation.[31] In it, the governor claimed all these territories because the French had enjoyed a long "uninterrupted possession of them." He maintained that this was renewed by sending a force of five hundred men there in 1749. Mitchell expressed bewilderment in regard to what he meant by "possession." He could only account for it by their expedition up the Ohio in 1729. Whatever they meant, however, there was little doubt that the French were about to implement their ambitions since they had sent such a force in spite of the later treaty. It was easy to understand their goal, since it would tie together their Canadian empire and that in Louisiana by means of the Mississippi basin.

The whole situation, Mitchell felt, was extremely complicated for

31. James Alexander, surveyor general of New York, sent remarks on the Canadian governor's letter and "some Extracts from the Indian register" to Colden on 29 August 1751. At the same time, he sent copies to Mitchell in London (LPCC 4:295).

the English. Neither New York nor Pennsylvania had shown great interest in the land beyond the mountains. The latter, being of Quaker persuasion, would, in no event, bear arms. Only Virginia appeared to have any reason for contesting this rich land with the French. Even they were apathetic to a certain extent and were often content to settle the southern rather than the western lands.

Much of his information Mitchell had received in conversation with a gentleman who had traveled all over the northern colonies, spending some time with the French at Niagara and at Fort Frederic (Crown Point). Although he did not name him, there is little doubt that he was Peter Kalm whom Mitchell had seen when he stopped in England on his way home from North America. Kalm had traveled widely in these areas. He had been received most cordially by the French in Canada and had remained there for some months. He had informed Mitchell that, in the last few years since the war, the French had been strengthening an old town, which they had seized from the Six Nations in 1701. It lay between Lakes Erie and Huron. This eventually became Detroit. Kalm said that the land was level and rich, which was an inducement to settlers discouraged by some of the barren Canadian farm land. To further populate the region, soldiers who had completed their service, were given land. Niagara had become a center for those passing from Canada to Detroit and its fortifications had been strengthened. It was from Niagara and Detroit that the threat of French encroachments was likely to come.

It would only be through amicable relations with the Indians that control of this country could be achieved, Mitchell believed. The French recognized this and had taken great care to regulate their trade with the Indians to insure such a state. On the other hand, no one had taken the trouble to instruct English traders from Virginia and Pennsylvania. As a result they had been taking advantage of the Indians and treating them most unfairly in their strenuous efforts to make a quick fortune. The Indians were not naïve and had plainly shown their feelings by seizing some of the traders, even threatening to murder them. Something had to be done to control the traders' frauds and abuses, or complete deterioration of English relations with the Indians would result. By just such practices the English had lost "Fort Albama" in Carolina to the French. This had given them possession of a vast land area, three hundred miles east of the Mississippi. It could easily happen at any place along the western settlements.

To land loss would be added serious competition in the rice and tobacco trade, as had happened already in sugar. The only reason that the French had not been producing both commodities in quantity before was that their northern colonies were unable to grow them satisfactorily and their Louisiana lands were "little better than Sandy Desarts." With the rich Mississippi Valley opening to them, tobacco and rice crops would be immense for that land was far more fertile than the worn-out fields of the Virginia and Carolina planters.

Mitchell stated that the reason for this account of his was to emphasize the importance of securing the Ohio River to protect English interests. It was his opinion that four steps were necessary in order to achieve this:

1. The boundaries of the various colonies should be established as soon as possible.

2. Pressure should be put upon the Ohio Company to lay off their grant immediately and to start their settlements. Until this was done, no other grants could be made.

3. To insure that this Ohio River area would soon be well populated, enticements (such as had been granted to the Ohio Company) should be offered. These would include forgiveness of quitrents and other charges.

4. A factory and fort similar to that at Oswego should be built to protect the Ohio Indians. It should be a joint project with Virginia, Maryland, and Pennsylvania all participating.

The wisdom of Mitchell's fourth recommendation was underlined in December of that year. Lieutenant Governor Dinwiddie then wrote that the Indians themselves desired the English to build forts all along the Ohio River. He had just entertained the Cherokee emperor and his family, who were now very loyal to the British. Mitchell's other suggestion, that the colonies should work together, gradually became apparent to all. The English hitherto had not encouraged such cooperation but, with the joint threat of Indian and French depredations, the colonies quickly realized their common interest. Undoubtedly, this was the beginning of a realization of the power there was in concerted action—a recognition which eventually led to the reaction to the Stamp Act and eventually to revolution.

Busy as he was during the first six months of 1753, Mitchell continued his custom of dining fairly often with the Duke of Argyll. Sometimes he and Dr. Stuart were the only guests but more often there were others. The Earl of Strafford, a close friend of Horace Walpole, was present twice. Another guest was Dr. Clephan, a member of the club of Scottish physicians in London. He and Mitchell should have been congenial for a friend described Clephan as "one of the most sensible, learned and judicious men I ever knew—an admirable classical scholar and a fine historian. He often led the conversation, but it was with an air of modesty and deference to the company, which added to the weight of all he said."[32]

In January, 1753, Collinson had received a bonanza in the way of mail from Bartram. There were three letters and seven boxes of seeds. To Mitchell's disgust, there was neither letter nor box for him, although he had ordered thirty-five pounds' worth of seeds for friends.[33] There was an explanation in one of the letters to Collinson. It seemed that Mitchell's orders had arrived too late in the season. Even Collinson was annoyed to find that Bartram had shipped one box separately and he wrote to his friend irascibly, "I wish they had been sent with the others for it takes up as much Time & Trouble & Expence to gett these from aboard through the Custom House as the seven boxes—if it is possible send all that I am concern'd in together next year—those for Mitchell or Powell or Williamson—as thou chooses—"[34]

Although Mitchell and others might neglect their correspondence, Collinson never did. He even tried to make up for their deficiencies in such matters. When he wrote to Jared Eliot, the Connecticut agriculturist, he gave him Mitchell's regards as well as the doctor's query as to the success of the potash.[35] To Franklin, he wrote in January that Mitchell was to report on the French map before the Royal Society.[36] When he wrote to him again in July, he asked him to remind Bartram of his eight boxes of seeds and Mitchell's order of the previous year.[37] In

---

32. Carlyle, *Autobiography*, p. 362.
33. 11 January 1753, Bartram Papers, 2:87, HSP.
34. 13 February 1753, ibid., p. 89, HSP.
35. 7 January 1753, Yale University.
36. 27 January 1753, *Papers of Franklin*, 4:414.
37. Ibid., 5:3.

June, he received several documents from Colden, to whom he replied: "Your Memorial & letter I had by my good Fr. Mr. Hill Secretary to the Board of Trade delivered into Lod Halifax's own Hands—but what will be done in it cannot saye for I have not the least Acquaintance with his Lordship—But Docr. Mitchell is Intimate with Him & I have acquainted Him with your Request & he has assured Mee he will do his best to Serve You. He gives his Service & wonders he has not a Line from You—"[38] Mitchell apparently had little time for social activity although he did go out to Cane Wood in mid-August. Whether it was merely for the day or for a longer visit, Bute did not say when he wrote to Collinson, suggesting that he join them.[39]

As busy as he sometimes may have been in 1753, Mitchell probably remembered that year as a time of leisure and peaceful work in comparison to the fourteen months preceding the publication of his map. None of his letters for this period survived and it may well be that he had no time for any. Neither did his friends speak of his activities. Argyll paid him seventeen and a half pounds in February,[40] probably for plants ordered from Bartram. Other than this and Collinson's reference to Mitchell's post office disappointment, there is no mention of him.

38. 10 June 1753, LPCC 4:393.
39. 10 August 1753, CLO 1:30.
40. Argyll's account, 11 February 1754, Ledger 28, Coutts & Company.

XIII ~ Cartographic Recognition

"Freeing himself from many traditions and drawing upon fresh sources of information, Mitchell produced a mother map which for forty years served as a model. . . ."

C. O. Paullin, 1932[1]

The map was proving a far greater task than Mitchell had anticipated and, as the English-French competition in the New World became more intense, there was tremendous pressure for its completion. As has often been said, the prospect of war is the best stimulus for cartography. When Mitchell commenced the redrawing of his first map in 1750, the immensity of the commissioners' archives and the new charts and surveys arriving from North America appeared eminently sufficient for all of his needs. However, as he began to study and compare all of his available materials, it was soon apparent to him that the most important feature of accurate cartography was, in many cases, lacking. While the general shape and figure of geographical subjects were available and from them could be adjudged the actual picture, there was no way at all to arrive at its actual location. Mitchell searched out and studied the available observations of specific places, but was still dissatisfied. He said, "I found the true Situation, or Latitude & Longitude of many places was undetermined or uncertain, & that in the principal Parts on the Coast."[2]

With his usual bulldog persistence, he finally discovered an answer to his problem. While it was not perfect, at least it was the best at the time. This was a study of the journals kept by His Majesty's ships of war at the Admiralty Office. From these he was able to make correc-

1. Charles Oscar Paullin, *Atlas of the Historical Geography of the United States,* ed. John K. Wright (Baltimore, 1932), p. 13.
2. Explanation of how he resolved some of the problems in drawing up the map was given by Mitchell in two blocks of text which appeared on the second edition of his map published in 1757, according to the British Museum. He also included an evaluation of some map makers and lists of the various references which he used.

tions and determinations of location. Even in these he had no great faith. In tabulating latitudes, he had three classifications of the journal observations: "good," "doubtful or uncertain," and those "without the Observations from Sea Reckonings." Of seventy-seven latitudes given, only ten were in the first category and fourteen in the second. Nevertheless, latitude determination was far more advanced than that of longitude. It was based on the use of an instrument which was the precursor of today's sextant and had been invented by two men simultaneously in 1731. One was John Hadley, vice-president of the Royal Society. The other was Thomas Godfrey of Philadelphia. When Hadley's report to the society of his invention was published, James Logan notified them that Godfrey's quadrant had already been tested by the mate of the sloop *Truman* on a voyage to Jamaica in 1730.[3] Perhaps Logan discussed the matter with Mitchell on his Philadelphia visit in 1744.

Much of the error present in maps Mitchell ascribed to the propensity of map makers to print old maps without questioning their accuracy. Perhaps the most flagrant example of this, Mitchell said, was Moll's publication of a map of New England and Nova Scotia, based on a draught by one Blackmore, "a feigned Survey by a pretended Surveyor General." In 1711, Blackmore was a lieutenant on the Man-of-war *Dragon*, stationed off that coast. About four years later, he applied to the Board of Trade for permission to survey it, accompanying his petition with a rough sketch of the area as he remembered it. It was this which had been used by Moll and referred to as an actual survey. Mitchell pronounced this extremely dangerous as "By this they make the whole Coast of New England from 10 to 25 Min. of Latitude too far North, which leads ships upon that dangerous Coast. . . ."

In order to arrive at a probable latitude, Mitchell used many references. He relied rather heavily on the observations of Jacques Nicolas Bellin (1703–72), a famous French geographical engineer, and Thomas Durrell, an English Navy captain. The latter had approached his surveying so scientifically that he even designed a sloop for that purpose, the *William Augustus*, built in Boston in 1721. Both men were well known for their careful work.[4] Lewis Evans's figures for the latitudes

---

3. Brown, *Story of Maps*, p. 193.
4. Don W. Thomson, *Men and Meridians: The History of Surveying and Mapping in Canada*, 3 vols. (Ottawa, 1966–67), 1:84 and 116.

of three places in Pennsylvania, Sandy Hook, and Oswego were used. The latter two may have originated with Colden, who assisted Evans in the New York portion of his map.[5] James Logan supplied the figures for Philadelphia and Colonel Fry for Ray's Town and Fort du Quesne and the source of the Potomac. For Nova Scotia, Mitchell had latitudes observed by Charles Morris, a native Bostonian, who had been sent there to survey in 1745 by the Massachusetts governor, William Shirley.[6] The careful observations of this area, made in a hydrographic survey of the coast by Joseph Bernard, Marquis de Chabert, in 1750–51,[7] were not available for the first issue of Mitchell's map. With the second issue, he included some of Chabert's information and made some few corrections. For some places, Mitchell could discover no accurate observations of latitude: Fort Antibis, Montreal, Fort Frontenac, Niagara, Detroit, Cherokee, Creeke, Fort Moore, etc. Typical of his insurmountable problem was Niagara's situation, which varied one whole degree: 43° to 44°—in other words, fifty-eight miles!

As mentioned before, longitudinal accuracy was then quite impossible, but had improved with the use of Harrison's clocks. As New York's location had been "pretty well determined by Dr. Bradley," Mitchell considered reckonings taken in "Short Runs & fair Winds" fairly reliable in giving the longitudinal difference between it and the coast to the south. Never before had there been any longitudinal observations in this area. He had some doubts about the accuracy of the South Carolina coast since the currents there are strong and unpredictable. The same type of strong currents in northern waters, around Cape Race and Cape Sable, posed the same problem. To this is added the strong tides at the Bay of Fundy. Mitchell wrote, "As the Coast is bold into these Northern Seas, they observe many Bearings and Distances of Places along Shoare, which if Justly taken would determine their true Situation more right than any thing. . . . Hence I have been at the tedious pains to Calculate the Latitudes & Longitudes to each Bearing & Distance observed in our Ships of War, taking the mean of several Observations as above, and allowing the Variation degree set down to each."

5. Henry M. Stevens, *Lewis Evans, His Map of the British Middle Colonies in America, A Comparative Account of Eighteen Different Editions Published between 1755 and 1814* (London, 1920), p. 2.

6. Thomson, *Men and Meridians*, 1:117.

7. Ibid., 1:89.

When one considers the innumerable problems of map makers today, it is astonishing that anyone had the courage to attempt a map 225 years ago. Lloyd Brown has recently noted that "a geometrical network of parallels of latitude and meridians of longitude spaced at intervals of one degree of arc" will provide 16,020 points where latitude and longitude intersect over the world's land surface. In 1740, the German astronomer, Johann Gabiel Doppelmayr, considered that only 116 had been correctly located. Even by 1817, there were only 6,000, most of which were in Europe. Brown writes "Running a line 58 miles long involves, among other things, over-the-horizon surveying (geodesy), taking into consideration the curvature of the earth and numerous other complicating factors." Mitchell was certainly aware of some of these weaknesses in eighteenth-century surveying. When he mentioned Gist's surveys of Fort du Quesne's location in comparison to that of Hazen, he referred to an allowance for the height of mountains. Even today there are thirteen different standards recognized internationally.[8] However, Gist's journals were of immense value to Mitchell for he carefully noted distances and courses every four or five miles which gave a truer approximation of places such as Logs Town and the Falls of the Ohio than had been known.

Christopher Gist, a Maryland surveyor's son, had been employed by the Ohio Company in 1750 to explore and survey the area around the Ohio River. He had made a second expedition in 1751–52 to investigate the possibilities of the southern bank of the river since the hostile Indians made settlement on the northern side impossible. One of Gist's friends was George Mercer, of Stafford County. It was to him that Gist attributed the description of an Indian festival which he included in his journal.[9] Both Mercer and his father, John Mercer, were members of the Ohio Company. One of the two made a copy of Gist's journal and sent it to Mitchell, knowing of what value it would be to him.[10]

About the same time, a map of some of this area was received by the

8. Brown, *Story of Maps*, pp. 10–11.

9. J. Stoddard Johnston, *First Explorations of Kentucky*, Filson Club Publications #13 (Louisville, 1898), pp. 85–103, 164.

10. Hazel Shields Garrison, "Letter of Lewis Evans, January 25, 1756," Notes & Documents, *Pennsylvania Magazine of History and Biography* 59 (July 1933):297. Garrison thinks that Mercer was probably Dr. Hugh Mercer, for whom Mercersburg, Pennsylvania, was named, although Johnston and Morton (*Colonial Virginia*, 2:652) seem certain that it was George Mercer.

lords commissioners. It was an enclosure in Dinwiddie's letter to them on 29 January 1754.[11] The previous October, the Virginia governor had sent young Major Washington to protest the French encroachments. The journal that he kept on the trip was printed in Williamsburg and manuscript copies went to England, along with a map showing the Ohio River and its tributaries. It also included the trail connecting the Potomac with the Ohio, various settlements, of which one was Gist's, "Log's Town," Venango, the village of Queen Aliquippa, and other places which Mitchell added to his map. It is a delightful example of the cartographer's art and lay undiscovered in the Public Record Office archives in London for almost 175 years, until it was found by Worthington Chauncey Ford.[12]

When fighting with the French and Indians broke out on the Virginia frontier in the late spring of 1754, Colonel Washington was dispatched to the Ohio Valley with a small force, which included Lieutenant George Mercer. The campaign was anything but successful. Later, Mercer sent back to England a map of the Ohio River Valley, including northern Virginia. On it are his manuscript notes, describing the movements of his company and of Gist's.[13] It probably arrived too late to be of any help to Mitchell in compiling his map although it may have been of some assistance.

Mitchell gave symbols for cities, towns, and villages, differentiating between the European ones and those of the Indians. Forts and fortifications were similarly indicated. Numbers denoted "the Variation of the Compass westerly with the years in which it was observed. no Date supposes the present time." Also given were the scales in English miles for latitude and degree, the number of English sea leagues to a degree as well as the French common league and the Dutch. Although Mitchell's map is large, three and a half by six feet, and does not include much of western North America, yet the eastern coastal area and some of the Ohio River country are so detailed that it is almost impossible to read.

Mitchell wanted to plot not only cities, towns, and villages, but also roads. These are of more than passing interest as they give indications

11. C.O. 5/14 f. 112, PRO.

12. Ford, "Washington's Map of the Ohio," *Massachusetts Historical Society Proceedings* 61 (1927–28):71–79.

13. "#12 shows the Ohio River Valley, and northern Va. with MSS notes by Hugh[?] Mercer on his Company's movements & Chr. Gists." Lawrence Martin, ed., *The George Washington Atlas* (Washington, 1932).

of the pattern of travel, the range of settlement, and the reaching out
into the wilderness by the scouts and traders. In the region that Mitchell knew best was the ancient trade route to Appomattox which continued on in a southwesterly direction. It was joined at Augusta by a
road marked "Route of Coll. Welch to the Mississippi since followed
by our traders 250 mi." There were roads from Fredericksburg to
Winchester and Alexandria, and to Williamsburg. This last continued
to Albemarle Sound, Beaufort, New Bern, Cape Fear, Charles Town,
Savannah, and on to St. Augustine, 140 miles beyond. Even there,
there could be found a trail to the west, ending at Pensacola. Another
road from Fredericksburg went to Fort Tobacco, Urbanna, Gloucester
Court House, Yorktown, Norfolk, and Edenton. There was a road
from Yorktown to Williamsburg and one from Chesterfield Court
House to Appomattox and west through Bedford to Otter River and
New River. Down the Valley of Virginia, a long established road took
settlers and traders along many rivers, the Jackson, the Calf Pasture,
the Cow Pasture, the Staunton, the Banister, and the Dan, ending
eventually in North Carolina. This was one of the roads that Bartram
used. Mitchell marked it "well settled," even the mountains along the
Holston River. From Keeowe a road led east to Charles Town. In the
northwest quadrant of Virginia lay "Gist's Route-Traders' Road," on
which was marked "Lower Shawnoah, an English factory 400 M. from
the Forks by Water; the Ohio is ¾ mi. Broad, deep & smooth with 5
or 6 feet water to the Forks." From Shawnoah there was also a road to
Logs Town from which branched another at Hockhocken going directly west to join Gist's route.

Pennsylvania, Maryland, and New York did not lack for roads either.
From Philadelphia, one could go west to Lancaster and south from
there to Winchester, in Virginia, or directly south to Fredericksburg
and Alexandria. There was a road to New Town, Annapolis, and the
Eastern Shore through Charles County, with a ferry across the Chesapeake to Stratford, Virginia. Going north from Philadelphia, the road
followed the Delaware River, eventually arriving at New York City.
There, a road followed the Hudson River north to Boston and Port-
land. New England's many small towns are shown along the Mer-
rimack and Connecticut Rivers and the Maine coast. It was well
populated, too, around many of the lakes: Winnipesaukee, George,
Champlain, and Sunapee. Unfortunately, the scope of his map limited

the number of roads which Mitchell would show in the crowded New England area.

In the section showing Louisiana, Mitchell marked the place where Ferdinand de Soto had discovered the Mississippi River: Ozier Point or Old Kappa. A road going east and west led to "Mexico and Mines of St. Barbeton." Bisecting this and going northwest was the "Road to New Mexico," south of which were "Wandering Savage Indians." The Colorado or Cane River and the Guadeloupe River as well as others are shown flowing into the Gulf of Mexico. The spot where La Salle settled in 1685 and the place where he was killed two years later are both noted. Considering the number of years the French had been in this general area, it was very poorly mapped. There are few details and many lakes in the vicinity of New Orleans have been omitted entirely.

For the land west of the Mississippi, Mitchell could find few descriptions and little information. He noted that the "Missouri River is reckoned to run westward to the Mountains of New Mexico as far as the Ohio does Eastwards." He could do little but list the various Indian tribes inhabiting the Missouri's environs: the Sioux, the Nadouesians, the Panis "with 40 Villages." For the Padoucas River, a Missouri tributary, Mitchell said "The Heads & Sources of these Rivers, and Country beyond the Bounds of this Map, are not well known." Where the river Hocheton joined the Mississippi, Mitchell remarked "Thus far the Mississippi has been ascended." He likewise noted that the source had not been discovered. Below the Cachia River is a road marked "Route of the French to the Western Indians." Still further south is an area of "Extensive Meadows full of Buffaloes." The Osages roamed south of here, where there was a "Country full of Mines." Southeast of the Illinois River was a copper mine and slightly down the Mississippi the "Mines of Marameg which gave rise to the famous Mississippi Scheme of 1719." The land south of the Ohio was "A Fine and Fertile Countrey of great Extent, by Accounts of the Indians and our People," Mitchell wrote. The same promising note is made about western Georgia which was inhabited by the Creeks and Alabamas.

When Mitchell drew the lands of New France, south and west of Hudson Bay, he said, "The long and Barbarous Names lately given to some of these Northern Parts of Canada and the Lakes we have not inserted, as they are of no use and uncertain Authority." He did show the

Lakes Erie and Huron inhabited by the Messesagues, who had been subdued by the Iroquois. The latter tribe was indeed warlike and had also subjugated the "Antient Hurons," who had been expelled. There were other tribes as well who had succumbed to the Iroquois. The southern boundary of Canada had the note that the limits were "according to De L'Isle, Du Fer, and other Geographers." In Nova Scotia, he delineated a few roads and many small towns along the coast. In Newfoundland, he remarked that "Cape of Point Rich." had been omitted entirely in the French maps, "seemingly because it is within the Bounds of their Privilege of Fishing which is extended from hence North round to Cape Bonavista." Little evidence of any towns is given.

In the upper lefthand corner, Mitchell inserted a new map of Hudson's Bay and Labrador, which had been recently surveyed. He said that "The Distance from Hudson's Bay to the South Sea appears from the late Discoveries of the Russians to be about 450 Leagues which makes a North-West Passage that way very improbable. . . . If there is a N. West Passage, it appears to be through one of these Inlets."

Since the primary purpose of the map from the government's viewpoint was to clearly delineate British claims in North America, Mitchell was meticulous in emphasizing these. To the north, he marked the "Bounds of Virginia and New England by Charters May 23, 1609 and Novr. 3, 1620, extending from Sea to Sea out of which our other Colonies were granted." This boundary is not very different from the present U.S.-Canadian border. South of this, the English claim, extending from the Atlantic Ocean to the Mississippi as far south as South Carolina, depended upon the land originally belonging to the Indians of the Six Nations. They had sold it to the English Crown in 1701 and had renewed the deed of sale in 1720 and 1744. It followed the 49th parallel along the St. Lawrence River. Mitchell marked it the "Extent & Limits of Conquests & Settlements before the Encroachment on Crown Point." On the southern shore of Lake Oswego, or Erie, he wrote Sandoski "usurped by the French 1751." Further west on the Miami River, he marked another fort taken over by the French. It was not far from Logs Town between Beaver and Buffalo creeks, where they join the Ohio. This had only been recently built by the English.

The whole general area from Niagara south and from Fort du Quesne, now Pittsburgh, west, lying on both sides of the Ohio River all the way to the Illinois River, was being desperately contested by France and England. The Six Nations had based their claim upon their subjection of the original Indian owners in 1672. The other tribes who then settled there were mainly the Shannoes, the Mohicans, and the Delawares, all of whom had long been friendly to the English. They were now known as the Ohio Indians. Much of this territory was labeled Virginia. In bolstering this claim by actual possession, Mitchell noted the first Virginia settlement on the Ohio River in 1725 at Allegheny, "Since which they have extended their Settlements from Shenango to Pickawillany." South of the Ohio, on the Cumberland River in what is now Kentucky, as previously mentioned, Mitchell had noted "Walker's, the Extent of the English Settlements 1750." It was Walker who gave the name Cumberland to the gap, river, and mountains in honor of George II's son, William Augustus, Duke of Cumberland, whom he had met in London.[14] Mitchell's was probably the first map to show the new name of the river.[15]

Below the "River of the Cherokees," (today's Tennessee River?), Mitchell remarked that this land to the south of the Six Nations' boundaries, had belonged to the Cherokees. They had "surrendered" it to the British "at Westminister in 1729." Further south, there were English towns and factories and the land of the Chickasaws "in Alliance and Subjection to the English." This is today's Georgia and Colonel Welch's and the traders' route lay through Augusta. The Creek territory showed English factories and settlements in many of their more important towns except Albamas "which was usurped by the French in 1715, but established by the English 28 Years before." Even when the French had been well settled for many decades, Mitchell had little compunction about pressing English claims. Thus, he marked the English Reaches which he had mentioned in his report to the board, on the southern part of the Mississippi River.

He went into great detail substantiating English claims in an article on the Batts and Fallam journal which he probably wrote about the time that he completed the map.[16] It was found among Sir Hans Sloane's collection of Royal Society papers, but there is no indication

14. Morton, *Colonial Virginia*, 2:575–76.

15. Emerson D. Fite and Archibald Freeman, *A Book of Old Maps Delineating American History* (New York, 1969, Dover Publications, originally published 1926), p. 183.

16. B.M. Sloane MSS 4452, f. 3.

in the society's journals that Mitchell ever gave the talk. Unlike the French, the English explorers had been negligent in printing their discoveries which naturally weakened English claims. The Society was certainly cognizant of the Batts and Fallam journal as the Reverend John Clayton had given them a copy and there was one by Dr. Daniel Coxe in the archives of the Board of Trade, now in the Public Record Office. Mitchell made a definite point that Robert Beverley, "a gentleman of note & Distinction," had given a brief account of these early discoveries in his history published in 1705, even if the Royal Society had not published it. It had assumed major importance as this Virginia expedition sent out by the trader Abraham Wood in 1671 preceded that of La Salle by nine years and the French were basing their claims on La Salle. It was far from the first western exploration by the English which had begun with Wood's and Edward Bland's travels to New Britain in 1650, and evidence of their prior expeditions as noted by Batts and Fallam. They crossed the Alleghenies and went as far as Wood River, part of the Ohio River watershed. They claimed all the land from there to the Mississippi for the British Crown.[17]

Mitchell's paper makes interesting reading. He noted that the expedition had started from Appomattox Town and followed the traders' route to the Wood River settlements shown on his map. He remarked that, while the explorers referred to Sapony River, this was the Staunton, which had been named in honor of Lady Gooch. Just after the running of the boundary line between Virginia and North Carolina, Mitchell said that the Sapony tribe had been removed southwards to the Pedee River as could be seen on Edward Moseley's 1733 map of North Carolina. The body of water that the explorers saw from the mountaintop near the Wood River and thought to be a sea, Mitchell believed was actually the same river further down. He based his assumption on a study of Gist's journal which indicated that he crossed the route of the earlier explorers at this point, viewed the same water, and later found it to be the Wood River. The salt-making Indians who lived

17. There are several printed versions of the Batts & Fallam expedition: Berthold Fernow, *Ohio Valley in Colonial Days* (Albany, 1890), pp. 220–29; *William and Mary Quarterly*, 1st ser. 15 (1907):234–41; D. I. Bushnell, Jr., "Virginia From Early Records," *American Anthropologist* 9 (1907):45–56; C. W. Alvord and Lee Bidgood, *The First Explorations of the Trans-Allegheny Region by the Virginians, 1650–1674* (Cleveland, 1912), pp. 183–95; Berkeley & Berkeley, *The Reverend John Clayton*, pp. 68–77; Dr. Coxe's version was published in *New York Colonial Documents* (Albany, 1853–87), 3:193–97.

on the "Great Water" beyond, about whom Batts and Fallam were told, Mitchell identified as the Chawanoes, who shortly afterwards were subjugated by the Iroquois. The "Great Water" undoubtedly was the Mississippi "which is so called from Mescha Ceke, two words in the Indians language that signify the *Great River* or *Water*." The distance of 338 miles which the expedition traveled was misleading and would make Wood River much farther west than it was known to be from the surveys made recently for the boundary line. This could be accounted for by their necessarily circuitous route. An actual straight line distance would measure 140 miles from Appomattox to Wood River. The present road, as shown on Mitchell's map, measured 160 miles between the two spots. Mitchell also referred to the evidence of the old expeditions sent out by Colonel Wood between 1654 and 1664: "These Discoveries are the more interesting at this Time, As those Parts are now claimed by the French merely & solely upon a frivolous Pretext of a prior Discovery by Mr. *La Salle* in 1680, who built the Fort of *Crevecœur* on or below the Lake *Pimiteoui*, in that year which seems to be the Lake Petite alluded to in the Extract of Mr. Clayton's Letter from a very imperfect Knowledge of it; which Lake upon the River Illinois is not less perhaps than a thousand miles beyond or to the westward of Fort *du Quesne* & the other places the French claim on the River Ohio in consequence of that Discovery as they call it."

Mitchell stated that the English had additional bases for validating their claims. In 1678, a group from New England had explored westward to the Mississippi and even beyond it. This was the area which La Salle claimed two years later. In fact, he said, the French, hearing of the vast western lands from the Indians who had accompanied the English, had employed them as guides.

There were other explorations in addition to these, Mitchell said. He referred to Spotswood's Golden Horseshoe expedition in 1714 over the Appalachians and the good road resulting. Mitchell, himself, had actual knowledge of this from talking to some of the men who had been with the governor. Not long after this, many settlements were started in the Valley of Virginia, particularly to the north, towards the Ohio River, extending to Logs Town "long before the later Encroachments & usurpations of the French there." In fact, Pennsylvanians, too, had made settlements in that area as early as 1725, as exhibited in various accounts, including the 1754 Treaty with the Indians at Albany. In

1736, this land had been surveyed as far as the source of the Potomac River. Salley and his group (1742), whose journals he had perused, went all the way to the Mississippi and down it. Then, too, the Ohio Company had offered to settle the lands where the Ohio River joined the Mississippi and even to defend it at their own expense. The government refused, as they "have alwaies prudently thought it more expedient to continue their settlements contiguous to one another than to suffer them to be straggling up & down in remote & uncultivated Desarts, as we see the French have done, in order thereby to seem to occupy a greater Extent of Territory, which in effect they hardly occupy any at all."

Perhaps Mitchell's most telling argument was his emphasis upon the English purchase of Indian land, some of which they had bought "three several times." In 1749, the English established a settlement at Pickawillaney, the Twightwee Indian town where lived George Croghan and other traders. This was five hundred miles west of Fort du Quesne. This they did at the Indians' own request made at the Treaty of Lancaster on 22 July 1749, Mitchell said. He ended his paper with a summary:

By this means we had several settlements all along the River *Ohio*, & all over the Countrey between that River & Lake Erie, & that long before the French ever set a foot upon it, or knew any thing about it, but by Hearsay. And on the South side of the *Ohio*, we are not only well settled on *Wood* River, that is described in this Journal, but likewise on Holston River that lies upwards of 150 miles to the westward of the Place that these People discovered on Wood River in 1671; and again on Cumberland River that lies as much farther to the westward of that; all which Places & Settlements you will see marked in our map above-mentioned.

As Mitchell neared completion of his map, interest in it was already apparent on both sides of the Atlantic. Franklin, who had encouraged the doctor's cartographic bent by sending him Evans's first Pennsylvania map, wrote to Richard Jackson in England on 12 December 1754: "We have a new Map going forward in Pensilvania, of the Western Country, or back Parts of our Province, and Virginia, and the Ohio and Lakes, &c. by Lewis Evans, who is for that purpose furnished with all the Materials our Country affords, and the Assembly have to encourage him given £50 towards the Expence. When that is done, Dr.

Mitchel's Map may be something improv'd from it, and I suppose it will be publish'd before spring. If the Dr's Map should afterwards be printed, I make no doubts but great Numbers would sell in America." By June, Franklin wrote to Collinson that he was anxious to see the map and that he would be glad to sell some for Mitchell.[18]

On 13 February 1755, the first issue of the first edition of the map was officially published.[19] It was engraved by Thomas Kitchin (1718–84), supposed to have been one of the more gifted men in that profession, but some errors crept in. Although little is known of Kitchin's life, the many maps which he drew are justifiably famous and he became "Hydrographer to his Majesty" by 1777, if not earlier.[20] In 1758, he drew a map of Connecticut, using Mitchell's, but added county and town lines.[21]

The publisher of Mitchell's map was the Scot, Andrew Millar, whose press had brought out the translation of Henckel's *Pyritologia*. Millar's name and address (Catherine Street) were misspelled in the first issue but these mistakes were shortly corrected in a new issue brought out the same year. One of Millar's publications was Dr. Johnson's *Dictionary* and of him Boswell said: "though himself no great judge of literature, has good sense enough to have for his friends very able men to give him their opinion and advice in the purchase of copy-right, the consequence of which was his acquiring a very large fortune with great liberality." In spite of this, he was considered very generous to authors themselves. Dr. Johnson remarked, "I respect Millar, Sir; he has raised the price of literature."[22]

Mitchell's completed map was not only large enough to show details

18. *Papers of Franklin*, 5:447–48; 26 June 1755, ibid., 6:88.

19. Surrounded by a fanciful and elaborate cartouche, the map title reads: *A Map of the British and French Dominions in North America With the Roads, Distances, Limits, and Extent of the Settlements, Humbly Inscribed to the Right Honourable The Earl of Halifax, And the Other Right Honourable The Lords Commissioners for Trade & Plantations, By Their Lordships Most Obliged and Very Humble Servant Jno. Mitchell.* There seems to be some difference of opinion as to the exact size of the map. Fite and Freeman record the second edition as being 40 x 72 inches (*A Book of Old Maps*, p. 181) while Dr. Walter W. Ristow states that it is "approximately 52 by 75 inches" (*A la Carte: Selected Papers on Maps and Atlases*, p. 107). In any event, because of its magnitude, the map was engraved in eight sheets, with a scale of approximately 32 miles to an inch.

20. Fite & Freeman, *A Book of Old Maps*, p. 181; Ronald Vere Tooley, *Maps and Map-makers* (London, 1952), p. 56.

21. Edmund Thompson, *Maps of Connecticut* (Windham, Conn., 1940), p. 33.

22. Nichols, *Literary Anecdotes*, 3:386–88, 441.

impossible in a smaller one, but was valuable in that it incorporated many of the latest and best colonial maps. Gipson is almost certain that Mitchell was allowed the use of John Patten's draught of the Ohio River.[23] Patten was an Indian trader in that area and his map was considered highly accurate. Richard Peters sent it to Thomas Penn with the suggestion that Lord Halifax should see it. This was probably one of those which Penn said that he showed to Mitchell. Evans's depiction of the Ohio River was so regular that Penn remarked that it was "much straighter than an intelligent Indian trader had it down, in a Draft he gave me from his own observations."[24] For Pennsylvania, Mitchell had used Evans's earlier map but did not have the benefit of his more recent and improved version. He had made good use of the Fry-Jefferson map.

Further south, he relied on a map made by Colonel John Barnwell by 1721, according to Dr. William P. Cumming. It was undoubtedly Catesby who had told Mitchell of the manuscript map, for he had used it himself in the preparation of his own map. Dr. Cumming adds that Mitchell was the first one to print the "valuable data collected by Barnwell over thirty years before."[25] As a result, Cumming said, "from the Appalachian region to the Mississippi, Mitchell's map marks a great advance in the printed cartographical knowledge. For the Atlantic coastal settlements Mitchell makes use of the Barnwell map, but more sparingly, for he evidently had later and fuller sources of information. Details of creeks, and their names, new settlements, and the position of roads for the 'improved part' of Carolina are fuller than in any other preserved map of this date and posit a use of the written reports to the Board of Trade to which he had access."[26]

Mitchell used Moseley's 1753 map for North Carolina but that area lacks detail. Cumming continued, "Some details are found which show that he does not rely even here upon printed maps; 'Brushy Mountains' is moved to the southwest slightly, and 'Pilot Mountain,' to the west of the Yadkin (and present Winston-Salem), is given. . . . The mountains of southwestern North Carolina and Tennessee are unimproved; he uses the detailed but faulty conception of the Barnwell

23. Gipson, *Lewis Evans*, pp. 58–61.

24. Penn to Richard Peters, 25 October 1755, Penn Letter Book, 4:177, HSP.

25. William P. Cumming, *The Southeast in Early Maps* (Princeton, 1958), p. 47. Cumming adds that in using so much of Barnwell's material, Mitchell preserved much of it, which has since become illegible on the original Barnwell map (ibid., p. 224).

26. Ibid., p 48.

map, in which the Tennessee River does not flow far enough south." Florida was only drawn to the 28th parallel. Cumming thinks that Mitchell was "evidently puzzled by the maps, following Nairne's 1711 map, which breaks southern Florida up into a kind of archipelago. This error is not given in Barnwell's map." On the other hand, Cumming said that it was one of the first times that Kissimee River appeared on a printed map.[27]

Among Mitchell's friends and acquaintances, there was great excitement. In England, Richard Jackson, a member of the Inner Temple and friend of Collinson, wrote to Jared Eliot in Connecticut that he would send the map the minute it was published, which would probably insure that Eliot would have the first one in North America. Jackson was as good as his word and shipped off a copy three weeks before official publication. Because of his haste it was neither colored nor on canvas. He wrote to Eliot that Mitchell

has had all the assistance the Board of Trade were capable of giving him but this makes but a small part of what his industry has procured for his purpose. As I have been a good deal conversant in Maps in general and am pretty well acquainted with America in Particular, I have some reason to assure you, that whereas till now we have had nothing that has deserved the name of a Map of America, this is superior to most of ye best Improved Maps of Europe. Yet you will not find it perhaps quite so perfect in New England as ye author wd. have made it had he been able to have got a sight of Dr. Douglas' Map of that Country, which ye Doctor's Directions in his will preventing his seeing.

In regard to the New England area, he added a note in his letter to Eliot on 13 August: "You will observe by Dr. Mitchels Ingravers Car[e]lessness notwithstanding the great pains ye Dr. took a few errors; among the[m] was the town of Worcester in Massachusetts is called Leicester so there are 2 Leicesters."[28]

A week after the map's publication, Thomas Penn wrote to the Reverend Richard Peters: "Dr. Mitchel is drawing a Map of North America here for several of which I shall subscribe, he has taken great pains, and

27. Ibid., pp. 47–49.
28. Carrier, "Dr. John Mitchell," *American Historical Association Report*, 1 (1918):207. The statement concerning Dr. William Douglass (1691–1752) is puzzling for his *Plan of the British Dominions of New England . . . Composed from Actual Surveys* was published by his executors in 1753.

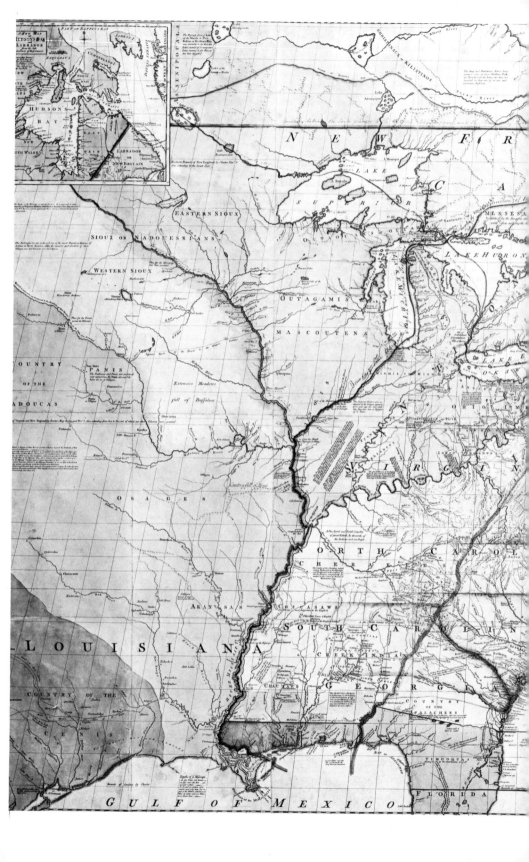

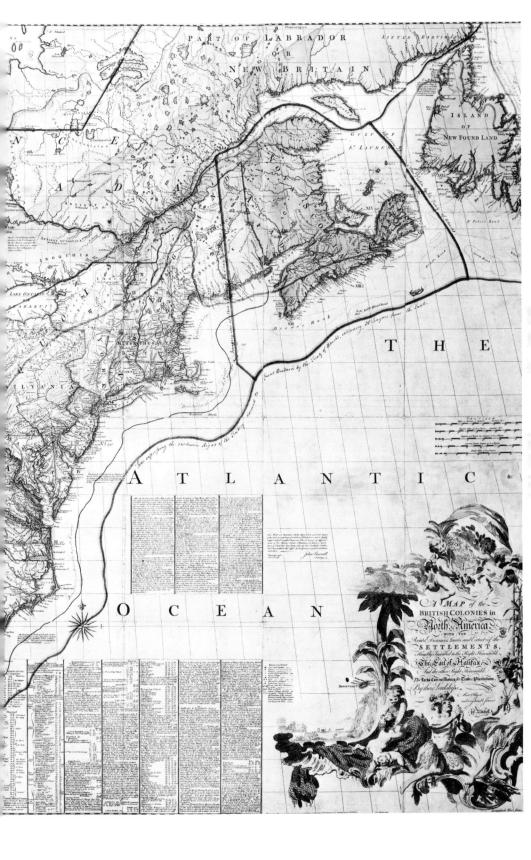

has been assisted by all the Drafts of the Board of Trade, and those of
several private people, what I have communicated to him, he lays down
all the principal Towns, Roads, distances, Rivers, etc. in our Colonys
that can be brought into Size—I shall be very pleased to see a better
of the Western frontiers, Maryland and Virginia, by Lewis Evans, and
desire you will send me half a dozen of them, and as many of Joshua
Fisher's Charts of the Bay. . . . Evans should have his Map printed
here."[29] Evans's map was published in London by Dodsley and pirated
by Kitchin not long after. However, Mitchell's map had long been
out, since the engraving of Evans's map, begun in November, 1754,
was not finished until the following June.[30]

Even France learned of Mitchell's map shortly after publication. Dr.
Matthew Maty mentioned it in his column, "From London," which
appeared in the *Journal Britannique*. He wrote thus for the March–April
issue:

A production, which at all times would have been well received, but which
deserves an especial prize in the present circumstances, is the new *Map of the
French and English Empires in North America, by Dr. Mitchell, Physician from
Virginia and Member of the Royal Society of London*. This Map is comprised of
eight sheets of very fine paper, & sells for a guinea in sheets, and a guinea
and a half colored & attached to rollers. It is based not only on the best observations, maps & surveys which have only just appeared here, but also on
various original Memoires which are found in the bureaus. This Map is very
detailed, & one can find there the roads which cross this great Continent.
The Author appears to be only determined on the best authorities and one
finds as well the case of his exactness and fidelity. Meanwhile, it seems that
two things should still be asked of him: the first would be an analytic note
on the case of those of Mr. Danville, which would give in detail the parts
which the Author has given in his work, & the reasons which he had had for
the choice which he has made; the second, would be a map which resembled
a single sheet, or even less, of the preceding eight sheets, which would make
it easier to judge the nearness and the boundaries of the various provinces.[31]

Little time was lost by the Board of Trade in forwarding copies of
Mitchell's map to all the provincial governors. William Alexander,

29. Penn Letter Book, 4:177, HSP.
30. Gipson, *Lewis Evans*, p. 63; Stevens, *Lewis Evans, His Map*, p. 14.
31. Copies of the *Journal Brittanique* were kindly loaned to the authors by Yale University Library.

secretary to Governor William Shirley for the Niagara expedition, ordered the best maps which he could find for the army. These included both Mitchell's and Evans's. As he was a surveyor and cartographer in a small way, he was an excellent judge of such things. The map became highly important to the colonies that spring as the scattered skirmishes with the French of the previous year were developing into a full-scale war.[32] As this came about, the general public was curious about the location of the British army's actions being reported in the papers. Cumming says, "The value of Mitchell's map was immediately recognized by other cartographers. Not only were foreign editions made of the map but also imitations without acknowledgment by European geographers appeared. Regional maps, such as those of the southern district in the *London Magazine* in 1755 and in *The American Gazetteer* in 1762, used Mitchell as their source."[33]

Reports of the popularity of the map seeped back to the colonies. Penn wrote to Peters that it was "esteemed here to be the best yet made."[34] Franklin proudly wrote to Eliot, "The Mitchell who made the Map, is our Dr. Mitchell."[35] In April, Collinson wrote to Linnaeus:

You desire to know our botanical people. The first in rank is the Right hon. the Earl of Bute. He is a perfect master of your method; by his letter to me you will see his sentiments, and those of another learned Botanist, on your *Species Plantarum*. Then there is Mr. Watson, Mr. Ellis, Mr. Ehret, Mr. Miller, Dr. Willmer, Dr. Mitchel, Dr. Martyn. These all are well skilled in your plan; and there are others. But we have great numbers of Nobility and Gentry that know plants very well but yet do not make botanic science their peculiar study.

Dr. Mitchel has left Botany for some time, and has wholly employed himself in making a map, or chart, of all North America, which is now published in eight large sheets for a guinea, and coloured for a guinea and a half. It is the most perfect of any before published, and is universally approved. He will get a good sum of money by it, which he deserves, for the immense labour and pains he has taken to perfect it.[36]

---

32. Theodore Thayer, "The Army Contractors for the Niagara Campaign, 1755–56," *William and Mary Quarterly* 3d ser. 14 (January 1957):37.

33. Cumming, *The Southeast in Early Maps*, p. 49.

34. 14 August 1755, Thomas Penn Letter Book, 4:142, HSP.

35. 31 August 1755, *Papers of Franklin*, 5:173.

36. 10 April 1755, CLO 1:33–34.

It is quite impossible to arrive at an actual figure in attempting to analyze Mitchell's income from the map. There is no record of his arrangement with Millar, so it is not known whether he sold the map rights to him or retained them himself. The only documented evidence there is of any transactions between the two men is the payment of £110 to Mitchell by Millar on 19 August 1755.[37]

It was not long before other cartographers took note of Mitchell's map. Some blandly based their own maps on his without any acknowledgment. Both G. Robert de Vangoudy and J. B. d'Anville published such maps the same year.[38] An anonymous publication, printed in Dublin, in 1756, was: *A Description of the English and French Territories in North America . . . Done from the Newest Maps published in London. And compared with Dr. Mitchell's, F.R.S. and every Omission carefully supplied from it.* The suspicion remains that the use of Mitchell's name in the title was purely a selling point, since there is no further reference to him.[39]

In 1755, R. &. J. Dodsley published *The Present State of North America* which appeared in two editions as well as one reprinted in Boston. Sabin remarked that it was "Principally taken from Dumont's *Histoire et Commerce des Colonies Anglaises.*"[40] According to the British Museum, the author was Ellis Huske, an Englishman who settled in New Hampshire and later moved to Boston where he became the publisher of the *Boston Weekly Postboy* as postmaster. (Some authorities consider Huske's son, John, to be the author.) Huske was an enthusiastic admirer of Mitchell's work and endorsed it wholeheartedly. He wrote:

But the French Geographers, D'Lisle, Du Fur, &c. have in their late Maps limited their Rights Northward, to a South West Line they have drawn from *Montreal* to Lake *Toronto*, where they also bound them to the westward, and allow them only the Country between this line and our Settlements. However, to point out the mistakes, or rather designed Encroachments of the maps of *America* published in *France*, of late Years by Authority, would be almost to copy the whole of them. Therefore it must give every

37. Account of Andrew Millar, Ledger 30, Coutts & Company Archives.
38. Cumming, *The Southeast in Early Maps*, p. 82n.
39. Map Division, British Museum.
40. Joseph Sabin, *A Dictionary of Books Relating to America*, 27 vols. (New York, 1885), 9:15–16.

Briton great Pleasure to see our Countryman Dr. Mitchel, F.R.S. detecting their Mistakes and designed Encroachments, and almost wholly restoring us to our just Rights and Possessions, as far as paper will admit of it, in his most elaborate and excellent Map of North-America just published; which deserves the warmest Thanks and Countenance from every good Subject in his Majesty's Dominions."[41]

In a footnote, he added, "Most, if not all, our maps also, preceding that by Dr. Mitchell, are very erroneous and injurious to his *Majesty's* Rights; and even the *Doctor* has not confined *Canada*, or *New-France*, and *Spanish Florida*, to their just Limits."[42]

There were definite exceptions to the warm reception of Mitchell's map. In 1755, Thomas Jefferys, Geographer to the Prince of Wales, brought out a publication entitled *Explanation For the New Map of Nova Scotia and Cape Britain, with the Adjacent Parts of New England and Canada*. The author was anonymous but is now known to have been John Green, alias Braddock Mead, a very remarkable character.[43] J. B. Hartley says Jefferys "probably owed a great deal to Green. Much of his best work appeared in this period."[44] His growing reputation was known in America and Fry and Jefferson and De Brahm all sent their maps to Jefferys for engraving.

Green was most specific in pointing out what he considered to be Mitchell's errors:

While I am writing this there is published a *New Map of the British and French Dominions in North America*, by Dr. Mitchel: From which ours differs much in many Respects; and particularly in the Part now under Consideration, especially the Coast from the North-entrance of *Kanso Gut* to *Port Royal*. This last Place is put 10 Minutes more South than in ours; and the first 10 Minutes more North, after Mr. *Robert*. Cape *Sambro* is situated 13 Minutes too low; and those of *Kanso* and *Sable* being placed four too high, the South-

---

41. Huske, *The Present State*, p. 27.

42. Ibid., p. 43.

43. See G. R. Crone, "John Green, Notes on a Neglected Eighteenth Century Geographer and Cartographer," *Imago Mundi* 6 (1949):85–91, and, by the same author, "Further Notes on Braddock Mead, Alias John Green, an Eighteenth Century Cartographer," ibid., 8 (1951):69–70. *The Whole Case and Proceedings in Relation to Bridget Reading, an Heiress . . . and of Her Pretended Marriage to Braddock Mead* (London, 1730) can be seen in the British Museum.

44. "The Bankruptcy of Thomas Jefferys; an Episode in the Economic History of Eighteenth-Century Map-making," *Imago Mundi* 20 (1966):40

coast of the Peninsula, instead of hollowing in towards the Middle, as it ought to do by the Remark, as well as Observations, of Mr. *Chabert*, bellies out considerably. Besides, as the Peninsula is very narrow in that Part, the Difference of Latitude between Cape *Sambro* and *Minas* being no more than 30 Minutes, or half a Degree, 13 Minutes make it by near one half broader than it is.

As to Longitude, he makes that of Cape *Kanso* 17 Minutes, and that of Cape *Sable* 1 Degree 5 Minutes, too much. The other Differences, with regard to the Figure of the Coasts, as well as Situation of Places in *Nova Scotia*, may be seen by comparing the Maps together, and inspecting the annexed Table; where our Work is supported by the many Observations made in these Parts by Mess. *Blackmore* and *Chabert* (especially this latter), as well as those of Mr. *Morris*; of which only, the Author of the New Map of *North America* seems to have made Use.

I judged it necessary to say thus much, to obviate any Objections which might be started against this Map, on account of its disagreeing so considerably with the other.[45]

The table to which Mead referred was most detailed. In it he gave the latitude and longitude for a number of cities and locations in this area, as given by various charts and cartographers: Southack, Durrell, Popple, Bellin, Danville (d'Anville), Robert, Blackmore, Chabert, and Mitchell, all compared with his own. In a final reference to Mitchell, he wrote "as that Gentleman has produced no Vouchers to support his performance, I presume what I have done that way will sufficiently justify mine."[46] Undoubtedly, Mead's criticism led Mitchell to add the several paragraphs to the second edition of his own map published in 1757. In these, he gave his references in great detail and explained how he arrived at his conclusions.[47] Mitchell's scathing remarks in regard to Blackmore were certainly in direct answer to Mead!

Today it is impossible to determine the comparative merits of Mitchell's and Mead's maps. Dr. Richard W. Stephenson, Head of the Reference and Bibliography Section of the Geography and Map Division, the Library of Congress, says, "We believe there is little to be gained by comparing the coordinates given in Green's table with today's ac-

45. *Explanation for the New Map of Nova Scotia and Cape Britain*, p. 18.
46. Ibid., pp. 18, 22.
47. See the second edition of Mitchell's map and Hunter Miller, *Treaties and Other International Acts of the United States of America* (Washington, 1933), 3:332.

curate calculations. In the mid-18th century, the determining of geographic coordinates was still a relatively inexact science."[48]

Recognition of the value of Mitchell's map was acknowledged by Zatta, who unembarrassedly pirated it in Venice in 1778. While Mitchell's name appears nowhere in the map's title, Zatta wrote in a note: "He who loves and knows the value of geographical things knows well the great map of the English and French possessions in North America, published by Mr. Mitchell in 1755, and worked out from many topographical drawings made by engineers who surveyed these provinces. The various copies made of it not only in France, but also in England, show clearly the approval given it, which is evident also from the fact that copies have become very rare, especially in Italy where a new edition has been desired for some time." Zatta also incorporated Mitchell's notes, rendered into Italian.[49]

At least twenty-one variations (editions and impressions) of Mitchell's map appeared between 1755 and 1791: seven in England; ten in France; two in Holland; and two in Italy. The recognized authority on the different versions of the map was the late Colonel Lawrence Martin, for many years (1924-46) chief of the Library of Congress Map Division. In the recently published book, A la Carte, Walter W. Ristow, the present chief, has compiled and edited Colonel Martin's published work on the Mitchell map. He writes: "Thanks to Lawrence Martin's diligent and persistent acquisition program, the Library of Congress has a most comprehensive collection of the several editions and impressions of Mitchell's map. For 19 of the 21 impressions the Library possesses originals and it has photocopies of the other two." A table for identifying these many versions of the map was begun by Martin and has been completed by Richard W. Stephenson. This, too, appears in A la Carte, a most attractive and interesting selection of papers on maps and atlases.[50]

48. Letter to the authors, 13 July 1971.

49. Lawrence Martin and Clara Egli, "Noteworthy Maps . . . Accessions," *Bulletin* #98, Division of Maps, LC, p. 20.

50. In the *Report of the Librarian of Congress* (Washington, 1926), Colonel Martin made perhaps the first attempt to list the various editions and to encourage a collection of them by the Library of Congress (pp. 107–22). Over the next several years, he continued this project and published his results (see ibid., 1927, pp. 90–91; 1928, p. 95; 1929, pp. 136–51; 1930, pp. 174–80; 1932, pp. 130–31). Martin, with Clara Egli, described several of the Library of Congress's acquisitions (see "Noteworthy Maps . . . Accessions,"

It would be interesting to know if Mitchell ever saw the letter that Lewis Evans wrote to his London agent, the printer Robert Dodsley, on 25 January 1756. Evans remarked on the large sale of his map in the colonies, many of which had been purchased by army officers to send to their families at home. If Dodsley had found the map equally popular in England, Evans would forward more copies. Although there were many copies of Mitchell's map in America, Evans said there were few who looked "into them for any place on our Borders."[51] He continued: "Mr. [William] Alexander, General Shirley's Secretary, who before he went to Oswego insisted I was wrong in the Longitude of it, has since told me that tho they had measured the greater Part of the Way beyond the Settlements, he does not think I am at all amiss, except in the Inflections of the Rivers, which could not be expected right, as they had never been surveyed. That though I make L. Ontario so much longer than Dr. Mitchel does, it is at least as full as long as I make it; for one of their Vessels saild West 50 Leagues and did not see Niagara. They think the Bearing and Distance of Frontenac right; but the Bay at the S East End is not so deep."[52] Evans was correct as to Oswego's longitude, but Mitchell's 168 miles was closer to the actual length of Lake Ontario (190 miles) than Evans's 240.

Perhaps what would have interested Mitchell most was Christopher Gist's reaction to the two maps, about which Evans wrote:

Since the Publication of my Map, Mr. Gist, whose Journal is made Use of in Dr. Mitchel's Map, was some Weeks in Philadelphia. When I shew'd him my Map, he could not well be persuaded at first but I had a Persual of his Draught because he could distinctly trace the far greater Number of Places he had been at, and it agreed so well with the Idea he had of the Country. I then shewed him Dr. Mitchel's Map, and his Route as laid down there-

Division of Maps, *Bulletin* 77, p. 19; 78, p. 20; 79, pp. 20–22; 80, p. 21; 81, p. 21; 92, p. 17; 93, p. 17; 94, p. 18; 95, p. 19; 96, p. 19; 97, p. 20; 98, p. 20; 99, pp. 20–21; 102, p. 20; 103, pp. 20–21; 104, p. 21; 105, pp. 21–22; 106, p. 22; 107, p. 22; 108, p. 22). Ristow, *A la Carte*, pp. 103–8. "Table for Identifying Variant Editions and Impressions of John Mitchell's Map of the British and French Dominion in North America," compiled by Richard W. Stephenson, ibid., pp. 109–13. Miller, *Treaties*, 3:331–33, gives a list of editions and impressions. Henry Stevens's and Roland Tree's list of editions was published in 1967 in *The Map Collectors' Circle*, #39, under "Comparative Cartography," pp. 342–43.

51. Garrison, "Letter of Lewis Evans," *Pennsylvania Magazine of History and Biography* 59 (July 1935):296.

52. Ibid.

on. The Route he said, had the Rivers he Crost, and the Creeks which he travelled upon; but the Map wanted the Shape his Idea represented to him. I asked him if Ohio was as crooked as Dr. Mitchel represented it; He said he had seen but very little of it, but could not well conceive it should, as neither the Traders who very frequently went up and down it, had never mentioned so remarkable Singularity; nor did he think the Land would admit it. He however confirmed me in a Suspicion I had of having placed the important Pass through the Ouasioto Mountain 30 or 40 Miles too far West. Mr. Gist imagined that his Journal became misrepresented in Dr. Mitchel's Map, by the Copy Dr. Mercer sent of it home from Virginia.[53]

For many years, Mitchell's map continued as an important reference (see chapter 17 for further discussion). Of it, Charles Oscar Paullin, author of *The Atlas of Historical Geography of the United States*, wrote the following evaluation:

It is the second large-scale map of North America made by the English in the eighteenth century and is much superior to the first—the Popple Map (Pl. 27). In some respects it is superior to the maps of the great French cartographers of this century, the Delisles, Bellin, and d'Anville. Freeing himself from many traditions and drawing upon fresh sources in information, Mitchell produced a mother map which for forty years served as a model, until it was succeeded by Arrowsmith's Map. Used by the Commissioners who negotiated the Treaty of Paris in 1783, it was the basic map in the disputes over the northeastern boundary of the United States. . . .

Mitchell's delineation of the drainage of the Atlantic seaboard is generally good with the exception of the upper river courses. The drainage of Texas, compared with earlier maps, is poor. The Great Lakes are somewhat after the Bellin model but an improvement on it, though many inaccuracies in their delineation still remain. West of the Mississippi River, the map adds little to our knowledge. The delineation of the Ohio River basin, one of the noteworthy features of the map, is superior to all that proceeded it.

Previous to the publication of his map Mitchell had lived for a time in America, and this may have had something to do with the excellence of his work. His map was highly regarded on both sides of the Atlantic. It was frequently reprinted, with changes; and French, Dutch, and other foreign editions were issued. In one form or another it was widely circulated and gained great popularity.[54]

53. Ibid., pp. 296–97.
54. Pp. 13–14.

Perhaps the most recent comments on the map were made by Don W. Thomson in his three-volume *Men and Meridians, the History of Surveying and Mapping in Canada*, published in 1966–67. He says that it "provides a fair representation of the courses" of the three great rivers, the St. Lawrence, the Ohio, and the Mississippi in addition to a fairly accurate outline of the Great Lakes. He adds that "The map was a highly useful part of the standard equipment of British officers during military campaigns preceding the formation of the United States. It became a much consulted reference work in the possession of international commissions deliberating over Canada-United States boundary lines. . . ." For the time in which Mitchell worked, Thomson considers his map "a first-class cartographical production although more extensive geographical knowledge was actually available at that time than Mitchell was able to obtain. His collection of details relating to eastern North America, and especially to the seaboard colonies is commendable but knowledge of the vast Canadian West was apparently so scanty that the map extends to just west of the Lake of the Woods and to just north of the Albany River system."[55] Not only was Mitchell's map extensively used in regard to boundary disputes between the states after the Revolution, but Thomson says that it was also employed in the case of the Province of Quebec's boundary around 1871.[56] Again, in 1926, it was used in evidence concerning the "location and definition" of the boundary between Canada and Newfoundland, according to Miller.[57]

55. 1:90.
56. Ibid., 2:272.
57. Miller, *Treaties*, 3:345.

XIV ❧ Mitchell, the Political Writer

"I am but too apprehensive indeed, that these our contests in America, and all accounts of them, are reckoned by many to be prejudiced to the greatest blessing any nation can enjoy, peace. It was this that has made me hitherto resist the frequent solicitations of many to give some account of those matters, that they were pleased to think I had some pains to be acquainted with."

John Mitchell, The Contest in America[1]

The first surviving records of any of Mitchell's financial affairs appeared in 1755 when Andrew Millar transferred £110 from his account with the bank later known as Coutts & Company, to one which Mitchell opened with the same firm on 19 August.[2] The bank had been founded prior to 1692, by a kinsman of the Duke of Argyll, one John Campbell. In 1755, it was owned by his bachelor son, George Campbell. Campbell's niece, who kept house for him, married James Coutts that year and he had taken the young man into partnership. Today, it is one of the oldest financial houses in England, with an illustrious history of prominent customers throughout the centuries both in Great Britain and on the Continent. Among them is the royal family, who have had an account with Coutts since the time of George III.[3]

From Virginia, Mitchell also received cheering financial news. His accounts with various patients, delinquent for ten years, were finally to be settled by Lancaster County Court order. The patients included the

1. *The Contest in America between Great Britain and France with Its Consequences and Importance* (London, 1757), p. 30.
2. Account of Millar, payment 19 August 1755, Ledger 30. In this same book, the opening of Mitchell's account is recorded (f. 201) with a deposit of £225. There is no indication as to the source of the £115 in addition to Millar's payment. He may very well have paid Mitchell the total amount, half of which was in cash.
3. M. Veronica Stokes, *Notes on the Origin and History of Coutts & Company* (London, 1968), pp. 1–3, 8–10. "The spirit that led Middleton to arrange for the repair of the Earl of Islay's house at Kenwood and Thomas Coutts to assist William Pitt the Elder when his Exchequer grants were in arrears, still survives" (ibid., p. 13).

recently deceased Jesse Ball, the William Dowmans, Richard and John Chichester, and their sisters. The case was finally decided 19 September, after fifteen months' litigation, and awarded Mitchell £71, which included interest from 15 January 1745.[4] Although court records do not indicate that Mitchell's half brother Robert brought the suit for him, there is every reason to believe that he did, as Mitchell was in England at that time.

In fact, the end of June he was dining at the Duke of Argyll's with a George Campbell, who assuredly was the owner of the banking-house, with whom he was shortly to open an account. From May on, Mitchell had again been free enough to accept the duke's dinner invitations. Lord Bute was sometimes among his fellow guests and another was a Mr. Hamilton, who may have been Gavin Hamilton (1723-98). He was an artist and archaeologist who spent much time in Italy and was responsible for the excavation of Hadrian's villa. At this time he was in London and a member of the commission to found the Royal Academy. Fletcher noted that Hamilton entertained them all, including Mitchell, on 26 June.[5]

The colorful Bubb Doddington was present twice with Mitchell at Argyll's dinner that summer. In December, he would be appointed treasurer of the Navy, a position he had held once before until he lost favor with George II by intriguing with Halifax and the Prince of Wales. With the death of the latter, he no longer enjoyed the king's patronage. His two London homes at Hammersmith and Pall Mall were described as "full of tasteless splendor" by a contemporary. His state bed was covered "with gold and silver embroidery, showing by the remains of pocket holes that they were made out of old coats and breeches. His vast figure was arrayed in gorgeous brocades, some of which 'broke from their moorings in a very indecorous manner' when he was being presented to the queen on her marriage to George III."[6]

The long labors and intense concentration necessary for the making and completion of his map had quite exhausted Mitchell and he welcomed a year's respite. However, with the coming of 1756, his thoughts turned to a new project. His friends had told him that he had been

4. Lancaster County Order Book #10, 20 June 1755, pp. 240, 269, 329, 361, and Lancaster County Record Book #15, 19 September 1755, p. 226.

5. Fletcher's "Catalogue," Box 435, Saltoun MSS, NL.

6. *D.N.B.*

recommended for the position of keeper of the newly created British Museum,[7] a brainchild of Sir Hans Sloane. Well before the old gentleman had died in January, 1753, he had conceived the notion as a means of keeping together his vast and curious collections and of making them available to the general public. In June, a Parliamentary Act ordered a lottery to raise £100,000. This would be used to purchase Sloane's collection for £20,000 and a manuscript collection, the Harleian, for £10,000. The act further provided that the principal librarian to be responsible for the museum should be appointed by the king from two nominees to be recommended by the archbishop of Canterbury, the chancellor of Great Britain, and the speaker of the House of Commons. To house these collections and the Cotton and King Libraries, Montagu House was bought, repaired, and furnished with shelves and cabinets. The remaining money was set up as a trust fund.[8]

Among the trustees appointed by Sloane was Horace Walpole, who viewed his responsibilities in irreverent fashion when he wrote to Sir Horace Mann: "You will scarce guess how I employ my time; chiefly at present in the guardianship of embryos and cockle-shells. . . . He [Sloane] valued it at four score thousand; and so would anyone who loves hippopotamuses, sharks with one ear, and spiders as big as geese. . . ."[9] When the act creating the museum was passed, a number of trustees were appointed and fifteen were to be elected.

Applications for keeper were not slow in coming in. When the trustees met on 11 December 1753, they had a great many to consider for that position and for assistants. The keeper or librarian was to receive £200 per annum, the underlibrarian, £100, and the three assistants, £50. Among the applicants were: George Whiston, the notorious John Hill who wrote five letters of application, John Henry Hampe, Richard Combes, Thomas Collet, Gowin Knight, F.R.S., Samuel Stonehouse, James Empson (Sloane's curator) for departmental librarian, Mitchell's friend, da Costa, for a similar position, as well as Matthew Maty, Dr. Moreton, and Joseph Ames. The successful applicants were to be in charge of 347 volumes of drawings and illuminated books, 3,516 vol-

7. Mitchell to Lord Hardwicke, 20 January 1756, B.M. Add. MSS 36,269, Letters & Papers Relating to the Establishment of the British Museum.

8. E. St. John Brooks, *Sir Hans Sloane: The Great Collector and His Circle* (London, 1954), pp. 218–23.

9. Ibid., p. 221.

umes of manuscripts, 50,000 books, as well as the vast collections.[10] For the next two years, the trustees made no decisions as to museum employees.

Thus it was that Mitchell wrote to Lord Hardwicke on 20 January 1756. The earl was a barrister who had been successively a member of parliament, solicitor general, attorney general, and finally lord high chancellor in 1736, a position which he still held. Of Hardwicke, Lord Chesterfield wrote: "He was a chearful and instructive companion, humane in his nature, decent in his manners, unstained with any vice (avarice excepted), a very great magistrate, but by no means a great minister. . . ."[11] To Hardwicke, Mitchell wrote: "Being informed that the Office of Keeper or Librarian to the British Museum is soon to be appointed, I humbly beg Leave to offer my Service for that Employment as I have spent most of my Time upon those Studies and have reason to believe, that I have been formerly recommended to your Lordship for that purpose, and have the Honour to be known to most of the Trustees."[12] It was certainly true that Mitchell knew a great many of them at this time, as can be seen by a list of sixteen of them: Duke of Argyll, Earl of Northumberland, Lord Charles Cavendish, Lord Willoughby of Parham, the Honorable Philip York, Esq., Sir George Littleton, Bt., Sir John Evelyn, Bt., William Sloane, Esq., Nicholas Hardinge, Esq., Charles Grey, Esq., William Sotheby, Esq., Dr. Thomas Birch, Dr. John Ward of Gresham College, and William Watson. With many of these he had dined at Argyll's. Others he had met at the Royal Society.

Having considered the various applications for two and a half years, on 17 May, the committee charged by parliament with recommendations to the king, sent the following letter to George II:

To the King's Most Excellent Majesty

May it Please your Majesty,

Whereas by an Act of Parliament made in the 26th Year of your Majesty's Reign for the purchase of the Museum or Collection of Sir Hans Sloane etc. It is Enacted That the Principal Librarian, to whom the Care and Custody

10. Lord Hardwicke's Papers regarding the Establishment of the British Msueum, B.M. Add. MSS 36,269.

11. Matthew Maty, ed., *Miscellaneous Works of the Late Philip Dormer Stanhope, Earl of Chesterfield*, 4 vols. (London, 1779), 2:52.

12. 20 January 1756, Letters & Papers regarding the Establishment of the British Museum, B.M. Add. MSS 36,269.

of the General Repository of the British Museum shall be chiefly Committed, Shall be Nominated and appointed in manner following Vizt. the Archbishop of Canterbury, the Chancellor of Great Britian and the Speaker of the House of Commons, or any two of them, shall recommend to Your Majesty two Persons, each of whom They shall judge fit to execute the said Office and such of the said two Persons so recommended as Your Majesty by Writing under Your Royal Sign Manual shall appoint Shall (after giving such Security as is required by the said Act) have and hold said Office during such Time as He shall behave well therein; We therefore most humbly Recommend to Your Majesty Gowin Knight Doctor of Physic and John Mitchell Doctor of Physic in pursuance of the said Act.
May the 17th 1756

> Tho. Carstairs
> Hardwicke C.
> At: Onslow Speaker[13]

Knight, two years younger than Mitchell, was a formidable opponent. He was an Oxford graduate with both M.A. and M.B. degrees and one of the more able scientists of the Royal Society. In addition to his income from his London practice, he had a steady increment from the sale of bar magnets. Although he had demonstrated them before the Royal Society, he had never revealed his methods of magnetization. This interest, plus his study of lightning's effect on ship's compasses, and the improvement of them, resulted in his close collaboration with the Royal Navy on the subject. His 1748 treatise on nature's attraction and repulsion hinted at today's molecular theories. Knight had been elected a Fellow of the Royal Society in 1745 and was awarded the Copley Medal two years later. He had lost out to Thomas Birch when he applied for the secretaryship of the society in 1752.[14]

It was probably no great surprise to Mitchell, even though a disappointment, when Carstairs, Hardwicke, and Onslow announced the king's nomination of Knight for librarian on 3 June. Other things being equal, a colonial usually stood less chance in competition with an Englishman nor was an Edinburgh alumnus considered in quite the same category as an Oxford man. That Mitchell had been one of the two men nominated is testimony to both the high regard in which he was held, and the influence of his friends. The underlibrarians appointed

13. State Papers Domestic, George III, vol. 134, f. 71, SP/36, PRO; Crown-copyright is acknowledged.
14. D.N.B.

were announced on 19 June: Dr. Charles Morton, Dr. Matthew Maty, and Mr. James Empson.[15] Mitchell's friend, da Costa, attributed his disappointment to his religion.[16] It seems unlikely that Mitchell would have been interested in the lesser posts.

William Watson, as a trustee, did not hesitate to write the archbishop his disapproval of the choice of assistants. He considered them "unexceptional" and thought each should have been an expert in a different field: natural history, antiquities, and books.[17] Even if the trustees' choices were not universally approved, the British Museum was in good hands. Dr. Knight was able to soundly establish it, although parliament was dilatory in providing funds other than those for salaries. Knight's own financial affairs likewise were bothersome. Unfortunate mining speculations forced him to borrow 1,000 guineas from Dr. Fothergill which he was never able to repay.[18]

While Mitchell must have been disappointed that he was not appointed librarian, he could rejoice in the preferment of his friend, Lord Bute, whom George II made "Groom of the Stole" in 1756. The king had just made provision for his grandson to have his own establishment, with Bute directing his education. There were many who envied Bute his unique position of influence on a future king, and influence he certainly had. Bute gave the young man a bitter disapproval of Whig corruption and a belief in a strong monarchy. The latter was reinforced by a reading of Blackstone's *Commentaries* in manuscript.[19] Bute had his problems, too, with the young man of nineteen, upon whom "the mother and the nursery always prevailed" up to this time. Inclined to be lazy, he was sometimes "sullen and silent, and retires to his closet," but there is little doubt of the very real affection which the prince developed for his mentor.[20] There is little doubt, too, that Bute rapidly achieved a position in which he would be able to realize his ambition when his young charge would come to the throne.

15. B.M. Add. MSS 36,269.
16. Da Costa to Mr. Turbevil Needham, 18 March 1760, B.M. Add. MSS 28,540, f. 93.
17. Letter attached to memoranda of meeting, 19 June 1756, B.M. Add. MSS 36,269.
18. Dr. Lettsom said that Dr. Knight had lost money "by some speculation in mining, more plausible than productive" (John Coakley Lettsom, *Some Account of the Life of Dr. Fothergill* [London, 1786], p. 109).
19. Lovat-Fraser, *Bute*, pp. 8–11.
20. James Earl Waldegrave, *Memoirs from 1754 to 1758* (London, 1821), pp. 8–10.

Preoccupation with the map had interrupted much of Mitchell's correspondence with North American friends. He had written to Franklin the previous April, requesting him to ask Bartram to ship five boxes of seeds.[21] When Collinson wrote to Bartram in February of 1756, he was in a quandary about them for Bartram had only mentioned them once and then dropped the subject.[22] Eighteen months later, on 25 September 1757, Bartram wrote to Collinson that he had had no further orders from Mitchell.[23] This appears to be the final reference to the relationship between the two men—or at least the only one that survives.

North American seeds did arrive for Argyll that spring. They had been sent from Virginia by Robert Dinwiddie in January.[24] The previous April, Mitchell had sent several copies of his map with a letter to the governor. One of the maps Dinwiddie had forwarded to the Maryland governor, Horatio Sharpe, who had requested it.[25] Dinwiddie did not reply to Mitchell's letter until a month after he had sent the seeds to Argyll:

Y'r L'r of the 18th Apr. I rec'd with the Maps. Those in Books are d'd to y'r f'd, the Atto. Gen'l, who no doubt writes you thereon. The Map appears to me to be the best we have. The People here say you have not laid down the count'y in y'r Dom'n properly tho' I think y't Mistake very trivial, and I hope every Person will support H. M'y's Rights to the interior Parts of Amer'a, from the No. to the So. Sea, agreeable to former Grants and Patents. We remain in a state of Uncertainty in reg'd to Peace or War, tho' we may justly say the Colonies are in a State of War, and many Robberies and Murders have been Committed on the Front's of most of our Colonies. The precipit'e March of Col. Dunbar encourag'd the Enemy. with y'r Ind's, to come over the Mount's and they have done much Mischief. I shall be glad to hear from You, with any views you have; none here y'ts agreeable.[26]

21. Bartram to Collinson, 27 April 1755, Darlington, *Memorials*, p. 198, and Bartram Papers, 2:35, HSP.

22. 18 February 1756, Bartram Papers, 2:93, HSP. This reference was omitted from the letter printed in Darlington.

23. Bartram Papers, 1:44, HSP. This reference was also omitted from the printed version in Darlington.

24. Box 415 (1756), Saltoun MSS, NL.

25. 3 October 1755, R. A. Brock, ed., *The Official Records of Robert Dinwiddie*, 2 vols. (Richmond, 1888), 2:232.

26. 23 February 1756, ibid., p. 238.

Peyton Randolph, the attorney general, to whom Dinwiddie referred, was the governor's bête-noir. In December, 1753, he had informed the Board of Trade that Randolph had been appointed by the burgesses to present their case in regard to the reforms which Dinwiddie had instituted to do away with the land abuses.[27]

On 20 June 1756, Mitchell was present at Argyll's for Sunday dinner with Charles Hope Weir, Sir Francis Dashwood, and several others with whom he had dined often: William Watson, Sir Harry Bellenden, Sir Hew Dalrymple, and Dr. Stuart.[28] Undoubtedly, Watson entertained the guests with a report on the substance from a burnt haystack which the duke had sent to the Royal Society for analysis. The matter had been referred to Watson who found that it was not potash as had been suspected.[29] Mitchell did not dine again with the duke until Sunday, 1 August, and again two weeks later. At the earlier dinner, Argyll's natural son, Captain William Williams, was present. Argyll had had no children by his wife, daughter of Mr. Whitfield, paymaster of the marines, who died in 1723, and he had a lasting liaison with Mrs. Anne Williams, "otherwise Shireburn," of Whittendean, Middlesex and Marlborough Street, London. To them was born this one son who eventually took the name Campbell after his father's death, and named his son Archibald. In 1739, he was appointed auditor of excise in Scotland. At this time, he was captain of the Third Regiment of Footguards, becoming lieutenant colonel in 1758.[30] Horace Walpole said that Argyll "was the only man of any consequence whom her Majesty did not make feel how injudicious it was (however novel) to prefer the interest of the mistress to that of a wife. . . . Duke Archibald was undoubtedly a dark and shrewd man. . . ."[31] Argyll must have departed for his annual Scottish visit shortly after this for Mitchell did not dine with him again until the end of November. He was present twice for Sunday dinner in December, once when Captain Williams was also present.

27. For a detailed account, see Morton, *Colonial Virginia*, 2:629–32. Also see C.O. 5/1328, ff. 77, 95, 167, 181, PRO.

28. Fletcher's "Catalogue," Box 435, Saltoun MSS, NL.

29. Watson's examination showed the sample to be principally earth and a minute quantity of a "lixivial salt," 13 May 1756, Royal Society Journal XXII, p. 362.

30. Argyll's will, 14 August 1760, Somerset House, London (f. 151); Paul, *The Scots Peerage*, pp. 380–81.

31. Walpole to Dalrymple, 10 February 1781, W. S. Lewis, Charles H. Bennett, & Andrew G. Hoover, eds., *Horace Walpole's Correspondence with Sir Davis Dalrymple* (London, 1952), pp. 152–53.

It was during 1756 that Mitchell seems to have enjoyed perhaps his greatest financial prosperity according to his Coutts's account. His expenses would appear to have been modest, averaging £21 a quarter or £83 a year. He may have had additional sources of income, either in other accounts, or from investments, or possibly from Argyll, although no record of the last appears in the duke's account with Coutts. In May, Millar transferred £29..1..6 over to Mitchell's account. In August, Coutts charged two shillings sixpence for "noting" John Spotswood's bill on Thomas Knox for £325..0..10. Of this, Mitchell appears to have taken a hundred pounds in cash, depositing £225, to which was added £21 a week later.[32] It is quite impossible to deduce the source of either transaction as none of the men whose names appeared would necessarily be involved with Mitchell. Due notes were exchanged freely as legal tender. It is quite possible that the Spotswood bill had a Virginia origin and was in payment of the money due to Mitchell from the Ball court case of the previous year and various other debts owing to him.

With his failure to become librarian of the British Museum, Mitchell's indefatigable disposition sought other interests. He may already have been involved in writing but now approached it with fewer distractions. However, it is impossible to agree with Lyman Carrier's conviction that Mitchell was the author of *A New and Complete History of the British Empire in America*, begun in 1756.[33] It was printed in a series of pamphlets of twenty-four pages. The only surviving copy appears to be at the Houghton Library at Harvard, although Sabin states that there is one at Brown University. It is bound in three volumes. The first deals with New England and the English possessions in Canada; the second continues on the subject of New England and then discusses New York, New Jersey, and Pennsylvania. Volume three deals with Maryland, Virginia, and North Carolina but ends abruptly in the middle of a sentence discussing a general assembly held at Edenton in April, 1741. There is no indication of a printer or publisher.

It is totally unlike any of Mitchell's known writing and would seem to be typical of many booksellers' publications of the time. In the first place, it is not an original composition but rather a potpourri of information, awkwardly put together, borrowed from many sources. In

32. Ledger 30, f. 201, Archives of Coutts & Company.
33. Carrier, "Dr. John Mitchell," *Annual Report of the American Historical Association*, I (1918):209-10.

many cases, the author did not bother to credit the original writers even when he used their actual phrases and sometimes even sentences. For instance, in the description of Williamsburg, Virginia, he thus cavalierly quoted from Robert Beverley, Hugh Jones, and Kimber.[34] At other times, he gave the proper attribution but was careless in delineating the extent of the quotation. He frankly said in his introduction:

> As the design of this work is to render it the most complete and perfect ever before published; to the whole shall be added a succinct history of the Spanish, French, Dutch, and Danish Islands in the West Indies, lately communicated to the publisher: and if any ingenious and learned gentleman, warmed with love for their Country, its trade and commerce, who have been resident in, or well acquainted with the civil and natural state of our Colonies and islands, or any part of them; or have any prospects, plans, of towns, forts, etc. or subjects of natural history, for the illustration of this Work, the insertion of them may be depended on.[35]

Even if one was unfamiliar with the publications from which the editor was quoting, the cursory descriptions of plant and animal life are not those of a scientist of Mitchell's caliber. One example alone is sufficient testimony: rattlesnakes are included among "stinging insects!"[36] Evaluation of land along the Atlantic coast is in direct contrast to Mitchell's view, as can be seen from comparing it with his book published in 1757. It is true that the writings of many of those referred to such as Colden, Kalm, Gist, and Dinwiddie had been the concern of Mitchell while making his map, but they were also completely available to others.

One of Carrier's strongest arguments for his thesis was his contention that the maps included were small-scale copies of Mitchell's. It is true that the anonymous author also used many of the same points as Mitchell did in regard to French encroachments in Newfoundland and Nova Scotia. But then again, the editor could have borrowed as freely from Mitchell's map as he had from the works of other people. As far as the sentiments concerning French activities are concerned, Mitchell's views were probably shared by many. From a careful comparison of these volumes and those known to be by Mitchell, there seems little reason

34. Mrs. Robert A. McGregor, Research Archivist of Colonial Williamsburg, assisted in identifying these quotations.

35. *A New and Complete History*, 1:xlvi.

36. Ibid., 3:160.

to consider him the author. One small supporting bit of evidence is that they are listed separately in the catalogue of Argyll's library: under Miscellaney "Dr. Mitchel, N. America"; seventeen pages later there appears "British empire in America. 2 vols. London" with no attribution.[37]

There is no doubt that Mitchell was the author of *The Contest in America between Great Britain and France with Its Consequence and Importance*, by an "Impartial Hand," London, 1757. It was published by the same man who printed Mitchell's map, Andrew Millar. The anonymous author of *American Husbandry* referred to *The Contest* as a "bulky pamphlet" written by Mitchell to accompany his map.[38] Although others have also thought that it was written merely as a supplement to the map, this was not the case. Mitchell gives his own explanation in the introduction: "I am but too apprehensive indeed, that these our contests in America, and all accounts of them, are reckoned by many to be prejudicial to the greatest blessing any nation can enjoy, peace. It was this that has made me hitherto resist the frequent sollicitations of many to give some account of those matters, that they were pleased to think I had some pains to be acquainted with." He concluded that now that the peace was broken, the best hope of restoring it was to fight with enthusiasm.[39]

In a lengthy introduction, Mitchell enumerated his several objectives: to make the colonies better known; to point out the dangers inherent in permitting the French to settle on the frontiers and to emphasize the colonies' value to Great Britain. They were worth five million to six million pounds a year, they furnished forty thousand to fifty thousand seamen annually, and they employed two thousand ships. "It is this that makes this nation both prosperous at home, and considerable abroad." Mitchell stated that England had grossly neglected her colonies until the French "opened our eyes about them."[40]

He had an answer to the French ambassador's often repeated accusation that "You have brought this nation into a war, for a port or two

37. *Catalogus Librorum ACDA* [i.e., Archibald Campbell, Duke of Argyll], (Glasgow, 1758), pp. 270 and 287.
38. Henry J. Carman, ed., *American Husbandry* (New York, 1939, originally published in London, 1775), pp. 205–7.
39. *The Contest*, p. v.
40. Ibid., pp. iv–xxxvii, quotations pp. vii and ix, respectively.

in Nova Scotia, or an Indian fort on the river Ohio." Mitchell stated that the area to which the Frenchman referred was no less than nineteen parts in twenty! If only Nova Scotia had been settled immediately after the Treaty of Utrecht, war would have been avoided. He considered the people as much to blame as the ministers. He also thought that the influential merchants were equally guilty since they were uninterested in inland America. They seemed unaware that the superb water-routes in that area were ideal for marketing the produce. Much prejudice against the colonies was the result of the fear of rebellion which was absurd since they were unable alone to resist even the French.[41]

Competition in manufactures was the basis of England's trouble with her colonies and he foresaw that the inevitable restrictions on colonial manufacture would be the source of the first rupture. To counteract this, he advocated encouragement in other endeavors such as the raising of Hemp, Flax, oil, wine, Indigo, Madder, pitch and tar, saltpeter, potash, naval stores, timber, and Currants.[42] Many of these same products had been suggested to the Royal Society of Arts in London by Dr. Alexander Garden of Charles Town. In fact, in the summer of 1757, Garden was attempting to form an agricultural society in South Carolina in order to encourage planters in raising such items.[43]

The wholesale planting projected by Mitchell required large land areas but the increasing constriction by the French, particularly in the northern colonies, was threatening this. As a result, New England land brought two to five pounds an acre while that in the south was only five to ten pounds for one hundred acres. Thus, northerners became farmers rather than planters and failed to produce the raw materials that Great Britain desired.[44]

Lack of cooperation between the colonies was the greatest weakness in their defense against the French, Mitchell felt. As a case in point, he cited Crown Point, a strategic fort seized by the French. They should have been unable to do this had New York not been so involved in a boundary dispute with New Jersey that she ignored the situation. Mitchell went into some detail over the dispute since it gave him the

41. Ibid., pp. ix–xxi.
42. Ibid., pp. xxiii–xxiv.
43. Berkeley and Berkeley, *Dr. Alexander Garden of Charles Town* (Chapel Hill, 1969), pp. 58–59, 100–103.
44. *The Contest*, pp. xxx–xxxi.

opportunity to answer some criticisms leveled at his map by the Council of Proprietors of East New Jersey.[45]

Their president, Andrew Johnston, had written to Mitchell on 22 August 1755, and his letter was subsequently published in the *Gentleman's Magazine* in June of 1756. Johnston noted the two boundaries which Mitchell gave: "limits claimed by New York" and those claimed by his own colony. He said that the former had never been claimed by New York. In fact, it was but a single person, Mr. DeLancey, the lieutenant governor, who was responsible and he quoted from the minutes of the New Jersey Council on 20 August 1755:

'It seemeth to us that his honour must have meant those *Forks of Delaware* which are about eighty miles below the station point; because we find on Dr. *Mitchell's* excellent map, published this year, that a line from thence to *Hudson's* river is laid down, and on it wrote *Limits claimed by New York*; whereas we never heard that any one of New York had publickly advanced such a claim, nor put his name to it, except his honour, nor even heard that he had gained a proselyte to his opinion in America; but it seems he has gained some in Great Britain, who have prevailed on Dr. *Mitchell* to publish that, his honour's claim, in his said map; but we think his own name ought to have been put upon that line instead of the words New York upon it, and that it would have been more just, and would still be a proper correction.'[46]

Johnston referred to various negotiations with New York and enclosed the necessary documents as proof.

In his answer to the complaint, Mitchell reviewed the history, too. By the 1719 agreement between the two colonies the boundary was to run from Yonkers to the "northern branch" of the Delaware River at 41° 40' latitude. Since there was no northern branch at that latitude, Mitchell thought that the Lecha River must have been meant. It was considered the most northern at the time the charter was granted and said to be in that latitude, although no surveys were run. Thus, Mitchell said, it was in the maps of "Vischer, DeWit, Allard, Dankers, Maurice, Speed, Seller, Keith, Lean and Senex's map of the bounds of Pennsylvania."[47] The map made by George Keith can still be seen at the Public Record Office. It was sent to London by De Lancey on 21 May 1754,

45. Ibid., pp. 19–25.
46. *Gentleman's Magazine* 26 (June 1756):288.
47. *The Contest*, pp. 26–27.

and was received there a month later, where Mitchell saw it.[48] Mitchell's New York claim therefore ran about the same place, marked as the Jersey line according to the grant given to Berkeley and Carteret by the Duke of York (on Keith's map roughly around 40°30'). The New Jersey limits claimed appear to be about 41°40'. In regard to the 41°40' mentioned in the charter, Mitchell said that if this latitude was a mistake, "it is no more than what must be expected, before we had any certain observations of the latitude. . . ." For this reason, he said, places were usually considered more distant than they actually were.[49]

The boundary debate lasted for many years. In 1767, a Royal Commission was finally appointed and a line surveyed five years later. It ran somewhat south of Jersey's claim but far to the north of New York's. Neither colony was satisfied and New Jersey still regrets the 150,000 acres which she considers that she lost.[50]

A triple union for cooperation was proposed by Mitchell: the northern district to include Nova Scotia, New England, New York, and New Jersey; the middle, Pennsylvania, Maryland, and Virginia; and the southern, the Carolinas and Georgia. These districts were composed of natural boundaries, similar soils and shared mutual interests. Only concerted efforts could meet the French threat.[51]

Meanwhile, the enemy was busy attempting to achieve their ambitions: to take over Nova Scotia and Cape Breton; to discourage British growth and expansion and to secure the lands which they had claimed. From Canada to Louisiana they were hastily building forts to join the two areas and had already completed twenty-four, most of which were on English soil. They well recognized the importance of the cheap water carriage extending from the St. Lawrence to the Gulf of Mexico. Mitchell compared British and French strengths to the former's detriment. English colonies were open and exposed while those of the French were protected by forts. Englishmen were scattered as farmers and planters, and disorganized. The French were well trained, many of them being former soldiers. They were united and most of them were in forts and garrisons. The English had hundreds of places to

48. C.O. 5/1066, PRO.
49. *The Contest*, pp. 28–29.
50. Richard P. McCormick, *New Jersey from Colony to State, 1609–1789* (Princeton, 1964), p. 76.
51. *The Contest*, pp. 38–40.

guard while two forts, Crown Point and Niagara, safeguarded the French. There were Indian allies for the French but there were none for the English.[52]

It was of the greatest importance that key points such as Crown Point, Niagara, and Fort du Quesne, should be in British hands. In the case of the last, Maryland, Virginia, Pennsylvania, and the Ohio Company shared an interest in the Ohio River environs which du Quesne commanded. Instead of working together, they often interfered with one another. Mitchell proposed that Great Britain should declare the St. Lawrence River a natural barrier and drive the French above it. Mitchell did not depend completely upon his own ideas but referred to various sources such as Sir Josiah Childs on *Trade*, La Salle, Dobbs, Washington's *Journal*, Cox's *Account of Carolina*, and Colden. His references included more French books than English.[53]

The Contest appeared in the late spring and was listed in the Register of Books under "Politicks" in the *Gentleman's Magazine* for June, 1757. It sold for three shillings, six pence.[54] In May, 1756, Millar had deposited twenty-nine pounds, one shilling, and sixpence to Mitchell's account.[55] This may have been for the sale of rights to *The Contest* or it could have been royalties from the map. Recently, in 1965, *The Contest* was republished under the auspices of the Social Science Research Council of Canada and others. As usual, Mitchell's friends would have been interested in his latest project, but only one mention of it remains. When Isaac Norris wrote to Franklin that November, he said that *The Contest* was one of several books sent to him by William Franklin.[56]

A review of *The Contest* appeared in the July, 1757, issue of *The Monthly Review*.[57] It was written by one Oliver Goldsmith, who had just been hired that spring to write for that magazine by the bookseller Griffith. In addition to his board and lodging, Goldsmith was to receive one hundred pounds per annum. He found this arrangement far from satisfactory and remained in Griffith's employ only about eight

52. Ibid., pp. 74–88, 137–39.
53. Ibid., pp. 150–89, 210.
54. Vol. 27, p. 291.
55. Ledger 30, Coutts & Company Archives.
56. 24 November 1757, *Papers of Franklin*, 7:281.
57. Pp. 172–75

months.[58] The first paragraph of his *Contest* review would hardly have encouraged readers: "An inequality of stile, a want of method, and a disgusting iteration of the same observations, manifestly betray too much the haste of the author in the present publication. The Author who engages in the transitory politics of the day, may be compared to a Sportsman shooting flying;—while he is taking aim, the object in view often gains too great a distance, and escapes the meditated blow. Such Writers are generally obliged to sacrifice ornament to opportunity, and in order to catch the present moment, give up all hopes with regard to posterity." In spite of this inauspicious introduction, Goldsmith summarized Mitchell's points in great detail and quoted from the book at length on the subject of tobacco. In conclusion, he wrote:

Let the foregoing abstract suffice for a general idea of a work that abounds with truths, hitherto, perhaps, not generally attended to, and with observations and proposals, that indicate the Author's knowledge of the subject, tho' his hints may not always be practicable, and his ardent zeal for the interests of Britain, tho' it often betrays him into national partiality.

One thing may be remarked, however, with respect to the French, because it would, perhaps, be equally true in regard to any other nation in the same circumstances, viz. that they will hardly ever let us be at rest in America, while we have so much to be robbed of there, and they have so little to lose.

Curiously enough, Sabin said that some people thought that Goldsmith himself was the author of *The Contest*.

Little is known of Mitchell's activities over the next two years. A number of small transactions are recorded in his account with Coutts. The year 1757 appeared to have been much less prosperous financially for him. He only deposited some fifty-two pounds in his account.[59] In the summers of 1757 and 1758, he still dined fairly frequently with

58. Arthur Freedman, ed., *Collected Works of Oliver Goldsmith* (Oxford, 1966), 1:3. The *Contest* review is reprinted in this same volume, 105–9.

59. In both April and June he paid £30 to himself but did not draw any more money until November when he took out £21. He did pay one Thomas Tucker five and a half pounds in September. In December, he cashed £31, leaving a balance of £75:14:8. In 1758, Mitchell was more restrained in his withdrawals: £10 in February; £26:5 in March; £10:10 in April; £15:15 in June; and £10:10 on August 1. On the thirty-first of that month, having "examined, adjusted & settled this account," he withdrew the remaining £2:4:8. No other entry appears under Mitchell's name until June of 1759. Ledgers 32 (f. 229), and 34 (f. 245), Coutts & Company Archives.

Argyll, often with Dr. Stuart and Colonel Williams.[60] The paucity of material regarding Mitchell at this period is curious. One might expect references to him in Franklin's correspondence but there are none. It may have been that he was exhausted from map making and writing and that his health had accordingly suffered. In this case, he may have sought a more beneficial climate where he could enjoy the warmth of the sun on the Continent or even in the south of England. Three years later, he would refer to the "necessity of my enjoying a warm climate again."

60. Fletcher's "Catalogue," Box 435, Saltoun MSS, NL.

XV ❧ Mitchell's Part
in the Early Days
at Kew

*"I also sent your List to the Princess of Wales Garden
at Kew—which is the Paradise of England; I may say of Europe—for from
all Parts of the World, flows in Vegetable Treasures every Year—all that
Art, or Expence, can do, is Here Exhibited—"*

Collinson to Trew, 30 June 1767[1]

The year 1759 began propitiously. Throughout January mild southern
winds blew and on only two days was there frost. By early March, the
Dogwood and Sweet Bay were in full leaf.[2] Such warmth was very
welcome to Mitchell and from February on he took many a Sunday
dinner, including Easter, with Argyll. There he was joined by old
friends: Dr. Stuart, Sir Henry Bellenden, Colonel Williams, Baron
Maule, Messrs. Adam, Ramsay, and Forrester, in addition to innumerable members of the Campbell family.[3]

The mild weather was auspicious for the start of a project with which
Mitchell was to be involved for the next two and a half years. It has
previously been noted that, in 1750, he had ordered seeds from Bartram
for Frederick, Prince of Wales, at the request of Lord Bute; also that in
that year Thomas Knowlton, a well-known gardener, had written to
Dr. Richard Richardson that Prince Frederick was planning a very large
hothouse and that Bute was corresponding with people in Africa, Asia,
Europe, and America to obtain plants for him. Unfortunately, Frederick caught cold while supervising the planting of trees and died of
pleurisy. Both Mitchell and Collinson wrote Bartram of this, and the
latter made an interesting comment: "Gardening and planting have
lost their best friend and encourager; for the Prince had delighted in

1. Trew Correspondence, ENU.
2. Collinson to Bartram, 10 March 1759, Bartram Papers, 2:97, HSP.
3. Fletcher's "Catalogue," Box 435, Saltoun MSS, NL.

231

that rational amusement, a long while; but lately he had a laudable and princely ambition to excel all others."[4]

It would appear that Frederick contemplated something on the order of a Royal Botanic Garden to excel all others in Great Britain, and that Bute was helping him to get it started. Since Bute was also very close to Frederick's son, George, it was hoped by Knowlton and others that George would carry on the project if anything happened to Frederick. George did not share his parents' enthusiasm for gardening, and the death of Frederick would have been the end of the botanic garden idea had it not been revived by his widow with encouragement from Lord Bute. In November, 1758, Dr. Stephen Hales wrote to John Ellis: "The Princess will build a hot green-house, 120 feet long, next spring at Kew, with a view to have exotics of the hottest climates, in which my pipes, to convey incessantly pure warm air, will probably be very serviceable. And as there will be several partitions in the green-house, I have proposed to have the glass of one of the rooms covered with shutters in winter, to keep the cold out, which will make a perpetual spring and summer, with an incessant succession of pure warm air. What a scene is here opened for improvements in green-house vegetation."[5] Hales, then an elderly man, was Clerk of the Closet to Princess Augusta, and had advised her concerning many botanical matters. An extremely versatile man, he had concerned himself with systems of ventilating ships, hence his reference to "my pipes." The Princess Augusta and Lord Bute have generally been credited with founding the now world-famous Royal Botanic Gardens at Kew, and they certainly deserve the credit for carrying out the idea. It would appear, however, that the plan originated with Frederick, and that he lost his life soon after starting to carry it out.

The Princess Augusta took up the idea of the botanic garden with enthusiasm. Lord Bute would be the principle manager of the undertaking. As chief gardener, she appointed twenty-eight-year-old William Aiton, who became part of her household. He was very knowledgeable for his age, having trained under Philip Miller at the Apothecaries' Garden at Chelsea. By 1766, Ellis was referring to him as the

4. 24 April 1751, Darlington, *Memorials*, p. 184.
5. 21 November 1758, CLO 2:41–42.

"best gardener for exotics in England."[6] William Chambers, the well-known architect, was employed to design the various buildings and stoves necessary to any eighteenth-century garden.[7]

As Groom of the Stole to the young prince, Bute had long been closely associated with his mother, in this connection as well as in affairs related to the garden. Consequently, gossip concerning their relationship was to be expected. James Earl Waldegrove, governor to the Prince of Wales, wrote in 1758 that the prince's father said that Bute was "a fine showy man, who would make an excellent ambassador in a court where there was no business . . . but the sagacity of the Princess dowager has discovered other accomplishments, of which the prince her husband may not perhaps have been the most competent judge."[8] The fact that Bute and Princess Augusta lived near each other gave further impetus to possible scandal for Bute had acquired a fairly old two-story house on Kew Green. Next to it was "a new detached brick building on one side of the garden, used by him in part for a library, and in part occupied by an under servant of the Royal Family." It must be remembered, too, that Bute, as a Scot, was strongly resented by many an Englishman for his great political influence, for his appointment of Scots, and for the great favor shown him by the Royal Family. All of these facts were likely to encourage gossip and scandal whether there was any basis for it or not.[9]

Having many obligations, Bute's time was too limited to supervise all the minutiae involved in establishing the botanic garden. To help him, he turned to his friend John Mitchell. The doctor would see that Bute's general orders were carried out. He would go to the nurseries and order plants, shrubs, and trees. He would tend to the bookkeeping involved in their payment. He would carry on the immense correspondence necessary to acquire seeds from all over the world, since the garden "was to contain all the plants known upon earth." Although Mitchell's successor considered one day's work a week sufficient to accomplish all this, the Virginian evidently thought it advisable to be on the spot. Certainly, at the very beginning, there was far more work

6. CLO 1:92.

7. W. T. Bean, *The Royal Botanic Gardens, Kew: Historical and Descriptive* (London, 1908), pp. 12–15.

8. Waldegrove, *Memoirs*, p. 39.

9. M. S. Johnston, "Kew Green," *The Journal of the London Society*, 298 (1948):45–48.

to be done in establishing the garden. Sometime early in 1759, Mitchell moved to Kew.[10] It is possible that he may have lived in Bute's "library" since his address there is not known.

Although only nine acres were available at the beginning, they presented a very real challenge in developing a garden. Four years later, Chambers described the situation: "The gardens of Kew are not very large. Nor is their situation by any means advantageous; as it is low, and Commands no prospects. Originally the ground was one continued dead flat; the soil was in general barren, and without either wood or water. With so many disadvantages it was not easy to produce any thing even tolerable in gardening: but princely munificence, guided by a diector [sic] equally skilled in cultivating the earth, and the politer arts, overcame all difficulties. What was once a Desart is now an Eden."[11] With unlimited funds it had been possible to accomplish such a transformation. Nevertheless, it required much hard work and supervision on the part of Bute and his assistant. Horace Walpole said Bute "raised hillocs to diversify the ground."[12] Just this topographic change was an immense undertaking and employed vast numbers of men and horses. Plans had to be made for a lake, designs for beds drawn up, the location of greenhouses determined, and methods of irrigation studied. Mitchell may even have helped with some of the planning.

He was certainly working hard that summer. On 12 June, five hundred and twenty-nine pounds, nine shillings were deposited to his account at Coutts and Company and within three days he was drawing on it. Whether Mitchell was paying bills as he made them or whether he had contracted for services and materials earlier is not known. Nothing is known, too, of the majority of the men who received payment from him that summer since there is no indication of what their service had been in Coutts's books, but only the bare note of the amount paid out. These included in June: £14..13 to Ben Clements on the fifteenth; £9..18 to "Tho. Ash" on the nineteenth; £13..19 to "Tho. Farr" on the twenty-second; £48..18..8 to John Williamson on the twenty-third;

10. Both in an article in *Philosophical Transactions* and in the Royal Society of Arts files, Mitchell's address is given as Kew in 1759 and 1760.

11. William Chambers, *Plans, Elevations, Sections and Perspective Views of the Gardens and Buildings at Kew in Surry* (London, 1763), p. 2.

12. Paget Toynbee, ed., "Horace Walpole's Journals of Visits to Country Seats, etc.," *Walpole Society* 16 (1927–29):23.

and £27 to Dr. John Heyler for "Payt. of 18 Currt. to Hen. Woodman on the 25th."[13]

A payment of £15..7 was made to one "Tho. Greening" on the twenty-fifth. This was probably H. T. Greening, the gardener at Kensington and St. James Palace. He is thought to have been a son of Thomas Greening, George II's gardener, who died in 1757. Greening had a contract to supply Kew with "glasses & Melon frames."[14] Four years later, there was some question as to his honesty.[15]

The largest sums which Mitchell paid that June were to well-known nursery-gardeners. On the thirtieth of June, he paid £107..12 to Christopher Gray. Gray's garden was at Fulham and it was there that Catesby had worked upon the acclimatization of North American plants to the English climate. In 1737, Gray had published *A Catalogue of American Trees & Shrubs That will Endure the Climate of England*. It included Catesby's drawing of *Magnolia altissima* and the plant list contained references to his *Natural History*. There is some question about how much of the publication Catesby was responsible for. He was definitely the sole author of another catalogue for Gray's garden, *The Hortus Britanno-Americanus*, published after his death in 1763. It was in this that Catesby referred to Mitchell's work on the Oaks. Gray had continued his interest in North American plants.[16] Through Ellis, he had sent a book to Alexander Garden at Charles Town, in return for which the doctor had sent several shipments of South Carolina seeds.[17]

Another large payment made by Mitchell went to Kennedy & Lee, £52..7..7 on the twenty-second. Little is known of Lewis Kennedy, who had an established business in Hammersmith when James Lee became his partner. Lee, a Scot, is said to have worked as a gardener at Whitton when he first came to England. There, the duke gave the ambitious lad free access to his fine library. J. C. Ludon was of the opinion that Lee had worked for Philip Miller and at Sion before he went to Argyll. Be that as it may, by 1759, he was well known in the natural history world as a conchologist, entomologist, and botanist. He was

---

13. Ledger 35, Coutts & Company Archives.
14. Thomas Worsley to Bute, 2 February 1761, Bute Papers Cardiff Public Library, subsequently referred to as CPL.
15. Worsley to Bute, 26 June 1763, Bute Papers, CPL.
16. Frick and Stearns, *Catesby*, pp. 41–42.
17. Garden to Ellis, 24 December 1755, CLO 1:359.

busy completing the first English translation of Linnaeus's *Philosophia Botanica*, which he incorporated in *An Introduction to Botany*, the following year.[18] Kennedy & Lee's nursery garden was one of England's finest. It specialized in rare and exotic plants, seeds for which were gathered from all over the world. It was responsible for the introduction of *Fuchsia* and the Tree Rose to England.[19] Unlike Miller's, the garden was open to all interested persons. Miller was so secretive that he was said to have thrown the papers in which his foreign seeds were sent into the Thames. Dr. Thornton, in his 1810 sketch of Lee, wrote: "and such is the ardour of Botany, although the acquisition was often to be swum for, these were fished for up again, and the names of the new plants when introduced, was thus known to Mr. LEE, and others, in a way which greatly surprised the author of the Gardener's Dictionary." Lee was equally generous in giving away duplicate plants and revealing his methods of propagation.[20]

Of the six men to whom Mitchell paid varying sums in July, August, and early September, four are unidentified: James Hewitt, who received £2..10; John Jeffrys, who received £5..8..9; Francis Hunt, who was paid £35..17; and Thomas Spyers, £34..18. From the larger amounts paid to Hunt and Spyers, it seems most likely that they were nursery gardeners. The other two were in that category. One was James Scott, who received £60..13. He was a friend of both Dr. Watson and Collinson. At his nursery at Turnham-Green, he had successfully raised the "Side-Sadle Flower" and published a cut of it in order to promote its sale.[21]

The largest sum paid by Mitchell was to James Gordon on July nineteenth, £159..2. It was his garden which he had visited with Andrew Fletcher in 1749. Collinson often shared with Gordon the seeds sent to him by Bartram, so he was well supplied with North American plants.[22] The esteem in which he was held was expressed by Ellis in a letter to Linnaeus in 1758: "If you want a correspondent here that is a

18. E. J. Willson, *James Lee and the Vineyard Nursery Hammersmith* (London, 1961), pp. 4–18.

19. Ibid., p. 1.

20. Dr. Robert John Thornton's sketch of Lee's life in James Lee, *An Introduction to the Science of Botany Chiefly Extracted from the Works of Linnaeus* (London, 1810), p. xv.

21. Thomas Knowlton to Richard Richardson, 21 July 1754, Turner, *Richardson*, pp. 418–19.

22. James Gordon to Bartram, 3 March 1750/51, Darlington, *Memorials*, p. 370.

curious gardener, I shall recommend you to Mr. James Gordon, Gardener, in Mile End, London. This man was bred under Lord Petre and Doctor Sherard, and knows systematically all the plants he cultivates. He has more knowledge in vegetation than all the gardeners and writers on Gardening in England put together, but is too modest to publish any thing. If you send him any thing rare, he will make you a proper return."[23] On 12 August, Gordon and Mitchell were fellow guests of Argyll.[24] In September, Mitchell checked the Coutts's account in his name, found it correct, and withdrew the remaining four pounds, five shillings.

With the coming of winter, he found that he now had more leisure. Life at Kew was very pleasant. The village was peaceful and remote from the clamor of London. The houses were built around a green where many a game of cricket was played.[25] Like an isolated island, at the eastern end of the green, stood the new church of St. Mary, built in 1714. At the western end, one could glimpse the palace with a windmill behind it. Opposite, there were great trees encircled by inviting seats.[26]

One of the things which Mitchell enjoyed most was seeing something of the brother of his old friend from Gloucester, Dr. John Symmer.[27] Robert Symmer, a fellow member of the Royal Society, was very much interested in electricity. In February, 1759, he presented a paper on his observations on electricity in the human body to the society. In it, he recounted experiments with silk and wool stockings. In a second paper in May, he spoke of his results in using black silk and white silk. This was followed by a third paper in June.[28] The subject enjoyed great popularity, and the Prince of Wales wrote to Bute in August that his mother was reading "The Doctrine of Stocking Electricity," which made it more fashionable than ever.[29]

One cold December Saturday, with the thermometer standing at

23. 25 April 1758, CLO 1:93.
24. Fletcher's "Catalogue," Box 435, Saltoun MSS, NL.
25. Frederick Scheer, *Kew and its Gardens* (Richmond, 1840), p. 29.
26. H. E. Malden, ed., *Victoria History of the County of Surrey* (Westminster, 1902), p. 486.
27. Dr. John Symmer to Sir Hans Sloane, n.d., B.M. Sloane MSS #4061, f. 158.
28. 1 February, 17 May, and 21 June 1759, Royal Society Journal Book XXIII, pp. 243, 371, and 419.
29. 6 August 1759, Register of Correspondence of the Earl of Bute, 1739–62, B.M. Add. MSS 36,796, f. 14.

32°F, Mitchell called upon Symmer.[30] For five or six days, it had been dry and clear, with an easterly wind, resulting in perfect weather for electrical experimentation. His host asked Mitchell if he would witness some experiments which he was about to make as he had just received some special silk stockings. They were of much heavier weight than those which Symmer had used before and the black pair had been twice dyed to insure perfect color, and weighed almost an ounce more than the white.

The two men began by performing Symmer's previous experiments with the lightweight stockings and found the results much as he had reported, as Mitchell was to write later: "that when the white stocking was put within the black, or *vice versa*, and both highly electrified, taking hold of the one, while a scale with weights was put to the other, we could raise seventeen ounces before the stockings separated." They varied the experiments, turning one stocking inside out and placing it in the other so that the rough sides were together. A twenty-ounce weight was necessary to separate them.

Symmer and Mitchell then turned their attention to the new stockings and were astonished to find that with the white stocking placed within the black, they could lift nine pounds. Even more amazing, when the rough sides were put together, it was possible to raise fifteen pounds. When they withdrew the white stocking, applying it to the exterior of the other, they could still raise one and three quarters pounds.

When the Royal Society met the next Thursday, Mr. Symmer gave his third paper, an extremely long one. To hear it, Mitchell had brought Dr. Patoun and a Mr. Hamilton, as guests. When it was over, a short review of the experiments which he had witnessed was given by Mitchell in the form of a letter to Dr. Birch. He ended by saying that he was not drawing any conclusions from the experiments but only describing them as a supplement to his friend's paper: "I consider the result of them, only, as a farther proof of the surprising degree, to which a power in electricity, which had not before been attended to, may be carried, in even the slightest substances, those of white and of black silk."

Symmer spent some time later reviewing their observations, and de-

---

30. For the following, see Mitchell's "Letter to the Reverend Dr. Birch, Secretary to the Royal Society concerning the Force of Electrical Cohesion," and the notes by Symmer appended to it, *Philosophical Transactions* 51 (1760):390–93.

cided that the thinner stockings had lost much of their former potency which had been present when he had first used them. He had the black ones re-dyed and the whites washed and bleached in sulphur fumes. As he had anticipated, their force was much improved. On a Wednesday, the ninth of January, the weather conditions were again as favorable as they had been on December fifteenth. With Mitchell present, Symmer repeated the experiments, and they found the lifting power much increased. Symmer was unwilling to specify what influence the sulphur might have had, since the hosier from whom he had bought the stockings new declared that they had never been exposed. He did think, however, that it did not contribute much. Alone, Symmer had done several other experiments. He found that when he had trimmed the loose threads and ends, that there was less cohesion rather than more which he had expected. He also discovered that the thinner stockings, being more pliant, actually had more force proportionately. Mitchell's letter was printed in the society's *Transactions* (Volume LI), accompanied by Symmer's notes of their further experimentations.

In mid-February, 1760, Mitchell's ire had been aroused by a letter to *The London Chronicle*, suggesting that England should restore Canada to France as part of a treaty of peace. He expressed himself strongly in opposition to such views in a letter to the *Chronicle* on February eighteenth.[31]

On 7 May 1760, Israel Wilkes proposed Dr. Mitchell, "of Kew," for membership in the Royal Society of Arts. This organization had been established some five years previously by Henry Baker, Dr. Hales, and nine other men in order to encourage English and colonial arts and manufactures. They had optimistically hoped that similar groups would flourish in the colonies. Mitchell was duly elected on 14 May, along with Lord Walpole, Colonel Tryon, Thomas Chippendale, and others. In the subscription book the "paid" opposite Mitchell's name has been erased and he appears to have taken no active part in the society.[32]

Mitchell was also a member of another such society for which specific dates of his membership are not known. This was the Gentleman's or Spalding Society at Spalding in Yorkshire. It had been founded

31. Dr. Gordon W. Jones kindly sent the authors a copy of this. It is not completely certain that Mitchell wrote the letter but it undoubtedly expresses his views.

32. Minutes of the Royal Society of Arts, 1760, p. 71; Subscription Book of the Society, 1754–63.

around 1710 by Maurice Johnson, primarily as an antiquarian society, but had broadened its interests to include the arts and sciences generally, especially natural history. The society met at times in part of the old monastery at Spalding, and also at a coffeehouse. Dues of twelve shillings per annum and a shilling per meeting provided funds for a society library. Its rather distinguished membership included at various times Sir Isaac Newton, Alexander Pope, Sir Hans Sloane, Dr. Richard Mead (His Majesty's physician), Sir John Evelyn, Martin Folkes, John Hill, Dr. James Parsons, George Edwards, and others.[33]

Lord Bute was ill in the late spring of 1760, which meant that Mitchell had more responsibility.[34] Nevertheless, he must have enjoyed his position. Gradually, the gardens were beginning to take shape although there were signs of activity in every direction.[35] The botanic garden was only a small part and the whole comprised some fifty acres. Everything was designed in relation to the palace. This was a very elaborate affair whose vestibule led to a two-storied "great Hall" with life-size portraits of William and Mary and two huge marble vases. The princess's apartments were on the right. Kent had decorated the picture gallery with blue wainscoting and gilt ornaments. He had also designed the ceiling over the great staircase. Four large "painted looking glasses" had been imported from China.

As one went from the palace into the garden, there was to be an orangery for which plans had been made. It would be built the next year. Next to the botanic garden was the original flower garden over which Frederick and Augusta had worked so long. Two stands at the entrance were reserved for rare flowers and formed one end of the garden. Tall trees enclosed two sides and the other end contained an aviary for both English and foreign birds. Walks divided the beds which were filled with flowering plants for most of the year. Nearby was a pool in which goldfish darted about. Beyond lay a walk to the growing menagerie whose cages encircled a small pond. In these, were exotic birds of all sorts, even Chinese and Tartarian pheasants. There was an island in the pond on which a pavilion designed by Chambers was being

33. Nichols, *Literary Anecdotes*, 6:6.

34. In spite of being busy, Mitchell managed to be present monthly at Argyll's Sunday dinner. Dr. Stuart was there each time. Although other guests varied, most were very familiar to Mitchell: Sir Harry Bellenden, Major General Campbell, Baron Maule, Mr. Millar, and Mr. Forrester (Fletcher's "Catalogue," Box 435, Saltoun MSS, NL).

35. The following is described in Chambers, *Plans*, pp. 1–4.

built. It was shaped after the Chinese Ting, a three-legged ceremonial bowl with two handles. From the menagerie, a path led to the lake. Nearby could be seen Chambers's Temple of Pan, already two years old. The Temple of Bellona was almost complete. These small decorative buildings were of wood and one had even been built in a single night in order to surprise the princess.

Chambers was also overseeing the completion of a typical eighteenth century garden device, the "Ruins of an Arch." It was to frame the Temple of Victory finished the previous year. A visitor five years later wrote, "The ruin is a very good one, & has a good effect; but the view of the temple of victory as you walk along through the Arch is affected & disagreeable. The ground on the left of the temple, seems ill laid out. The 3 hillocks give an unpleasant regularity to it. From the Temple of Victory you have a beautiful view to the house over the lawn; only the temple of Bellona is affectedly seen between two trees."[36]

Mitchell's immediate concerns naturally lay with the botanic garden. Here he would check to see how many of the plants which he had purchased from Lee, Gray, Gordon, and others had survived the winter. Here he would look over the precious seedlings raised from the rare seeds which had been procured not only with great trouble and expense, but sometimes with danger, from far-off lands. It was tremendously exciting to see what would develop from these tiny bits of life. Almost every ship brought more of these interesting seeds and would for many years to come. In Bute's correspondence can still be seen many letters announcing their shipment. Lieutenant Colonel Campbell Dalrymple sent both seeds and shells from Guadeloupe. Montaud shipped seeds via Bordeaux. Lady Bute's relative, E. Wortley Montagu, wrote from Turin that Dr. Allione, professor of botany, had offered to send Alpine and other flowers to Bute for the Kew garden or for his own. George Johnstone sent plants to Kew from Pensacola, Florida. Seeds and plants were not the only objects of interest collected for Bute. A Mr. Sullivan sent Chetajong fowls, with a note instructing that they ate Barley. It is hard to differentiate between gifts meant for Kew and those for Bute personally. Some were certainly meant for Bute alone, such as the turtles which he received. One, sent by Walter Pringle from St. Christopher's, weighed over three hundred pounds.[37]

36. "Misc. Notes Gilpin," fols. 77–78, MSS Eng. Misc. e. 522, Bodleian Library, OU.
37. Dalrymple to Bute, 14 April 1761; Montagu to Bute, 24 April 1762; Johnstone

Hearing that young William Molleson was going to the Orient as ship's surgeon, Sir Henry Erskine asked him to collect seeds of all the different species of trees that he could find. He also told him to note carefully the type of soil in which they grew and the type of climate in which they lived as well as any special instructions for their cultivation. After Molleson returned to England, it required five months for him to extract his seeds from India House and send them to Mrs. St. Clair (whose husband Erskine considered a second father). On 16 August, Molleson wrote to Erskine his sad saga. He said that the seeds "have not only been pilfered some out of each paper at the Warehouse, but have also taken off the upper wrapping paper on which the different names were wrote in English as the Chinese ones were on the under one, which will be a considerable inconvenience unless we can procure some person who understands the Characters . . . they will be of little use to the Thief, as he knows not the Soil they are to be cultivated in, nor the manner of cultivating them." Since Mrs. St. Clair had told Molleson that they were meant for Bute, he said he would be delighted to wait upon the latter when it was convenient.[38] When Erskine informed Bute, he told him that he would not send the surgeon to call upon him as it might be a nuisance. However, if Bute wished further information "Your Lordship, will by that means be able to obtain all the satisfaction which he can give by sending Dr. Mitchel to him."[39]

This must have been a time of great satisfaction for Mitchell. With vast sums of money being spent, with innumerable laborers and gardeners to call upon, and with inestimable resources for seed and plant gathering all over the world, no botanist could have asked for greater happiness. In addition to the excitement of new plant varieties, there was always the feeling of creating something new and very worthwhile.

Only one payment was made from Mitchell's account with Coutts in 1760 which might have been in connection with Kew. This was one for £70 to an unidentified Will Reeves, on 15 December. Mitchell had reopened his account on 27 September with a deposit of £125, which

---

to Bute, 2 June 1765; Sullivan to Bute, 13 September 1761; Edward Hanley to Bute, 21 June 1763, sending a turtle; and Pringle to Bute, 28 May 1760; all among the Bute Papers, CPL.

38. Bute Papers, CPL.

39. Erskine to Bute, 24 August 1760, Bute Papers, CPL.

was supplemented by another £40 in December. It seems likely that these may have been in payment for his own services for his other deposits around this time were two notes, Robert Baldwin's for £25 and James Richardson's for £16 on 3 January 1761.[40]

On 25 October 1760, George II died and, with the accession of George III to the throne, Bute and his Scottish friends became extremely influential. In fact, it was not long before Buckingham Palace was referred to as Holyrood. Mitchell may have been present on 13 November when the young king received the Royal Society. They had met at the house of the president, the Earl of Macclesfield, in St. James Square at ten o'clock. From there, they went to St. James where George III received them at three and signed their Charter Book as patron.[41]

With the coming of the new year, two projects must have concerned Mitchell as well as the men responsible for them since they directly involved the botanic garden. One was a powerful engine for raising water to the lakes and ponds. It was designed by John Smeaton (1724–92), who played an important part later in the industrial revolution. His "engine" at Kew employed two horses and was capable of raising 3,600 hogsheads of water in twelve hours.[42]

For the germination of seeds, the propagation of rare plants, and the cultivation of exotic ones, several hothouses were necessary. The largest one of these Chambers completed in 1761. It was to be the biggest of all those in England and it would be interesting to know what suggestions of Hales, Bute, and Mitchell might have been incorporated into its design. Chambers described it in detail and it certainly was most elaborate for its day:

Its extent from east to west is one hundred and fourteen foot: the center is occupied by a bark stove sixty foot long, twenty foot wide, and twenty foot high, exclusive of the Tan-pit, and the two ends form dry-stoves, each twenty five foot long, eighteen foot wide, and twenty foot high. The dry-stoves are furnished with stands for placing pots on, made in the form of steps. They have each three revolutions of flues in the back wall; and one of them hath likewise a flue under the pavement.

The bark-stove in the center is heated by four furnaces: two of these serve

40. Ledger 37, Archives of Coutts & Company.
41. Royal Society, 13 November 1760, Egerton MSS 2381, ff. 142–43, B.M.
42. Chambers, *Plans*, p. 4.

to warm the flues under the pavement, and two to warm those in the Back-wall, of which there are five revolutions. The flues are all of them 9 inches wide, and two foot high. Those in the back-wall are divided from the house by a brick-on-edge wall, and separated from each other by foot-tiles. Between some of them are placed air-pipes, for the introduction of fresh air, which by that means is warmed in its passage, and becomes very beneficial to the plants. The tan-pit is ten foot wide, and three foot six inches deep. It is surrounded on three sides by flues, being separated from them by a fourteen inch wall. The walks are three foot wide, paved with foot-tiles; and there is a border before the back-flues twenty inches wide, with a treillage for creepers, placed within six inches of the flues. The roof-lights are divided in to three heights and run on casters; so that they are moved up and down with great ease; from a boarded passage over the flues, between the treillage and the back-wall. The front lights slide in grooves. On the outside of the bark-stove, in front, there is a border covered with glass for the bulbous roots, which by the assistance of the flues under the pavements of the stove, flourish early every year.[43]

Mitchell's involvement with Kew had left little time for visits with Argyll. Almost a year had passed since Mitchell had dined with him, when word came to him that his seventy-nine year old friend had died on 13 April in London. The duke had appeared as usual at dinner but had died peacefully in his chair a few hours later. His many friends were greatly saddened. Collinson wrote a note in eulogy: "Great was his benevolence for he gave to everyone to encourage planting and raised plants on purpose to oblige the curious . . . he was a great chemist, natural philosopher, mechanic, astronomer and mathematician. He was a wonderful amiable man, plain in his dress, without pride or ostentation. . . ."[44] Argyll's body was taken to Scotland where it lay in state in his family's apartments at Holyrood, attended by most of the nobility, gentry, and city officials. "The crowds which filled every avenue gave proof of that singular importance and consideration which this great man had acquired, more by his abilities, and the lustre of his public conduct, than even by the nobility of his birth, or the eminence of his station."[45] This view was by no means universal. There were many who had disliked him intensely.

With the exception of a few bequests, the duke left his whole estate

43. Ibid., p. 3.
44. Norman G. Brett-James, *The Life of Peter Collinson* (London, n.d.), p. 59.
45. *The Edinburgh Evening Courant*, 16 May 1761.

to Mrs. Williams of Whitton Dean, Middlesex, and Marlborough Street, London. He added a proviso that it would eventually go to their son, Colonel Williams, in the event that his mother named no heir. Mitchell was not mentioned in the will, but there is a payment of £71..15 by James Coutts, one of the executors, to him on 12 August, which is puzzling.[46] Lord Bute told the banker that he would like to purchase his uncle's library if he could arrange it. Colonel Williams, who told Coutts that his mother would agree with his decision, said that he was perfectly willing to sell. Thus it was that this magnificent collection of books was lost, since it burned when Bute's house (not Cane Wood, which had been sold in 1754) was demolished by fire some years later.[47] The plant catalogue which Mitchell had prepared for Argyll undoubtedly was included in the holocaust.

Some of the duke's plants were more fortunate. In the spring of the following year, many of his rarest trees and shrubs were moved to Kew.[48] As late as 1908, several of these could be seen: "the fine cedar of Lebanon, the Turkey oak, and, perhaps the fine Persimmon and the old Robinia Pseudocacia."[49] Even today, one or two of these survive. It is well that they do for the beautiful gardens at Whitton Place have long been gone. George Gosling, who bought the house at Argyll's death, sold it to William Chambers. He reserved for his own use the conservatory which he converted to a house. Both eventually disappeared.[50] The Gothic Tower did survive into the 1960s but at last its crumbling remains were removed. All that remains today is a small, barren park, whose only clue to its history are several handsome Cedars of Lebanon. It is surrounded by the usual depressing, closely built-up suburbs adjacent to any large city. When William Aiton published his three-volume *Hortus Kewensis* in 1789, he took pains to interview James Lee, who remembered "the gardens of Archibald duke of Argyle, at Whitton near Hounslow, cultivated with much care and liberal expence. . . ." Lee gave Aiton a list of the trees which had been introduced by Argyll: *Ilex opaca* (1744) and *Itea virginica* of the same

---

46. Will dated 14 August 1760 at Somerset House; Ledger 38, Coutts & Company Archives.

47. Bute to James Coutts, 26 June 1761, Bute Papers, CPL.

48. Lambert, "Notes Relating to Botany," *Transactions of the Linnean Society* 10 (1811):275.

49. Bean, *The Royal Botanic Gardens*, p. 16.

50. Bate, *And So Make a City Here*, p. 211.

date; *Dirca palustris* (1750); *Guilandina dioica* (1748); *Andromeda pani-culata* (1748); *A. angustifolia* (1748); *Crataegus glandulosa* (1750); *C. aurea* (1746); and *Ilex prinoides* (sometime before 1760). It is very likely that Argyll can be credited with many more.[51]

Illness probably again plagued Mitchell in the late spring of 1761, causing him to seek the healing waters of Bath. Bath was, and still is, a charming town centered around springs whose curative qualities had been revered by the Romans. Their baths still can be seen and the waters themselves continue to be popular. In the eighteenth century, they were extremely fashionable and a stay at Bath was as much a holiday as a cure.

While at Bath, Mitchell sought out the apothecary, Thomas Haviland. He was a friend of da Costa and had been recommended to him by the gardener, Thomas Knowlton. Haviland probably introduced Mitchell to his friend, "Mr. Robins," who was a gifted botanical illustrator. Da Costa had taken some of Robins's drawings back to London with him where they had been greatly admired. Collinson had acquired some as well.[52] Little is known of "T. Robins," but Wilfred Blunt, after studying the hundred or so of his paintings which still exist, considered his work of very high caliber: "One is struck immediately by the modernity of the technique: a casual observer might well attribute the work to an artist of the twentieth century.... The drawing is exceptionally sensitive and delicate, and the brushwork crisp; the treatment decorative, but without sacrifice of naturalism."[53]

Another of da Costa's friends whom Mitchell must have seen was Dr. Ralph Schomberg (1714–92). He was then practicing medicine in Bath. The author of eighteen books and many poems, he has been unkindly referred to as "long a scribbler, without genius or veracity." Da Costa, writing on 1 June, asked Schomberg to tell Haviland that he had received his message but still had not heard from Mitchell nor received the package of drawings which he had sent, presumably by Mitchell.[54]

It may have been that Mitchell stayed at Bath for several months.

---

51. 3 vols. (London, 1789), 1:x, 169, 277; 2:27, 56, 69, 70, 169, 170; 1:69.
52. See correspondence of Haviland and da Costa, B.M. Add. MSS 28,538, ff. 62, 90.
53. *The Art of Botanical Illustration*, p. 152.
54. B.M. Add. MSS 28,538.

While he had drawn on his Coutts's account lavishly in February, almost eighty pounds, and another ten and a half in March, no other payment was made until October.[55] He was far from well and, as fall approached, he continued ailing. He knew that his health would be unable to withstand another cold winter. With great reluctance and regret, he wrote to Lord Bute on 29 September: "I sent the key of the Gardens by Dr. Blair, as your Lordship desired, and send some things herewith that belong to your Lordship. I am sorry I cannot leave this place with your lordship's approbation (which the necessity of my enjoying a warm climate again obliges me to) but that shall never hinder me to have the most gratefull sense of all your Lordship's favours, and of ever acknowledging myself Your Lordship's Most obliged & faithfull humble Servant."[56]

Necessary as it was, leaving Kew must have been a difficult decision for Mitchell. He would miss watching the planting develop and carrying out future projects. He would miss the excitement of receiving unknown seeds from abroad and the thrill of watching them grow. Yet, as a sick man, none of this was possible, so again Mitchell had to bow to his state of health and change his whole pattern of life. He would probably visit Kew from time to time and he must have been pleased with the small part he had played in its development.

What Mitchell had helped to start was already being admired by many. In 1766, Collinson wrote of it: "The *Stuartia* flowered for the first time in the Princess of Wales' Garden, at Kew, which is the Paradise of our world, where all plants are found, that money or interest can procure. When I am there, I am transported with the novelty and variety; and don't know which to admire first or most."[57] The following year, Henry Jones published *Kew Garden, A Poem*. For forty-five pages, he employed the most extravagant phraseology to describe its glory. In his phrase, "Hail fragrant guest!" he referred to the numerous imported plants such as Rhododendron, Mountain Laurel, "latifolia," Pimento from Jamaica, Bananas, "Saccharum rich," "Gardenio florido,

---

55. Ledger 37, Coutts & Company Archives.

56. Archives of the Earl of Bute, Rothesay, Isle of Bute. Miss Catherine Armet, Archivist, kindly sent the authors a photocopy of this letter. The Reverend John Blair was chaplain to the Princess of Wales at Kew.

57. Collinson to Bartram, 21 August, Darlington, *Memorials*, p. 282.

the Cape's rich jessamin," Magnolias, Bay Trees, red and white Azaleas, and Camphor Trees.[58] Lord Bute continued as head of Kew for many years until succeeded by Sir Joseph Banks in 1772. John Hill apparently was appointed to Mitchell's former position.

58. London, 1767, pp. 13–19 (Gough Survey 30, Bodleian Library, OU).

XVI ꧁ Mitchell on Colonial Economy

"... a particular Account of The Dearth and Scarcity of the Necessaries of Life in England; the Want of staple Commodities in the Colonies; the Decline of their Trade; Increase of People; and Necessity of Manufactures, as well as of a Trade in them hereafter. In which the Causes and Consequences of these growing Evils, and Methods of preventing them, are suggested; the proper Regulations for the Colonies, and the Taxes imposed upon them, are considered, &c."

John Mitchell, The Present State, 1767[1]

Three days after Mitchell sent in his resignation to Bute, he drew out five and a half pounds from his account. He had told Bute that he must seek a more favorable climate, possibly Bath where he had been before. It was certainly well away from London, for when he again needed money in late November, he requested Coutts to pay a "Bearer," ten and a half pounds from his account. He was back in London on Christmas Eve but did not remain long. In January, he was again receiving his money by bearer. By March, he considered it was safe to return.[2]

Any thought of going abroad at this time had been dismissed by Mitchell, for the war with France continued. Bute was extremely anxious for peace. For this reason, he accepted the position of prime minister in May. While he achieved his objective, the Treaty of Paris being signed less than a year later, Bute has been considered by some one of the worst prime ministers in English history. He was extremely unpopular with his peers, for they resented his partiality for Scots and his own kinsmen, when making important appointments. No indication has been found that Bute saw Mitchell after he left Kew. So little is known of Mitchell's subsequent life that there is no way to discover whether his abrupt resignation offended Bute or whether they saw each other from time to time but left no record of their meetings.

1. Title page of *The Present State of Great Britain and North America* (London).
2. Ledger 38, Coutts & Company Archives.

In the summer of 1762, Mitchell repaired to Tunbridge Wells. For over a century, this had been a fashionable watering place as well as a resort for invalids. It was particularly popular in the summer when both London and life in the country tended to be dull. From May to October was the popular "season" there. A well had been dug around the chalybeate springs, and the bank leveled to form the Upper Walk, paved with pantiles (Flemish paving stones) and shaded by a double row of Lime and Elm trees. On the walk's upper side was a colonnade in front of long rows of shops and coffeehouses. There was a Lower Walk as well, where farmers brought their produce to the market.[3]

Beau Nash, the celebrated master of ceremonies, had left his mark upon Tunbridge Wells and all visitors tended to follow the routine which he had laid out. From seven to nine was the water-drinking period, followed by breakfast and chapel. The morning's amusements consisted of country strolling, horseback riding, and browsing in the bookshops. After a midday dinner, everyone changed into formal wear and repaired to the walks. There they sought out the assembly rooms where there was the choice of tea, gambling, or dancing minuets and country dances, with a short intermission for supper. There were also lectures and a theater.[4]

The end of September saw Mitchell back in London. In November, he was one of the signers of a certificate proposing a gentleman from Cambridge University for membership in the Royal Society. He was George Wollaston, M.A., a fellow and lecturer in mathematics at Sidney Sussex College.[5] For the next three years, no mention of Mitchell's activities remains until 25 May 1765. On that date, he withdrew nineteen pounds one shilling from Coutts' & Company, closing out his account completely and finally.[6]

On 9 April of that year, Mitchell had been interested to learn that Collinson had been successful in his efforts to have John Bartram appointed King's Botanist at the munificent salary of fifty pounds a year. Mitchell may well have played a part in this appointment through Bute. Collinson wrote to Bartram that he should leave as soon as pos-

---

3. Martyn Hepworth, *The Story of the Pantiles* (Tunbridge Wells, 1956), pp. 8–9.
4. Ibid., pp. 13–14.
5. Royal Society Journal Book XXIV, p. 484.
6. Ledger 42, p. 278, Coutts & Company Archives.

sible on an exploration of Georgia and the newly acquired territory of Florida, examining "Plants, Fossils, Ores, etc."

Bartram compiled a regular journal as a report on his findings. It was approved by the Florida governor and sent to the Board of Trade and Plantations. Mitchell was fascinated by the tale of his friend's adventures in contrast to his own somewhat sedentary life. The board ordered the journal to be published to counteract some criticism in England that the newly acquired territory of Florida was a worthless, sandy desert. In America, feeling was much stronger. The colonials were extremely bitter. While England had acquired Canada from the French and the Floridas from the Spanish by the 1763 Treaty of Paris, she had infuriated them by a proclamation the same year forbidding the purchase of land beyond the Alleghenies. This was to be reserved for the Indians. Realizing the mounting criticism, the board considered that Bartram's journal, suitably edited, would be an excellent antidote and would encourage settlers to go to Florida rather than beyond the mountains. It was to accompany a Chamber of Commerce type publication by William Stork, who spared no complimentary adjectives in praising the glories, beauties, and possibilities of Florida.[7]

Mitchell was indignant about the way in which Bartram's account had been edited. He later wrote that the "rich lands" on the St. John River were actually forty to fifty miles of swamps, and the river choked with pond weeds causing it to flood badly according to Bartram. The Quaker had also reported that where the pine-barrens were not swampy and the low grounds located between the barrens and swamps, there were only small areas of sand.[8] Mitchell gave Bartram's manuscript journal as his reference, remarking "which passage we do not find in the edition that is published; although it is the most material of the whole, as it contains a general description of the country, and the author's opinion of it, after he had viewed it; but as this is not in favor of the country, it was not deemed fit to print."[9]

The book from which these quotations were taken is the only evi-

7. Stork's publication was duly noted in 1766 under "Books Published" in the *Gentleman's Magazine* (36:487) and a note followed: "To this Account of *East-Florida* is added a journal of *John Bartram of Philadelphia* which can afford entertainment only to a *botanist*, and to a *botanist* not much."

8. Mitchell, *The Present State*, pp. 199–202.

9. Ibid., p. 202.

dence of how Mitchell occupied himself between 1762 and 1767, the year in which it was published. It was entitled *The Present State of Great Britain and North America with Regard to Agriculture, Population, Trade and Manufactures, Impartially Considered.* It was printed by Becket and DeHondt and sold for five shillings. Andrew Millar, who had published Mitchell's *Contest,* had retired that year and was living at Kew Green. One of his assistants had been Thomas Becket, who later went into partnership with P. DeHondt, so it was quite natural that Mitchell turned to them for publication of his new book.[10]

Carrier has said that Mitchell was so disgusted with Bute's and George III's policy of "peace at any price," by which they had bartered all the land west of the Mississippi River for Canada and Florida, that he wrote the book.[11] This may well have influenced him, but there was much more involved than that and the book is an appropriate finale to Mitchell's varied life. In spite of being somewhat disorganized, and written in Mitchell's usual verbose style, it is interesting from many aspects. From it can be learned something of his character and philosophy. Perhaps the most unusual part of his character revealed is his social conscience, an extremely advanced one for his day, even though it was tied to practicality. There were few who had been born into comfortable circumstances and who had spent the greater part of their adult lives among the very wealthy, who had any real sympathy for, or knowledge of the manner in which the majority of people lived in the eighteenth century. Undoubtedly Mitchell's many years spent in the democratic colonial atmosphere as a doctor prepared his mind to view the English social scene with eyes not blinded by tradition. However, others with similar background did not have the same reaction. It must have been an innate part of Mitchell's personality which enabled him to view the whole scene with impartiality to any class, combining a strong feeling of common sense and a sympathetic heart. His views, social and economic, are often strangely modern.

Mitchell was in the unique position of being able to understand both the colonial and the English viewpoint. He felt that it was his duty to point out the various present and future problems as well as their solutions as he saw them. He was convinced that cooperation between

10. Nichols, *Literary Anecdotes,* 3:387–88.

11. "Dr. John Mitchell," Annual Report of the *American Historical Association,* 1 (1918):211.

the two was not only possible but necessary and that with it both segments of Great Britain would prosper. He wrote that England was suffering from a serious lack of provisions, due to several causes.[12] The Industrial Revolution had resulted in a great movement into the cities, which caused a reduced birth rate, decreased food production, idle farms turned to pasture, and small ones incorporated under absentee landlords. He understood the wretchedness of many in the cities for, he said, "Upon land, people only want through negligence, but in towns they starve for want of employment."

There were other reasons for the scarcity. Mitchell felt that it would be far wiser to use oxen, as the French did, rather than horses, which were a strain on the provisions and provided no meat and little manure. In 1588, there had been only 1,700 horses in London, but now he thought that there might be "a horse for every house in the kingdom."[13]

Others had suggested various solutions to this problem of scarcity. One had been to cut down on the planting of wheat for export but Mitchell felt that doing so would be injurious to trade. Some thought that removing the bounty on wheat would be beneficial, but he said it would only result in a sharp increase in price. It would be more sensible to lower the price of manufactured goods in order to compete in the world market and continue the subsidy by a tax on horses and possibly dogs. These two taxes would provide approximately 625,000 pounds which would allow taxes on the necessary items such as "beer, candles, soap, salt, leather and coals" to be dropped. These only amounted to £540,000 and were especially hard on the poor.[14]

As a starter, Mitchell advised the planting of Oats, Rye, Barley, Peas, Beans, and Buckwheat on the poorer lands. He particularly recommended the first as they were considered a valuable crop in the northern colonies. He had had experience with them himself: "Having mowed it for several years, I am well assured, it is the best fodder that grows, except the blades of Indian corn." While Wheat produced but one crop, a second could be garnered from Barley, Oats, or Buckwheat. If the poor were encouraged to eat them rather than wheat there would be more of the latter to export and more food for the

12. Mitchell, *Present State*, pp. 5–46.
13. Ibid., p. 32.
14. Ibid., pp. 54–56.

hungry. As an inducement, the poor should be given land on which to cultivate such crops, perhaps the commons. Oatmeal was especially suitable for Scotland and Potatoes for Ireland.[15]

In discussing the importance of raising more hogs than horses, he suggested in a footnote, the raising of Artichokes for their fodder, particularly since this would also improve the land: "I never knew the experiment tried but once, but it was with very great success. A piece of poor sandy land that would hardly bear anything upon it, they turned it up to the very bottom, and made it like a *hog-stye*; by that means it bore good tobacco, which required the richest land of any thing that grows. . . ."[16]

As subsequent growth of Great Britain was naturally dependent upon a reliable supply of raw materials from the colonies, Mitchell thought it was important to examine the situation there. Along the eastern seaboard, only the area from New York to middle North Carolina was favorable for agriculture, both in soil and climate. Further south, the maritime parts were extremely unhealthy and malaria was endemic. The Pine barrens could support no crops and the pastures were either marshes or covered by broom straw. In spite of inducements by England, the south was not suitable for raising Grapes and cochineal insects and the coastal area was too wet for silkworms. Even the indigo raised was not of prime quality. Mitchell saw little future for the colonists in Florida. Influenced by Bartram's unfavorable report and those of French and Spanish writers, he considered the best solution was for the Indians to settle Florida for they were the only people who would. In New England, early frosts and smut were only too apt to ruin the crops. There, people were turning to manufacture since the 1763 Proclamation forbade their seeking new lands to the west. Soon, they would be competing with the Mother Country.[17]

Many of the crops then raised in the colonies were unwise in such a restricted area as they exhausted the soil: Tobacco, Indigo, Hemp, and Flax. Great Britain should not continue to encourage the last two unless new lands became available on the Ohio and Mississippi rivers. The gradual breaking up of the Tobacco plantations in order to raise Wheat, cattle, and sheep would be very helpful to Great Britain, particularly

15. Ibid., pp. 68–79.
16. Ibid., pp. 79–80.
17. Ibid., pp. 127–38.

the resulting wool. That from the south was very like the choice Spanish wool. It would be a good substitute for it if the Spanish turned to manufacturing their own cloth and ceased to export the wool.[18]

For the southern colonies, Mitchell felt that the real answer was Cotton, which they were already planting on a small scale, and already manufacturing as much as wool in England. He said, "I have made several manufactures of it, which were the best of the kind I have seen. . . . The Cotton I have used there grew in the latitude of *Smyrna*, and parts adjacent, from which the *Turkey* Cotton is brought to *England*; it is the same kind with that but is of a much better and longer staple, if it is rightly cultivated; the staple indeed is not so long as the *West India* Cotton, but it is whiter, and wears white, when the other turns yellow, as I have found by experience with many others. Some of this Cotton from *Virginia* was sent to *Manchester* in the Year 1746 . . ." where it was sold at the highest price and reported to be as good as any which they had. Although the English factories offered to take all the colonists would raise at premium prices, little was being planted.[19]

Mitchell must have been very conscious of the increasing bitterness in the colonies. In conclusion, he presented a long, thoughtful argument against the evils that the repealed Stamp Act had proposed. He stressed the troubles it might cause and added, "There could not be a more effectual way to ruin the interest of *Great Britain* in *North America.*"[20]

Not relying on his own opinions and ideas solely, Mitchell annotated many statements. His citations include at least thirty-seven books and ranged from Sir Matthew Decker's *The Causes of the Decline of Foreign Trade* to Kempfer's *History of Japan* and Sir Josiah Child on *Trade*. He used two of Duhamel's books on agriculture and Jared Eliot's *New England Husbandry* as well as works by Dr. William Douglass. On his list, too, were many French authors and one Spanish.

In the *Monthly Review*, there was a lengthy review of Mitchell's book, which required space in both the May and June issues. Most of it was a detailed summary of the book's contents.[21] The reviewer concluded:

18. Ibid., pp. 138–43.
19. Ibid., pp. 147–48.
20. Ibid., p. 309.
21. Vol. 36 (1767):387–93, and 429–35.

Upon the whole, the Author of this Treatise appears to be well acquainted with the true interest, nature, and state of most of our different colonies; in some of which he is supposed to have resided many years, though at present in England. His style is somewhat too diffusive, at the same time that he is guilty of innumerable tautologies; which have both together protracted the work to a much greater length than would, otherwise, have been necessary.— We the rather mention these circumstances, as he seems to hint at giving the Public some farther thoughts, in regard to the same subject; in which it might be well to avoid every thing that may have a tendency to weary the attention, in the perusal of such arguments, as would carry the greater weight, if drawn up in fewer words.[22]

The final statement is of peculiar interest since it may have given rise to the widely held, but probably erroneous, opinion that Mitchell was the author of *American Husbandry*, a book published by J. Bew, in London, in 1775, some years after Mitchell's death. Mitchell had said:

To form a better judgment concerning the colonies it would be necessary to give an account of every one of them in particular: to consider the nature of the soil and climate and what it produces or is fit to produce for the benefit of the nation, this we have endeavored to supply by a few notes in order to explain many things which appear to be but little understood. But as these can give but an imperfect idea of many subjects treated of in them a more particular account shall be given in a second part of this discourse if we find that design is approved of. We may then also consider more particularly the several staple commodities that may be made in the plantations for the benefit of the nation and the ways of making them and give a more particular account of what they now make or of the produce of the colonies as well as their exports and imports.[23]

Carrier, one of the chief proponents of Mitchell as the author of *American Husbandry*, stated several reasons for his opinion. He thought the literary style was similar, being of direct quality though often repetitious and involving a thorough discussion. The author, like Mitchell, was well trained in science, had lived both in North America and England, but knew Virginia and Maryland agriculture best. For these reasons and the fact that there were so few serious errors, Carrier was

22. Ibid., p. 435.
23. Mitchell, *The Present State*, p. xiv.

certain that Mitchell was the author, although someone else had edited the manuscript.[24]

In 1939, Harry J. Carman edited *American Husbandry* which he considered "the most accurate and comprehensive account of the English colonies in North America and gives by far the best description of their agricultural practices. The recommendations for the improvement of farming compare favorably with those of any modern textbooks on the subject and are much superior in style and presentation to any other English or American agricultural books of the eighteenth century."[25]

Although Carrier said that Arthur Young could not have been the author since he was ignorant of North American agriculture, Carman considers it was much more likely that he was responsible than Mitchell. Carman found no evidence in Young's correspondence to indicate that he was the author but there was one suggestive letter to Young from John Reinhold Forster, who translated Kalm's *Travels* into English in 1770–71. He suggested that Young would be interested in the North American agricultural practices as described by Kalm: "I do not doubt you are best capable to superstruct upon these observations of my Author, the best Instructions for the Improvement of your Fellow-Subjects beyond ye Atlantic, who will be desirous to receive them as benefactions, what they really are. . . ."[26]

American Husbandry does include quotations from Kalm. Moreover, a review of the book called the author "a pretended Yankee," which would fit Young. In a footnote, there was a direct intimation that Young was the author and there was no refutation of this in his magazine during the next two years.[27] Carman also said that it could have been Dr. John Campbell. He had written a book on Barbadoes at Bute's suggestion. However, Carman thought this was unlikely as were similar suggestions that it might have been written by either William or Edmund Burke.[28]

All of these men (with the exception of William Burke), as well as many others, are referred to and quoted freely in *American Husbandry*.

24. Lyman Carrier, "*American Husbandry*, A Much Overlooked Publication," *Journal of the American Society of Agronomy* 2 (1918):206–11.
25. (New York, 1939), p. xl.
26. Ibid., pp. xlii and lvii.
27. Ibid., pp. lvii–lix.
28. Ibid., pp. lix–lx.

There are at least seven quotations from Arthur Young's *Political Essays*, published in 1772. There are two quotations from Kalm's *Travels*, but the greatest number from any one author is from Mitchell's works. There are some sixteen references and citations from his *Contest* and from his *Present State*, many of them extremely lengthy. The unknown author confirmed Mitchell's authorship of these books which had been anonymous:

> Upon occasion of the last war Dr. Mitchel was employed by the ministry to take an accurate survey of all the back countries of North America, most of them being then but little known except to the French, who were in possession of a line of forts through all North America. No person could have been more properly appointed, for he was not only able to lay down the country with exactness, but being well acquainted with practical agriculture in Virginia and Pennsylvania, he was able to understand the nature and value of those countries he should traverse. This was the origin of his map of North America, the best general one we have had; at the time it was published, it was accompanied by a bulky pamphlet, written by the Doctor and entitled, *The Contest in America*, in which he enters into a full elucidation of the importance of the back countries, and of the fatal effects which must flow from leaving the French in possession of their encroachments. Among others he considers particularly the territory of the Ohio, and shews of how much importance it is to the planters of Virginia. . . . Dr. Mitchel, in another work published in 1767 (*The Present State*), gives other particulars concerning this territory. . . .[29]

The author does not hesitate to be less than flattering to Mitchell on one occasion. In discussing the importance of the acquisition of Canada, he said that he thought Mitchell understood it "but he wrote in so confused a manner, that it is difficult to gain his meaning."[30]

One point which Carrier made against the possibility of Mitchell being the author was his modesty, evident from the fact that he seldom said anything about himself. To this he might have added the incontrovertible fact that it was published long after Mitchell's death and included much material published in the seventies and the misspelling of his name throughout the entire book.

On 4 February 1768, John Heathcote, Esquire, of Berkeley Square, was proposed for membership in the Royal Society. His certificate was

29. Ibid., pp. 205–6.
30. Ibid., p. 17.

signed by Lord Hardwicke, "J. Mitchell," and others.[31] This is the last mention found of Dr. Mitchell before his death on the twenty-ninth of that month. Announcement of his death appeared in the London papers, then in the March issue of the *Gentleman's Magazine*, and eventually in colonial papers, such as the *New York Gazette* or *Weekly Postboy* (25 April) and the *Virginia Gazette* (12 May). On the thirtieth of November, a list of the members of the Royal Society who had died since the previous St. Andrew's Day was read. Mitchell's name appeared along with those of Dr. John Huxham, Dr. John Tennent, Francis Fauquier, and Peter Collinson. In none of the obituaries is there any indication as to where Mitchell was living at the time, or where he was buried. All identify him simply as the man "who made the new map of North America."[32]

In spite of prolonged search in all likely places, no Mitchell will has been found. It may be that he was living on an annuity which stopped at his death, or he may have been living some distance from London. In that event, his will would have been probated there and not in the city nor its adjoining counties. His library, however, did come up for sale in London the following year. It had been purchased by the bookseller Thomas Payne, from whom Mitchell had bought books himself. Payne's shop was next to the Mews Gate, in Castle Street, St. Martin's. For over forty years Payne enjoyed "the highest reputation." His brother is credited with conceiving the idea of printing catalogues for book sales.[33] In 1769, there appeared *A Catalogue of Twenty Thousand Volumes, Containing the Libraries of R. Thornton, Esq., Dr. John Mitchel, Dr. T. Hayes, of Chester, Deceased; And of several other Collections lately purchased.*[34] In the list of books there is no indication of original ownership, so the extent, or composition, of Mitchell's English library can not be determined.

31. Royal Society Journal Book XXVI, pp. 443–44.
32. Ibid., p. 554.
33. Nichols, *Literary Anecdotes*, 3:655–56, and 6:439–40.
34. There is a copy of this catalogue in the British Museum.

XVII ⚜ An Ingenious Man

> *"In reviewing the busy life and work of one of Virginia's most distinguished botanists, we cannot fail to be impressed with his modesty, his scholarly attainments and his range of knowledge. He must indeed have been, as Bartram said, 'an ingenious man!'"*
>
> *Wyndham B. Blanton, 1931*[1]

The introduction to this biography is headed by a quotation from Theodore Hornberger, who considered that "few men rival Mitchell as a key to the problems of the intellectual life in the colonies," and accorded him high praise for his contributions to scientific knowledge, to cartography, and to politics. Yet Hornberger preceded this statement with another: "of all the men of science who resided in British America prior to the Revolution the most puzzling and the least likeable was John Mitchell (1690?–1768). Had he the opportunity, Mitchell would probably object to being classed as a colonial. He showed scant respect for his American contemporaries, complained bitterly about the American climate, believed in a strict mercantilist economy which allowed no nonsense about permitting the Americans to go about their business in their own way."[2] All of these statements are approximately as accurate as the date given for Mitchell's birth. In fairness to Hornberger, it must be said that neither the date nor the place of Mitchell's birth had been established when he wrote his study of Mitchell's scientific ideas. It is nonetheless difficult to understand how he could have arrived at such an estimate of the man in the face of a wealth of evidence to the contrary.

There seems to be little reason to refer to Mitchell as puzzling, except with reference to his date and place of birth, which were long in question. His contemporaries were probably better judges than we can be of whether or not he was a likable person, and they clearly found him to be a person of great personal charm. On one brief visit to Philadelphia he made friends with whom he corresponded for much of the remainder of his life. When he went to England and arrived there in

---

1. *Medicine in Virginia in the Eighteenth Century*, p. 141.
2. "The Scientific Ideas of John Mitchell," *Huntington Library Quarterly* 10 (1947):277.

what Linnaeus described as a destitute condition, he found acceptance in both scientific and social circles. It is true that he had little patience with what he regarded as medical quackery, but his correspondence with Colden, Franklin, Bartram, and others shows little evidence of lack of respect for his contemporaries. His unfavorable commentary on American climate was largely limited to that of coastal areas which he and many others found very unhealthy at that time. His extreme concern for the welfare of the colonies and their protection from the depredations of the French, as well as for their harmonious relations with England, are amply supported by his extensive writing on the subject, and by his map. It is true that circumstances largely beyond his control caused him to spend many years of his life in Scotland and in England. If he felt uncertain whether or not to consider himself a colonial, it is readily understandable, although he did not have much to say on the subject. The suggestion that he would have objected to being considered a colonial seems to have little foundation.

Mitchell had all of the attributes of an able scientist—an inquiring mind, a passion for accuracy, and a willingness to devote long periods to patient study. He acquired at Edinburgh a deep respect for the experimental method in science. Like many eighteenth-century scientists he was broad in his interests. He was thus able, as Hornberger pointed out, to make some contribution to scientific knowledge in "botany, zoology, physiology, medicine, cartography, climatology and agriculture."[3] All of this was accomplished as a private citizen, not associated with any educational institution. He made no great or fundamental scientific discoveries in any of these fields, but his ideas were respected by his contemporaries in all of them, and to a great extent still are. Comparatively few scientists in any age have shown this degree of versatility.

Throughout his life Mitchell seems to have been plagued by miserable health, but he never let this prevent him from making a substantial contribution to the intellectual life around him. When illness finally drove him to leave Virginia for England he might easily have dropped out of sight. Instead he was very soon elected to membership in the Royal Society of London, perhaps the most prestigious scientific society in the world, and began to make contributions to its deliberations. There seems to be no reason to doubt that he was respected and liked

3. Ibid.

by at least many of its members who soon became his friends. As one of colonial birth, with no apparent family connections of social consequence in England, he might have been expected to have a very limited social activity there. Yet, in a comparatively short time he became intimate with many of the most influential men in public life. All of this suggests a man of unusual personal charm, as well as a scholarly mind.

While Mitchell achieved some reputation as a scientist and a writer, his name has been, and is likely to continue to be, most often associated with his map. Miller has called it "the most important and most famous map in American history."[4] Its importance is due to its use on so many significant occasions. Lengthy treatises have been written about these. The subject is peculiarly fascinating as an exposé of the devious methods often employed by diplomacy. A certain gentlemanly cloak-and-dagger aura has been associated with the map. Even now there is still uncertainty as to the exact events. The story has been retold so often and there are so many fine accounts of what transpired, that only a brief and superficial summary is presented here.

During the Revolution the map was used by both American and British forces.[5] Under the Treaty of 1783, Great Britain acknowledged the United States' independence. During the treaty negotiations (1782–83), it was Mitchell's map that was used in establishing the boundaries between the two countries and also between French and Spanish possessions in North America. The line established at that time, which was to cause so much dissension later, was that defining the extent of Nova Scotia and the states of Maine and Massachusetts. It was referred to as the Northeast Boundary line, and was described as follows: "From the North-west angle of Nova Scotia, viz. that angle which is formed by a line drawn due North from the source of St. Croix River to the Highlands; along the said Highlands which divide those Rivers that empty themselves into the River St. Lawrence from those which fall into the Atlantic Ocean, to the North-westernmost head of Connecticut River . . . East by a line to be drawn along the middle of the River St. Croix from its mouth in the Bay of Fundy to its source, and from its source directly North to the aforesaid Highlands, which divide the Rivers that fall into the Atlantic Ocean from those which fall into the River St.

---

4. Miller, *Treaties*, 3:349.

5. Lyman H. Butterfield, ed., *Adams Family Correspondence*, 2 vols. (Cambridge, Mass., 1963), 2:90–91.

Lawrence."[6] This represented a concession on the part of the Americans, as the province of Massachusetts had claimed that her eastern line was delineated by the St. John River. Although the British representative had accepted this in tentative Articles of Agreement on 8 October 1782, it was subsequently changed in the final treaty, as the Americans realized there was little basis for the claim when studies were made of the old charts.

Copies of Mitchell's map had been used by the negotiators (Benjamin Franklin, John Jay, and John Adams for the United States and Richard Oswald, a well-known merchant, for Great Britain). Unfortunately, no copy of the map was appended to the treaty. All of the maps used mysteriously disappeared. Two eventually came to light many years later, under such circumstances as to make it impossible to determine with certainty which copies had been used at the actual signing of the treaty in Paris. A note was appended to the treaty stating that the true line of the Northeast Boundary would be settled as soon as possible. This turned out to be a matter of sixty years. The first meeting between commissioners for the two countries occurred thirteen years after the treaty was signed and lasted two years. It was known as the St. Croix Commission and was to determine "the uncertain source of an uncertain river."[7] This was the St. Croix. Its identity was established and a monument placed at its source. There was some mention of the boundary during negotiations preceding the Treaty of Ghent but the idea was dropped except for a clause providing for meetings on the subject later. This commission met in 1816 and concluded its discussions in 1822 with nothing accomplished.

Under the Treaty of Ghent, arbitration was to be sought if no agreement had been reached. Accordingly, the case was presented by each party before the king of the Netherlands whose decision, given in 1831, was known as the "Dutch Award." Award was an appropriate designation as far as the British were concerned. A letter to the English Foreign Secretary, Lord Aberdeen, representing Britain, explained their position. He was advised to try to "persuade the arbiter that the intentions of the negotiators were really in our favour and that any apparent

6. Dudley A. Mills, "The Ashburton Treaty: Development of the Boundary Line," *United Empire, The Royal Colonial Institute Journal*, n.s. 2 (1911):683.

7. The quotation is a note made in the margin of the draft of the Treaty of 1783 when it was being considered by the Cabinet of Shelburne in November, 1782 (ibid, p. 685).

conflict between our claim and the wording of the Treaty is due to the inherent obscurity of the subject, which it would be waste of time to clear up."[8] Aberdeen was successful and the arbiter, whom he admitted was "notoriously under our influence,"[9] recommended a compromise due to the vagueness of the 1783 treaty. President Jackson was quite ready to accept it but the state of Maine, represented by the judge of the state supreme court, William Pitt Preble, was not. The loss of 4,000 square miles was anathema to him as to all Maine citizens.

Negotiations continued for ten years. Feeling often ran high in the disputed territory and, at one point, was little short of war. When Aberdeen became foreign secretary in 1841, he appointed Alexander Baring, Lord Ashburton, to represent England, so that the ancient argument could be finally settled. Ashburton, whose wife was the daughter of Senator William Bingham of Pennsylvania, was quite familiar with the area in question. Secretary of State Daniel Webster was anxious to successfully settle the boundary dispute once and for all. When he went to discuss it with the Maine governor, he took with him Judge Sprague and the historian Jared Sparks. The latter had with him two maps which so influenced the governor that he and the legislature, to whom Sprague had talked, agreed to appoint commissioners. These, too, were shown the maps and were likewise influenced. With four representatives from Maine, three from Massachusetts, negotiations began with Ashburton on 18 June.[10]

The history of the two maps which Sparks produced is interesting. In checking the archives of the French foreign office, Sparks had discovered a letter from Franklin to Vergennes, written 6 December 1782. In it, he said that he was returning his map on which he had marked the boundaries decided upon in the preliminaries by a "Strong Red Line." When Sparks found a 1746 map of North America by d'Anville marked in such a manner, he was convinced that this was the one to which Franklin referred and it has since been known as the "Red Line Map." Unfortunately, the boundaries shown went beyond the British claims. Sparks reproduced this line on one of the maps which he took

8. The quotation is Mills's summary of a letter written by Stratford Canning to Aberdeen, 15 September 1829 (ibid., p. 688).

9. The quotation is from a letter of Aberdeen to Croker, 25 February 1843, quoted by Mills (ibid., p. 688).

10. Ibid., pp. 690-91.

to Maine. More recently, it has been found that Vergennes was using a French edition of Mitchell's map as had been the practice of the French foreign office since 1779. In fact, Sparks himself later discovered four or five maps with similar annotation. It is now thought that the "Red Line Map" might have been used to demonstrate the French claims prior to the Seven Years War with Great Britain.[11]

The other of Sparks's maps is known as the Steuben-Webster Copy. In 1838, John W. Mulligan, a New York lawyer trained in Alexander Hamilton's office, offered it for sale to the British consul, Buchanan. He had inherited it from Baron Steuben, whose secretary he had been. The boundary line drawn on it supported the British claims. The consul, naturally, was very anxious to acquire this map but, after much correspondence with Viscount Palmerston, Buchanan was forced to give up the idea, as the former refused to authorize payment of anything but an insignificant amount and Mulligan was well aware of its value to the British. Webster learned of the map and, like Buchanan, realizing its importance, purchased it from Mulligan for a stiff price.[12]

Lieutenant Colonel Mills has said, "The strategy of Webster was not only justifiable but brilliant. He desired above all things a settlement with Great Britain. Maine was intractable. With the misleading maps he frightened the Governor of Maine into appointing Commissioners, and then later on these Commissioners themselves into concurring with the proposed settlement." In spite of some remaining reservations on the part of the men from Maine, which made them difficult for Ashburton to deal with, a treaty was finally hammered out. Five thousand square miles of New England territory became British. Maine and Massachusetts received $300,000 compensation from the United States. Great Britain gave this country forty square miles in the area of Rouse's Point. She gave up several doubtful claims and acceded certain navigational rights on the St. John River. There were additional provisions dealing with Slave Trade & Extradition. Neither side felt unhappy since they both were extremely anxious to have the boundary question finally settled.[13]

While the Americans were congratulating themselves on their prac-

11. Ibid., pp. 702–3.
12. Miller, *Treaties*, 3:339.
13. Mills, "The Ashburton Treaty," *United Empire*, n.s. 2 (1911):691.

tice of sophisticated European diplomacy to deceive the British, the British had employed the same to delude their own diplomats and the Americans. On 27 March 1839, Sir Charles Grey said in parliament that he had seen in the British Museum a copy of Mitchell's map on which were marked boundaries. Lord Palmerston immediately queried the librarian, Mr. Panizzi. He replied that they had several Mitchell maps, on one of which the boundaries as "described by Mr. Oswald" were marked. It had come from the collection of George III in 1823 and he had put it in a locked cupboard away from prying eyes. He wrote Palmerston that Oswald, who had represented England in the original negotiations with Franklin, Jay, and Adams, was strongly suspected of prejudice towards the United States. He had lived there; he was a friend of Franklin and his bail had delivered Henry Laurens from the Tower of London.[14]

The map was removed to the foreign office, where neither Aberdeen nor Ashburton was shown it, or even knew of its existence until the negotiations were completed. The Americans had shown Aberdeen their maps when the treaty was a certainty. This must have given him a feeling of confidence that he had been justified in demanding the New England territory although he must have entertained some misgivings at the time due to Maine's intransigence. When he finally saw the George III map, it must have been a relief that he had not known of it for he could never have argued with such conviction nor would he have so impressed the Americans with his sincerity.[15]

The real irony of the situation has been that Ashburton's name became anathema in Canada for many years and generations, due to the treaty. Mills said the " 'Losing by neglect' is the charge on which British statesmen have been arraigned. 'Attempted theft' was their real crime." He further states, "The more the case is studied the clearer becomes the answer—the British claim had no foundation of any sort of kind." The word "attempted" could very well be omitted. Evidence supporting the George III map is borne out by the Mitchell copy known as the Jay Map, which had been in that family's possession from 1783 to 1843. Still more corroborating evidence is the French 1783 edition of Mitchell's map. On it is printed *"En Mars 1783 on a tracé sur cette Carte*

14. A. Panizzi to Lord Palmerston, 29 March 1839, B.M. F.O. 5:340; Miller, *Treaties*, 4:409.

15. Mills, "The Ashburton Treaty," *United Empire* n.s. 2 (1911):699.

Les Limites des États unis et des autres puissances selon le dernier Traité de paix."[16]

Mitchell's map has continued to be of use and to be reproduced. Copies of it were made in whole or in part by U.S. and Canadian historical and geographical societies and appeared in their journals. Official reproductions were made jointly by the British foreign office and the provinces of Quebec and Ontario, Canada in 1910 and again in 1926. The United States has likewise reproduced it as have the states of Maine, Maryland, Massachusetts, and Virginia. The U.S. Geological Survey made a half-scale copy in 1923. It was used in a Library of Congress exhibit in 1926.[17]

In 1861, Colonel McDonald gave a report on the boundary between Virginia and Maryland, in which he cited Mitchell's map. When the joint commission finally met in 1873, Virginia gave the map in evidence but Maryland did not.[18] In 1910, the Court of Arbitration at the Hague heard the North Atlantic Fisheries Case where a Mitchell copy was again used in evidence. In 1925, Michigan employed it in arguments in the Wisconsin-Michigan boundary decisions. It was important in two cases in 1926: in the Great Lakes level case and the Canada-Newfoundland one. The last known use was made of it in 1932 when New Jersey-Delaware boundaries were determined.[19]

There can be little doubt that John Mitchell, a country boy from Tidewater Virginia, had significant influence on important events of his own day, or that his accomplishments and influence have extended well beyond his own time. While still a very young doctor, only a few years out of medical school, he made studies that impressed older physicians and other scientists of London's Royal Society. These included the anatomy and reproduction of the o'possum, a marsupial hitherto little known to science, and studies of the nature of the pigmentation of human skin. During this same early period of his life he made extensive studies of the nature and cause of what he thought was yellow fever. In addition to this, during the same period, he not only discov-

16. Ibid., pp. 684, 687, 699–700; Lawrence Martin and S. F. Bemis, "Franklin's Red-Line Map Was a Mitchell," *New England Quarterly* 10 (March 1937):108.

17. Lawrence Martin's article in *D.A.B.*

18. Earl G. Swem, "Maps Relating to Virginia in the Virginia State Library," *Bulletin, the Virginia State Library* 7 (July 1914):230.

19. H. Garth Hamilton, "Mitchell's Map of North America, February 13, 1755," paper given in a Diplomatic History class, Alderman Library, University of Virginia.

ered and described a number of new genera of plants, but he proposed a new system of plant classification.

As a more mature man in England, Mitchell was clearly respected by the scientific men of the time, and also by prominent political figures of the day. His scientific interests ranged from the production of potash and the nature of electricity, to plant introduction and economic botany. He became an influential interpreter of the problems of the colonies to England and, in addition to the years which he devoted to the making of the map, he wrote extensively on the economy of England and her colonies.

Clearly John Mitchell was endowed with a superior mind, capable of making valuable contributions in many fields. It was well said of him by Blanton that "we cannot fail to be impressed with his modesty, his scholarly attainments and his range of knowledge. He must indeed have been, as Bartram said, 'an ingenious man!' "[20]

20. See note 1

Bibliography

I. MANUSCRIPT COLLECTIONS

Adam Papers. General Register. Edinburgh.

Bartram Papers, Gratz Collection, and Thomas Penn Letter Books. Historical Society of Pennsylvania.

Berkeley Papers and Paper by H. Garth Hamilton. University of Virginia.

Marquess of Bute Collections. Mount Stuart, Isle of Bute.

Bute Papers. Cardiff (Wales) Public Library.

Coutts & Company (London) Archives.

Da Costa Papers, Sloane Manuscripts, and Other Additional Manuscripts. British Museum.

John Evelyn Papers. Christ Church College, Oxford University.

Laing Manuscripts and University Archives. University of Edinburgh.

Lancaster County (Virginia) Court Records.

Linnean Correspondence. Linnean Society of London.

Middlesex County (Virginia) Court Records.

Public Record Office. London.

Public Record Office Transcripts and Other Manuscripts. Library of Congress.

Rappahannock County (Virginia) Court Records.

Richmond County (Virginia) Court Records.

Royal Botanic Gardens (Kew) Archives.

Royal Society of Arts (London) Archives.

Royal Society of London Archives.

Saltoun Manuscripts. National Library of Scotland.

Sherard Manuscripts, Bodleian Western Manuscripts, MSS English Miscellaneous, and Stukeley Correspondence. Bodleian Library, Oxford University.

Dr. Christopher Jacob Trew Papers and Jean Ambrose Beurer Papers. Erlangen-Nurnberg University.

Westmoreland County (Virginia) Court Records.

II. PRINTED MATERIALS

"Account of a Journey into Scotland." *Gentleman's Magazine* 36 (May 1766):211.

Aiton, William. *Hortus Kewensis*. London, 1789.

Alston, Charles. "On the Sexes of Plants." *Gentleman's Magazine* 24 (1754):465–66.

American Husbandry. London, 1775.

Bate, G. E. *And So Make a City Here*. Hounslow, 1948.

Bean, W. T. *The Royal Botanic Gardens, Kew: Historical and Descriptive*. London, 1908.

Berkeley, Edmund, and Berkeley, Dorothy Smith. *Dr. Alexander Garden of Charles Town*. Chapel Hill, 1969.

———. *John Clayton: Pioneer of American Botany*. Chapel Hill, 1963.

————. *The Reverend John Clayton: A Parson with a Scientific Mind.* Charlottesville, 1965.

Blake, John B. "Yellow Fever in the Eighteenth Century." *Bulletin of the New York Academy of Medicine*, 2d ser. 44 (June 1968):673-86.

Blanton, Wyndham B. *Medicine in Virginia in the Eighteenth Century.* Richmond, 1931.

Blunt, Wilfred. *The Art of Botanical Illustration.* London, 1950.

Booker, J. Motley. "Mitchell Family Bible." *Northern Neck of Virginia Historical Magazine* 14 (December 1964):1280.

————. "Old Wills in the Northern Neck and Essex Counties." *Northern Neck of Virginia Historical Magazine* 14 (December 1964):1319.

Boswell, James. *The Journal of a Tour to the Hebrides with Samuel Johnson, LL.D.* Edited by Jack Werner. London, 1956.

Brett-James, Norman G. *The Life of Peter Collinson.* London, n.d.

Bridenbaugh, Carl, ed. *Gentleman's Progress: The Itinerarium of Dr. Alexander Hamilton.* Chapel Hill, 1948.

Brock, R. Alonzo, ed. "Journal of William Black, 1744." *Pennsylvania Magazine of History and Biography*, 1 (1877):117-32; 233-49; 404-19; 2 (1878):40-49.

————. *The Official Records of Robert Dinwiddie.* 2 vols. Richmond, 1888.

Brooks, E. St. John. *Sir Hans Sloane: The Great Collector and His Circle.* London, 1954.

Broughton, Mrs. Vernon Delves, ed. *Court and Private Life in the Time of Queen Charlotte: Being the Journals of Mrs. Papendiek.* London, 1787.

Brown, Lloyd A. *Early Maps of the Ohio Valley.* Pittsburgh, 1959.

————. *Map Making: The Art That Became a Science.* Boston, 1960.

————. *The Story of Maps.* New York, 1949.

Burton, John Hill, ed. *The Autobiography of Dr. Alexander Carlyle of Inverask, 1722-1805.* Edinburgh, 1910.

Butterfield, Lyman H., ed. *Adams Family Correspondence.* 2 vols. Cambridge, Mass., 1963.

Byrd, William. *Histories of the Dividing Line Betwixt Virginia and North Carolina.* Introductions by William K. Boyd and Percy G. Adams. New York, 1967.

Carlyle, Alexander. *Autobiography of the Rev. Alexander Carlyle.* Edinburgh, 1860.

Carman, Harry J., ed. *American Husbandry.* New York, 1939.

Carrier, Lyman. "*American Husbandry*, A Much Overlooked Publication." *Journal of the American Society of Agronomy* 2 (1918):206-11.

————. "Dr. John Mitchell, Naturalist, Cartographer, and Historian." *Annual Report of the American Historical Association* 1 (1918):199-219.

Catalogus Librorum ACDA. Glasgow, 1758.

Catesby, Mark. *Hortus Europae Americanus.* London, 1767.

————. *The Natural History of Carolina, Florida and the Bahama Islands.* 2 vols. London, 1729-47.

Cecil, Russell L. ed. *A Text-Book of Medicine by American Authors.* Philadelphia and London, 1934.

Chacellor, E. B. *The Annals of the Strand.* London, 1912.

Chamberlayne, G. S. *The Vestry Book of Christ Church Parish, Middlesex County, Virginia, 1663-1767.* Richmond, 1927.

Chambers, William. *Plans, Elevations, Sections, and Perspective Views of the Gardens and Buildings at Kew in Surry.* London, 1763.

Chowning, Carroll C. "Some Colonial Homes of Middlesex County." *William and Mary Quarterly*, 2d ser. 22 (April 1942):142–60.

Clayton, The Rev. John. "A Letter from Mr. John Clayton . . . Giving an Account of Several Observables in Virginia, and in His Voyage Hither, More Particularly Concerning the Air." *Philosophical Transactions* 17 (1693):781–89.

Clayton, John, and Gronovius, John Frederic. *Flora Virginica.* Leiden, 1739 & 1743, 1762.

Cohen, I. Bernard. "Benjamin Franklin and the Mysterious 'Dr. Spence.' " *Journal of the Franklin Institute* 235 (January 1943):1–25.

Colden, Cadwallader. "Cure of Cancers." *Gentleman's Magazine* 20 (1751):306–8.

———. *Letters and Papers of Cadwallader Colden.* 9 vols. New York, 1920.

Collinson, Peter. "Remarks on the White or Weymouth Pine." *Gentleman's Magazine* 25 (November 1755):503–4 and (December 1755):550–51.

Comrie, John D. *History of Scottish Medicine.* 2 vols. London, 1932.

Cowan, John Macqueen. "The History of the Royal Botanic Garden, Edinburgh." *Notes from the Royal Botanic Garden* 19 (1933):1–62.

Cumming, William P. *The Southeast in Early Maps.* Princeton, 1958.

Da Costa, Mendez. "Notices and Anecdotes of Literati, Collectors, Etc. from a MS by the Late Mendez da Costa, and Collected Between 1747 and 1788." *Gentleman's Magazine* 82, pt. 1 (1812):205–8.

Darlington, William, ed. *Memorials of John Bartram and Humphry Marshall.* Philadelphia, 1849.

Dictionary of American Biography. S.v. "Mitchell, John," by Lawrence Martin.

Dillenius, John Jac. *Historia Muscorum.* London, 1768.

Dorman, John Frederick, and Lewis, James F. "Doctor John Mitchell, F.R.S., Native Virginian." *Virginia Magazine of History and Biography* 76 (October 1968):437–40.

Druce, C. Claridge, and Vines, S. H. *The Dillenian Herbaria.* Oxford, 1907.

Ducarel. *A Letter from Dr. Ducarel, FRS and FSA to William Watson, MD, FRS, upon the Early Cultivation of Botany in England and Some Particulars about John Tradescant.* London, 1773.

"Duke of Argyll's Windmill." *Gentleman's Magazine* 19 (June 1749):249–50.

Dutens, Louis. *Memoirs of a Traveller Now in Retirement.* 5 vols. London, 1806.

Eberlin, Harold Donaldson, and Hubbard, Cortlandt Van Dyke. *Portrait of a Colonial City, Philadelphia, 1670–1838.* Philadelphia, 1939.

Edinburgh, University of. *A Catalogue of the Graduates in the Faculties of Arts, Divinity and Law, of the University of Edinburgh since Its Foundation.* Edinburgh, 1858.

Edinburgh University: A Sketch of Its Life for 300 Years. Edinburgh, 1884.

Edwards, Averyl. *Frederick Louis, Prince of Wales 1707–1751.* London, 1947.

Edwards, George. *Natural History of Birds.* 2 vols. London, 1747.

Evans, Lewis. *Geographical, Historical, Political, Philosophical And Mechanical Essays.* Philadelphia, 1755.

Ewan, Joseph, ed. *A Short History of Botany in the United States.* New York, 1969.

Ewan, Joseph, and Ewan, Nesta. *John Banister and His Natural History of Virginia, 1678-1692.* Urbana, 1970.

Fite, Emerson D., and Freeman, Archibald. *A Book of Old Maps Delineating American History.* New York, 1969.

Ford, Worthington Chauncey. "Washington's Map of the Ohio." *Massachusetts Historical Society Proceedings* 61 (1927-28):71-79.

Fox, R. Hingston. *Dr. John Fothergill and His Friends.* London, 1919.

Franklin, Benjamin. *The Autobiography of Benjamin Franklin.* New York, 1955.

———. *The Papers of Benjamin Franklin.* Edited by Leonard W. Labaree. New Haven, 1960-.

———. *The Works of Benjamin Franklin.* Edited by Jared Sparks. 10 vols. Boston, 1856.

Frick, George Frederick, and Stearns, Raymond Phineas. *Mark Catesby: The Colonial Audubon.* Urbana, 1961.

Garrison, Hazel Shields. "Cartography of Pennsylvania Before 1800." *Pennsylvania Magazine of History and Biography* 59 (July 1935):255-83.

———. "Letter of Lewis Evans, January 25, 1756." *Pennsylvania Magazine of History and Biography* 59 (July 1935):295-301.

"Genuine Anecdotes of the Life of the Late Peter Collinson, F.R.S." *Annual Register* (1770):57.

Gipson, Lawrence Henry. *Lewis Evans.* Philadelphia, 1939.

Gordon, Charles. *Oldtime Aldwych, Kingsway and Neighborhood.* London, 1903.

Grant, Alexander. *The Story of the University of Edinburgh.* 2 vols. London, 1884.

Guthrie, Douglas. *The Medical School of Edinburgh.* Edinburgh, 1959.

———. "The Three Alexander Monros and the Foundation of the Edinburgh School." *Journal of the Royal College of Surgeons of Edinburgh* 2 (September 1956): 24-34.

Hall, George Birbeck, ed. *Boswell's Life of Johnson.* 6 vols. Oxford, 1950.

Hart, Albert Bushnell, ed. *Hamilton's Itinerarium Being a Narrative of a Journey.* St. Louis, 1907.

Heiser, Charles B., Jr. "Taxonomy." In *A Short History of Botany in the United States,* edited by Joseph Ewan. New York, 1969.

Henckel, J. F. *Pyritologia: or a History of the Pyrites, the Principal Body in the Mineral Kingdom.* Translated by John Mitchell. London, 1757.

Henderson, Andrew. *Considerations on the Questions, Relating to the Scots Militia . . . Among Which, A Faithful Character of Archibald Late Duke of Argyle.* N.p., 1761?

Hepworth, Martyn. *The Story of the Pantiles.* Tunbridge Wells, 1956.

Hill, John. *A Review of the Works of the Royal Society of London.* London, 1751.

———. *Vegetable System.* 5 vols. London, 1762.

Hill, Mrs. John. *An Address to the Public by the Honble Lady Hill Setting Forth the Consequences of the Late Sir John Hill's Acquaintance with the Earl of Bute.* London, 1788.

Hindle, Brooke. *The Pursuit of Science in Revolutionary America, 1735-1789.* Chapel Hill, 1956.

Hirsch, August. *Handbook of Geographical and Historical Pathology.* Translated by C. C. Creighton. London, 1883-86.

Horn, D. B. *A Short History of the University of Edinburgh.* Edinburgh, 1967.

Hornberger, Theodore. "A Letter from John Mitchell to Cadwallader Colden." *Huntington Library Quarterly* 10 (1946–47):412–13.

———. "The Scientific Ideas of John Mitchell." *Huntington Library Quarterly* 10 (1946–47):277–96.

Jarcho, Saul. "Cadwallader Colden as a Student of Infectious Disease." *Bulletin of the History of Medicine* 29 (March–April 1955):99–115.

———. "John Mitchell, Benjamin Rush and Yellow Fever." *Bulletin of the History of Medicine* 31 (1957):132–36.

Johnston, J. Stoddard. *First Explorations of Kentucky*. Louisville, 1898.

Johnston, M. S. "Kew Green." *The Journal of the London Society* 298 (1948):45–48.

Jones, Gordon W. "Dr. John Mitchell's Yellow Fever Epidemics." *Virginia Magazine of History and Biography* 70 (1962):43–48.

———. "The Library of Doctor John Mitchell of Urbanna." *Virginia Magazine of History and Biography* 76 (October 1968):441–43.

Kalm, Peter. *Kalm's Account of His Visit to England on His Way to America in 1748*. Edited by Joseph Lucas. London, 1892.

———. *Peter Kalm's Travels in North America*. Edited by Adolph B. Benson. 2 vols. New York, 1937.

Keith, Theodore. "Scottish Trade with the Plantations before 1707." *Scottish Historical Review* 6 (1908):32–48.

Kerkkonen, Matti. *Peter Kalm's North American Journey, Its Ideological Background and Results*. Helsinki, 1959.

Lambert, Aylmer Bourke. "Notes Relating to Botany, Collected from the Manuscripts of the Late Peter Collinson." *Transactions of the Linnean Society* 10 (1811):273.

La Roche, R. *Yellow Fever Considered in Its Historical, Pathological, Etiological and Therapeutical Relations*. 2 vols. Philadelphia, 1855.

Lee, James. *An Introduction to the Science of Botany Chiefly Extracted from the Works of Linnaeus*. London, 1810.

Lettsom, John Coakley. *Some Account of the Life of Dr. Fothergill*. London, 1786.

Lewis, W. S., Bennett, Charles H., and Hoover, Andrew G., eds. *Horace Walpole's Correspondence with Sir Davis Dalrymple*. London, 1952.

Lewis, W. S., and Brown, Ralph S., Jr., eds. *Horace Walpole's Correspondence with George Montagu*. 2 vols. New Haven, 1941.

Lewis, W. S., and Smith, Robert A., eds. *Horace Walpole's Correspondence with George Selwyn, Lord Lincoln, Sir Charles Hanbury Williams, Henry Fox, Richard Edgcumbe*. London, 1961.

Lovat-Fraser, J. A. *David Balfour's Duke of Argyll*. Inverness, 1928.

———. *John Stuart, Earl of Bute*. Cambridge, England, 1912.

McCormick, Richard P. *New Jersey from Colony to State, 1609–1789*. Princeton, 1964.

McDonnell, Ann Chilton. "Chilton and Shelton, Two Distinct Virginia Families." *William and Mary Quarterly*, 2d ser. 10 (January 1930):56–63.

Malden, H. E., ed. *Victoria History of the County of Surrey*. Westminster, England, 1902.

Martin, Lawrence. "Mitchell Editions." *Report of the Librarian of Congress*. Washington, D.C., 1926, 1927, 1928, 1929, 1930, 1932.

——— ed., *The George Washington Atlas*. Washington, D.C., 1932.

Martin, Lawrence, and Bemis, S. F. "Franklin's Red-Line Map Was a Mitchell." *New England Quarterly* 10 (March 1937):105-11.

Martin, Lawrence, and Eggli, Clara. "Noteworthy Maps . . . Accessions." Division of Maps, Library of Congress. *Bulletins* 77, p. 19; 78, p. 20; 79, pp. 20-22; 80, p. 21; 81, p. 21; 92, p. 17; 93, p. 17; 94, p. 18; 95, p. 19; 96, p. 19; 97, p. 20; 98, p. 20; 99, pp. 20-21; 102, p. 20; 103, pp. 20-21; 104, p. 21; 105, pp. 21-22; 106, p. 22; 107, p. 22; 108, p. 22.

Maty, Matthew, ed. *Miscellaneous Works of the Late Philip Dormer Stanhope, Earl of Chesterfield.* 4 vols. London, 1779.

Maxwell, Gordon Stanley. *Highwayman's Heath.* London, 1935.

Miller, Hunter, ed. *Treaties and Other International Acts of the United States of America.* Washington, D.C., 1933.

Miller, Philip. *The Gardener's Dictionary.* London, 1752.

Mitchell, John. "An Account of the Preparation and Uses of the Various Kinds of Pot-ash." *Philosophical Transactions* 48 (1749):541-63 and *Pennsylvania Gazette* (18 and 25 December 1750).

———. "Account of the Yellow Fever in Virginia, 1741 and 1742." *Medical Museum* 1 (1804):1-21.

———. *The Contest in America between Great Britain and France with Its Consequences and Importance.* London, 1757.

———. "Dissertatio Brevis de Principiis botanicorum et Zoologorum de que novo stabilende naturae rerum congruo cum Appendice Aliquot Generum plantarum recens conditorum . . ." *Acta Physico-Medica Academae Caesarae . . . Ephemerides* 8 (1748):188-224.

———. "Essay on the Causes of the Different Colour of People of Different Climates." *Philosophical Transactions* 43 (1744):102-50.

———. "Letter to the Reverend Dr. Birch, Secretary of the Royal Society, Concerning the Force of Electrical Cohesion." *Philosophical Transactions* 51 (1760):390-93.

———. "Mitchell on the Fever of Virginia." *The American Medical and Philosophical Register* 4 (1814):181-215 and 378-87.

———. *The Present State of Great Britain and North America.* London, 1767.

Morton, Richard L. *Colonial Virginia.* 2 vols. Chapel Hill, 1960.

A New and Complete History of the British Empire in America. London, 1756.

Nichols, John. *Literary Anecdotes of the Eighteenth Century.* 9 vols. London, 1812.

Packard, Francis R. "The Manuscript of Dr. John Mitchell's Account of the Yellow Fever in Virginia in 1741-42, Written in 1748." *Proceedings of the Charaka Club* 9 (1938):45-46.

Paul, James Balfour. *The Scots Peerage.* Edinburgh, 1904.

Paullin, Charles Oscar. *Atlas of the Historical Geography of the United States.* Edited by John K. Wright. Baltimore, 1932.

Pennant, Thomas. *Arctic Zoology.* 2 vols. London, 1784.

Price, Jacob M. "The Rise of Glasgow in the Chesapeake Tobacco Trade, 1707-1775." *William and Mary Quarterly*, 3d ser. 11 (April 1954):179-99.

Pringle, John. *Observations on the Diseases of the Army.* London, 1768.

Pulteney, Richard. *Historical and Biographical Sketches of the Progress of Botany in England*. 2 vols. London, 1790.

Pye, Henrietta. *A Short Account of the Principal Seats and Gardens in and about Kew*. Brentford, c. 1760.

Rhind, William, ed. *The Scottish Tourist*. Edinburgh, 1845.

Ristow, Walter W., ed. *A la Carte: Selected Papers on Maps and Atlases*. Washington, D.C., 1972.

Rousseau, G. S. "The Much Maligned Doctor, 'Sir' John Hill (1707–1775)." *Jama* 212 (April 1970):103–8.

Rush, Benjamin. *An Account of the Bilious Remitting Yellow Fever as It Appeared in the City of Philadelphia in the Year 1793*. Philadelphia, 1794.

———. *Letters of Benjamin Rush*. Edited by Lyman H. Butterfield. 2 vols. Princeton, 1951.

———. *Sixteen Introductory Lectures, to Courses of Lectures Upon the Institutes and Practice of Medicine*. Philadelphia, 1811.

Sabin, Joseph. *A Dictionary of Books Relating to America*. 27 vols. New York, 1885.

Scheer, Frederick. *Kew and Its Gardens*. Richmond, 1840.

Shackleton, Robert. *The Book of Philadelphia*. Philadelphia, 1918.

Smallwood, William Martin, and Smallwood, Mabel Sarah Coon. *Natural History and the American Mind*. New York, 1941.

Smith, James Edward, ed. "Remarks on the Generic Character of Mosses, and Particularly of the Genus Mnium." *Transactions of the Linnean Society of London* 7 (1804):262.

———. *A Selection of the Correspondence of Linnaeus and Other Naturalists*. 2 vols. London, 1821.

Stanard, W. G. "Major Robert Beverley and His Descendants." *Virginia Magazine of History and Biography* 2 (1894):405–13; 3 (1895):47–52, 169–76, 261–71, 383–92.

Stearns, Raymond Phineas. "Colonial Fellows of the Royal Society of London, 1661–1788." *William and Mary Quarterly*, 3d ser. 3 (April 1946):209–68.

———. *Science in the British Colonies of America*. Urbana, 1970.

Stearns, Raymond Phineas, and Frick, George Frederick. *Mark Catesby: The Colonial Audubon*. Urbana, 1961.

Stevens, Henry, and Tree, Roland. "Comparative Cartography." *The Map Collectors' Circle* 39 (1967):342.

Stevens, Henry M. *Lewis Evans, His Map of the British Middle Colonies in America, A Comparative Account of Eighteen Different Editions Published between 1755 and 1814*. London, 1920.

Stokes, M. Veronica. *Notes on the Origin and History of Coutts & Company*. London, 1968.

Stroud, Dorothy. *Capability Brown*. London, 1950.

Summerson, John. *The Iveagh Bequest, Kenwood, A Short Account of Its History and Architecture*. London, n.d.

Swem, E. G. *Brothers of the Spade: Correspondence of Peter Collinson of London, and of John Custis of Williamsburg, Virginia, 1734–1746*. Barre, Massachusetts, 1957.

————. "Maps Relating to Virginia in the Virginia State Library." *Bulletin, the Virginia State Library* 7 (July 1914):230.

Thatcher, Herbert. "Dr. Mitchell, M.D., F.R.S. of Virginia." *The Virginia Magazine of History and Biography* 39 (1931):126–35, 206–20; 40 (1932):48–62, 97–110, 268–79, 335–46; 41 (1933):59–70, 144–56.

Thayer, Theodore. "The Army Contractors for the Niagara Campaign, 1755–56." *William and Mary Quarterly*, 3d ser. 14 (January 1957):31–46.

Thistleton-Dyer, W. T. "Historical Account of Kew to 1841, Royal Gardens, Kew." *Bulletin of Miscellaneous Information* 16 (December 1891):287–89.

Thompson, Edmund. *Maps of Connecticut*. Windham, Conn., 1940.

Thomson, Don W. *Men and Meridians: The History of Surveying and Mapping in Canada*. 3 vols. Ottawa, 1966–67.

Tooke, Horne. *Petition of an Englishman*. London, 1765.

Tooley, Ronald Vere. *Maps and Map-Makers*. London, 1952.

Toynbee, Paget, ed. "Horace Walpole's Journals of Visits to County Seats, etc." *Walpole Society* 16 (1927–28):23–29.

Turner, Dawson, ed. *Extracts from the Literary and Scientific Correspondence of Richard Richardson*. Yarmouth, 1835.

Van Doren, Carl. *Benjamin Franklin*. New York, 1938.

————. *Benjamin Franklin's Autobiographical Writings*. New York, 1945.

Verner, Coolie. "The Fry and Jefferson Map." *Imago Mundi* 21 (1967):70–94.

Von Haller, Albrecht. *Bibliotheca Botanica*. 2 vols. London, 1771–72.

Waldegrave, James Earl. *Memoirs from 1754 to 1758*. London, 1821.

Walpole, Horace. See Lewis, W. S., and Toynbee, Paget, eds.

Warren, Henry. *A Treatise Concerning the Malignant Fever in Barbadoes and the Neighboring Islands*. London, 1740.

Watson, William. "Some Account of the Remains of John Tradescant's Garden at Lambeth." *Philosophical Transactions* 46 (1749):668–69.

Weiss, Harry B., and Kemble, Howard R. *They Took to the Waters: The Forgotten Mineral Spring Resorts of New Jersey and Nearby Pennsylvania*. Trenton, 1962.

Willson, E. J. *James Lee and the Vineyard Nursery Hammersmith*. London, 1961.

Wilson, J. Gordon. "The Influence of Edinburgh on American Medicine in the 18th Century." *Proceedings of the Institute of Medicine of Chicago* 7 (1929):129–39.

Winsor, Justin, ed. *Narrative and Critical History of North America*. 8 vols. Boston, 1887.

Wyndham, Henry Penruddocke, ed. *The Diary of the Late George Bubb Doddington, Baron of Melcombe Regis, From March of 1749 to February 6, 1761*. London, 1809.

Zirkle, Conway. *The Beginnings of Plant Hybridization*. Philadelphia, 1935.

————. "Plant Hybridization and Plant Breeding in Eighteenth-Century American Agriculture." *Agricultural History* 43 (January 1969):25–39.

Index